the weekend baker

also by abigail johnson dodge

Great Fruit Desserts

The Kid's Cookbook

Dessert

Kid's Baking

the
weekend baker

irresistible recipes, simple techniques, and
stress-free strategies for busy people

photographs by gentl & hyers/edge

abigail johnson dodge

w. w. norton & company
new york • london

Copyright © 2005 by Abigail Johnson Dodge
Photographs © 2005 by Gentl & Hyers

For information about permission to reproduce selections from this book, write to Permissions,
W. W. Norton & Company, Inc., 500 Fifth Avenue, New York, NY 10110

Manufacturing by Maple-Vail Book Manufacturing Group
Book design by Urbain Design
Production manager: Julia Druskin

Library of Congress Cataloging-in-Publication Data

Dodge, Abigail Johnson.
    The weekend baker : irresistible recipes, simple techniques, and stress-free strategies for busy people /
Abigail Johnson Dodge ; photographs by Gentl & Hyers/Edge.
    p. cm.
    Includes index.
    ISBN 0-393-05883-2 (hardcover)
1. Baking. I. Title.
    TX765.D63 2004
    641.8'15—dc22

                                                                                        2004015023

W. W. Norton & Company, Inc., 500 Fifth Avenue, New York, N.Y. 10110
www.wwnorton.com

W. W. Norton & Company Ltd., Castle House, 75/76 Wells Street, London W1T 3QT

1 2 3 4 5 6 7 8 9 0

For Darv, Tim, and Steve

Through the best and worst of times,
humor has been our bond and salvation.
Thanks for always making me laugh so hard that I cry.
With all my love.

contents

acknowledgments

Cookbooks are born from years of collaboration and teamwork, and I am endlessly grateful to all the brilliantly creative and generous people who have shared and shaped my life, encouraged me to follow my own path, and helped create this book.

Lucetta Clark, Maggie Daly, Tommy Mays, Sally Powel, and Moonie Wallace – through the years you have protected, guided, inspired, and encouraged me, and, most of all, you mothered me when the real one was no longer able to.

Chris, Alex, and Tierney – I love you all so much. Thank you for patiently tasting endless versions of recipes, adding your thoughts and comments and, especially, putting up with wacky old me. Your steadfast support and love made this a wonderful journey that we took together.

Tom Connor – thanks for pushing me to actually write this book rather than simply talk about it. It truly wouldn't have happened without you. I'm lucky to have such a trusted friend.

Maria Guarnaschelli – bless you and thank you for leading me through one of the best experiences of my life. Your guidance, wisdom, and instincts were always right on. You believed in me and shared my passion for this book and for that I am eternally grateful.

Claire Van de Berghe – head of *The Weekend Baker* test kitchen. Thank you for your endless enthusiasm, unwavering support, and patience. Your testing and tasting comments were invaluable to me.

Stacey Glick – my endless gratitude for immediately grasping the book's concept and pushing me to always do better. Your keen instincts, clear thinking, and constructive criticism have served me well. Thanks for being in my corner!

Amy Albert – you have done so much, it's hard to know where to start. All the times that I was sure I couldn't write this book, you were there to pick me up, dust me off, and push me forward. I'm grateful for your friendship.

Li Agen – how can I thank you for answering all of my endless (and I do mean endless!) questions with humor, patience, and accuracy? Li, you are truly a goddess!

The photography team – and what an all-star team it was! Andrea Gentl and Marty Hyers are two of the most gifted photographers around. Your talent and vision are matched only by your grace and humor. Thanks to you and your stellar team, shooting this book was a pleasure, and the results are an author's dream come true.

Michael Pederson and Tracy Harlor created the gorgeous foods that grace the photographs and did so with unmatched style and grace.

Sabine Tucker and Kim Ficaro pulled together a glorious collection of props to complement the recipes.

Thanks to Kate Sears, Jill Ruchala, and Tali Magal for making everything look easy!

Nowhere is teamwork more brilliantly executed than at W. W. Norton. I am indebted to Jeannie Luciano, Drake McFeely, Starling Lawrence, Nancy Palmquist, Susan Sanfrey, Louise Brockett, Debra Morton Hoyt, Julia Druskin, and Bill Rusin. Your generous attention to this book means everything. Thank you for your faith in this project and in me.

Thanks to Erik Johnson for so graciously tolerating my endless questions and patiently explaining things over and over!

My sincere thanks to Kim Urbain for her stunning book design. It's just gorgeous!

Sharon Silva – This is the fifth project we've worked on together, and your copyediting skills never fail to amaze me. Thank you for gently leading me through the English language and for keeping all the recipes on track.

Doris Hardiman – I handed you pages and pages of recipes and you willingly and effortlessly went to work on them. Your wonderfully methodical mind made sense of them all and gave me tremendous peace of mind. You are a dream!

Richard Lerner and Aresel Marketing – guiding me through the world of the Internet, Web design, and business building might just be the most horrible job in America. I'm so thankful that you are willing to put up with me!

To "The Friends" – Ann, Betsey, Hats, Jen, Sarah – thanks for remembering who I was when I finally came up for air, and the answer to the oft-asked question is "Yes, the book is DONE!"

Spic and Span Market – I know my family agrees that without this gem of a store, our dinners would have been chosen from my daily baking results. Thanks to Greg, Lori, Jim, Glenn, and Jay for keeping the Dodges fed in such fine fashion and making me laugh along the way.

Kudos to the Dianon Systems Crew – my chief tasters. Thanks for lending your palates to *The Weekend Baker*. Your thoughtful comments were instrumental and greatly appreciated!

Katherine Seeley – thanks for sharing your testing time, taste buds, and food wisdom. How you found time to do this while raising two babies and starting a business with Lou, I'll never know.

My deepest thanks to Martha Holmberg, Susie Middleton, and the staff of *Fine Cooking* magazine for producing such a wonderful magazine and for putting up with a more than distracted contributing editor. Thanks for so patiently waiting for me to resurface!

And, last but not least, my deepest thanks to all the gifted chefs, editors, writers, and readers whose thoughts, suggestions, and questions continue to inspire me.

introduction

One day years ago, when I was working as the test kitchen director at *Fine Cooking* magazine, a reader – I'll call him Doug – phoned the kitchen's direct line. Doug loved to bake, and he had his heart set on a particular recipe for a dinner party he was giving that Friday. But he was worried about being able to bring it all together. "I don't get home until six," Doug said, sounding overwhelmed even though the party was four days away. "How am I ever going to make the dessert, much less dinner for six, by eight p.m.?"

Anyone can freak out before a dinner party, and Doug could well be me on any given day. So, I proceeded to tell him what I'd do for myself – break the recipe down into parts, spread it out over the next three evenings, and create a manageable, low-stress plan. By scripting out the recipe in this way, I was able to take the fear and anxiety out of an activity that Doug was clearly passionate about. He got to bake his dessert and enjoy it too.

In my diverse roles as food editor, cooking teacher, recipe developer, and test kitchen director, I've received countless calls like Doug's. They're the inspiration for this book. Just like those callers, and just like you, I am a Weekend Baker. I juggle family, friends, work, social life, exercise, community service, and household – and I bake. It's a passion I refuse to give up just because I'm busy. You too can bake without giving up anything else in your life.

Throughout this book, I share personal experience backed by my professional training about how you can fit baking into everyday life – how you can be a Weekend Baker. It only takes a little planning.

who is a weekend baker?

Anyone who loves to bake, but avoids doing it, believing that it's too time-consuming, is a Weekend Baker. If you're a lapsed home baker, I'm here to show you how to head back to the kitchen despite a time-pressed schedule. You'll see that baking can be broken down into doable parts so that it can slip into time pockets between carpools, work, school, errands, and children's naps. *Weekend* is a loose term. The streamlined recipes I offer in this book are great for the weekends, but they're also right for weekdays and any time you have some extra minutes. Whether you need a dessert an hour from now or in a few days, you'll find recipes to suit your palate and lifestyle – and the results will delight you.

how i fell in love with baking

I've always been a baker, starting at age four when my mom gave me my first cookbook, *Mud Pies and Other Recipes: A Cookbook for Dolls* by Marjorie Winslow. Granted, recipes like Pine Needle Upside-Down Cake weren't exactly bakery or dinner-party fare, but I spent hours under the pine trees diligently following their directions. Even then I was a stickler for the right ingredients and amounts, one of the telltale traits of a baker. I would be remiss if I didn't mention my Easy-Bake Oven. I consider it my starter set to the real thing. I was an avid user and would feed everyone (dolls and dog included) my creations. It wasn't long before I graduated to real desserts, and my mom would clip recipes from magazines to satisfy my endless curiosity. Floating island with vanilla custard began appearing at our Sunday-night family dinners. I believe my desire to make desserts arose from the fact that I enjoyed eating them so much.

As a teenager, I devised a summer job that was much more than a way to earn some money. With my good friend Harriet "Hatsy" Mays, I started a catering business called Four Hands. Resplendent in our Austrian dirndl costumes (the height of fashion), and armed with our limited menu of recipes pinched from our mothers' recipe boxes, Four Hands enjoyed several successful summers. Nothing fancy, mind you, but, by the end of our run Hatsy and I had really learned how to pull together good meals in little time. That experience is the genesis of my Weekend Baker motto, "Keep it simple – make it great."

After college, I shipped myself off to France with the goal of learning the classics and making a career in the food business specializing in desserts. Studying in Paris at Anne Willan's Ecole de Cuisine La Varenne was a dream come true. My mom often told me that I should choose a profession I was passionate about. "You'll be working for the rest of your life, so you might as well enjoy whatever it is" were her words. Lucky for me, I listened.

how i became a weekend baker

After studying and working in France and then in the States, I set my sights on the editorial side of the food business. I freelanced at many magazines until I joined the staff of *Woman's Day* magazine. Then I went on to *Parents Magazine* and, after a husband and two kids came along, I founded *Fine Cooking* magazine's test kitchen and was appointed a contributing editor. My experiences up until then had been in professional kitchens, and I was lucky enough to learn from a retinue of gifted chefs who were true artists. Working at the different magazines, listening to the concerns of the readers, solving their problems, and writing articles for them put me in direct contact with the needs of the home cook. In the process, I acquired a clear view into the kitchens of folks who have to cook for their families and themselves day in and day out.

As my kids grew, my days became even more hectic. I thought I was busy when I was chasing toddlers. Little did I know that as my children got older, I'd have even less freedom. This meant setting aside my vocation, baking. But I loved taking in the scent of cookies baking, frosting a banana cake for my husband's birthday, making a batch of rice pudding and spooning it straight from the pot into a warm dish. Luckily, being the stubborn type, I was determined to find a way to fit baking into my schedule. Over the years, I learned that the secret is organization, and an awareness of one's time constraints. From there, it's a piece of cake.

how to use *the weekend baker*

I designed this book with efficiency in mind, because I myself choose desserts based on the amount of time I have available. To make the most of this book, all you need to do is:

• First, figure out when you need to serve the dessert. Do you need cupcakes for Cub Scouts in an hour? A dessert for Saturday night's company? Or a treat for an unexpected guest who has just dropped by?

• Next, decide how much time you have to make it. Do you need to take the dog to the vet for shots, plus answer an hour's worth of e-mail before your guests arrive, leaving you just about an hour to bake brownies, a pudding, or scones? Or do you have a couple of hours to make a mousse cake or ice cream sandwiches that can sit beautifully in the fridge or freezer for a few days?

• Now, turn to the table of contents. You'll see that I've divided the recipes into three categories: Baker's Express, Baking in Stages, and Productions. Go to the section that fits your time specifications.

baker's express consists of recipes that can be prepared in a hurry. Time-pressed bakers or anyone caught off guard who needs a dessert fast will benefit from these streamlined recipes. The speedy techniques and shortcuts will put dessert on the table, any day of the week, in short order. Although the recipes can be executed quickly, this section isn't a speed test. Keep in mind that the first time you try a recipe is always a get-acquainted experience. The second and third time you do it, you'll know it better and putting it together will go even faster. Some recipes mix up in no time (10-Minute Mocha Pots de Crème, page 98) and some are ready to serve in 20 minutes (White Chocolate Cream with Crushed Amaretti, page 110).

baking in stages includes uncomplicated recipes that can be made in stages and/or prepared in advance. It's the section to turn to when you know ahead of time that you'll need a dessert and can plan for it. With an emphasis on the "do some now, do some later" approach, recipes like Chocolate-Macadamia Biscotti (page 142) and Old-Fashioned Berry Icebox Cake (page 185) can be made in manageable steps spread over three days. The recipes are broken down into brief segments that can slide into any crowded schedule. Read through the Do Aheads section at the beginning of each recipe. That's where you'll find out which components of a recipe can be made ahead of time and how best to store them.

productions contains recipes for occasions when you can plan ahead, have extra time, and want to pull out all the stops. But don't confuse elaborate presentation and recipe length with difficulty. The recipes in this section consist of simple parts that yield creations exciting enough to attract ambitious, advanced bakers and still easy enough for the first-timer. Chocolate-Chip Brownie Double-Deckers (page 263) are made of two simple components. Both batters – chocolate chip and brownie – are a cinch to prepare. The process takes only a bit longer than baking them separately. The Strawberries-and-Cream Layer Cake (page 309) looks as if it were prepared by a professional. No one else at the table needs to know how undemanding the recipe is. The cake layers can be baked a month in advance and the vanilla filling and frosting are nothing more than whipped cream with a bit of gelatin added for stability. As in Baking in Stages, study the

Do Aheads section at the beginning of each recipe to learn which steps can be done in advance.

No matter what your time frame, I urge you to set realistic goals. Trying to cram too much into too small a time slot will make you cranky (and crazed), produce results that are unsatisfactory, and, worse, most likely cause you to be late for work, appointments, classes, or school pickup. I've learned this from trying too many times to squeeze 10 minutes into 5. It doesn't work. Just ask my daughter Tierney about the time I was very late picking her up from summer beach camp because I had to wait for my banana bread to finish baking. I now know that the Supermoist Banana-Nut Muffins (page 81) would have been better suited to the time I had.

So, what are you waiting for? Turn to the section and chapter that suits both your schedule and your taste buds, select a recipe, and start baking!

postscript

As I worked to complete this book, I spent days on end sitting in front of the computer. When I headed back into the kitchen to finish developing and testing the recipes for the Productions section, baking the Chocolate-Chip Brownie Double-Deckers was the first task on my list. Melting, stirring, and layering the batters was effortless. What's more, I had fun doing it. As the double-deckers baked, the house filled with warmth and the chocolate aroma wafted through the air and into my office. I could barely wait for them to cool.

They tasted every bit as good as they smelled, and the entire experi-ence gave me great satisfaction. After all that computer time, making the double-deckers reminded me how much I love to bake, how gratifying baking is to the soul and the stomach, and why I wanted to share this experience with you in hopes that you too will discover (or rediscover) the rewards of baking.

the
weekend baker
basics

Pantry Essentials: On-Hand Ingredients

Here's a checklist of vital items for Weekend Bakers to have on hand, a basic guide to help new or born-again bakers set up shop. You'll be amazed by what you can whip up with the everyday stuff that most of us have in our kitchens. If you're a seasoned baker, some items might seem obvious, but you also might discover a few new things to add to your list of indispensable ingredients.

flour

All-Purpose Flour

All-purpose flour is the most common and versatile flour, and it's what most of us have in our cupboards. Sure, other flours exist, but for ease and consistency, all but a few of the recipes in *The Weekend Baker* call for all-purpose flour. Because cake flour requires the extra step of sifting before measuring and mixing, it is called for only in the Productions section of the book. The few cakes there benefit from the softer, finer texture that cake flour produces. My favorite brands are King Arthur for all-purpose flour, and Softasilk for cake flour (not self-rising).

Cornmeal

Different grinds exist, but for baking I recommend finely ground cornmeal. The coarse stuff makes terrific polenta, but produces a gritty texture in shortbreads and cakes.

Leaveners

Most baked goods call for leaveners, such as baking powder, baking soda, or yeast. I keep a packet or two of instant yeast (Fleischmann's Rapid Rise,

Red Star's Quick-Rise, or SAF Instant) in the fridge and a container of double-acting baking powder and a box of baking soda in the pantry.

salt

For baking, I use table salt, not kosher or other coarse salts (I save those for my savory cooking). The finer grains make for a more accurate measurement and disperse more evenly in a batter or dough.

sugar

Granulated Sugar

It's in your sugar bowl, and again, it's what most of us have on hand.

Light and Dark Brown Sugar

I love brown sugar for the subtle butterscotch flavor it imparts. It might seem picky to stock both, but each produces different results – different intensity. I store brown sugar in a Tupperware container to keep it moist. Once it's hard and lumpy, it is no longer usable.

Superfine Sugar

Finer in texture than granulated, superfine is what I use for meringues and other desserts that require a quick-dissolving sugar. Having a box on hand saves a step, but superfine sugar can be made simply by pulsing granulated sugar in the food processor until it's finely pulverized. Measure the sugar for a recipe after processing. For those mixologists out there, superfine is also known as bar sugar – it's what bartenders use for mixed drinks.

Confectioners' Sugar

Also called powdered sugar, this super-superfine sugar is mixed with a small amount of cornstarch to keep it from lumping. Once opened, it's important to keep it away from moisture, so store the sugar in a zipper-top bag or a small Tupperware container in your cupboard.

dairy

Milk

I tested these recipes with whole milk. So, keep whole on hand for consistently great baked results. If you're a skim person, save it for your cereal or low-fat latte.

Heavy Cream

Most heavy cream in the supermarkets is ultrapasteurized. If you come across heavy cream that's simply pasteurized, so much the better for flavor. In general, heavy cream and whipping cream can be used interchangeably. However, I prefer to use heavy cream because it has a slightly higher fat content (usually 6 percent or more) and will whip up faster and firmer than whipping cream.

Unsalted Butter

It's a control thing: when you bake and cook with unsalted butter, you know exactly how much salt is going into your recipe, because you're the only one adding it. If you really like the taste of salted butter, save it for dinner rolls and savory cooking.

As far as brands go, I tested every *Weekend Baker* dessert with Land O'Lakes unsalted butter or my grocery-store brand. They're not fancy butters, but I think they're just perfect. For those occasions when you want to indulge, try Cabot or Vermont Butter & Cheese Company brands, and save them for recipes that don't call for strong flavors like spices or chocolate. This way the fresh butter flavor really stands out. Whichever brand you purchase, I recommend stocking up on it when it's on sale and storing it, well wrapped, in the freezer. Butter freezes beautifully for three months, retaining its fresh, clean flavor.

Buttermilk

Buttermilk adds a unique tang to cakes and muffins. Luckily, it has a long shelf life, and occasionally I come upon pint containers. I've found no difference between low-fat and nonfat versions. In a pinch, I substitute 1 teaspoon lemon juice mixed into 1 cup whole milk and then measure out the amount called for, but real buttermilk is better.

Eggs

All the recipes in *The Weekend Baker* were developed and tested with large eggs. Substituting jumbo, extra large, or medium will alter the finished results. Buy the freshest eggs you can find and, before putting them in your cart, check each one for cracks. If you come upon a cracked egg, select another carton.

flavorings

Extracts

Pass over the imitation stuff and spend the extra dollar or two on extracts labeled "pure." I keep vanilla, almond, and lemon on hand.

Pure Vanilla Bean Paste

I always keep a bottle of pure vanilla bean paste on hand. This fragrant, viscous syrup is made of vanilla extract and vanilla bean seeds. Substitute the same quantity of the paste for extract as called for in the recipe. It's a flavorful addition to whipped creams, toppings, and vanilla cookies.

Coffee

Instant coffee granules or espresso powder, decaffeinated or regular – no coffee lover I know drinks them, but all bakers I know agree that they carry great coffee flavor.

Spirits

Keep a few bottles around. They're a great way to sneak more flavor into fruits, desserts, toppings, and sauces. If you don't keep a fully stocked bar, buy small bottles (which get used up more quickly). Here are a few I like to have on hand: Grand Marnier or other orange-flavored liqueurs, Kahlúa or other coffee liqueurs, Sambuca or other anise-flavored liqueurs, Chambord or other raspberry-flavored liqueurs, Dark rum, such as Myers's or Mount Gay.

Chocolate

I've tested these recipes with Ghirardelli brand chocolate, which I buy in the grocery store. Nestlé's semisweet chips are also tucked in my pantry. If you want to splurge, Lindt 70 percent bittersweet, Callebaut, or Valrhona, a French brand, have a more distinct chocolaty taste.

Unsweetened Cocoa

With this ingredient, I can build in potent chocolate flavor. Unsweetened cocoa powder is what remains when much of the cocoa butter is removed from the chocolate liquor and the solids are then pulverized. Dutch-process, or alkalized, cocoa refers to a process that reduces the acidity in the cocoa, making the color darker and the chocolate flavor mellower. Natural, or nonalkalized, cocoa hasn't undergone this process. It imparts a stronger, slightly acidic flavor and is lighter in color.

Years ago, I developed recipes with only natural cocoa, because Dutch-process cocoa wasn't then sold in most grocery stores. I came to prefer natural cocoa's stronger, slightly sharp chocolate flavor. Nowadays, however, both types are widely available and most bakers stock both in their pantries. I use natural cocoa in recipes leavened with baking soda, like the Emergency Blender Cupcakes (page 72), and the resulting flavor is deeply chocolaty.

Dutch-process cocoa delivers a smoother, more polished flavor and is what I reach for when I'm looking for a subtler chocolate finish. The mousse in the Layered Chocolate Mousse Cake (page 299) is laced with Dutch-process cocoa and, as a result, has a more refined taste. Unless you're an experienced baker, follow the recipe exactly and use the type of cocoa specified. Because of the difference in acidity, different types and amounts of leavening agents (baking powder and baking soda) are used and the results can vary depending on the type of cocoa used.

spices

My basic list of spices includes cinnamon, cloves, ginger, and nutmeg. If you don't use them frequently, consider buying small containers instead of the larger jars. While they might cost a bit more, your desserts will benefit from the fresher, more intense flavors. Replace spices if they're more than six months old.

fruit

Keep some on hand, as there's always a use for it. Stone fruits (peaches, plums, nectarines, apricots), mangoes, apples, pears, and berries can become the building blocks to delectable last-minute desserts. For the best taste, buy what's ripe and in season.

ingredients to store frozen

Think of the freezer as an extension of your spice cabinet, one where you can store the following:

Fruits, especially those that enjoy a short season – strawberries, blueberries, blackberries, cherries, raspberries, cranberries – are prime candidates for freezing. Most of these can be found in the freezer section of the grocery store (make sure to buy them unsweetened), but it's simple to freeze your own. Cranberries are easy – just toss a bag or two in the freezer. Spread blueberries, raspberries, strawberries, and blackberries in a single layer on a half sheet pan (or plate, depending on how many you have), slide them into the freezer, and leave them until they are frozen. Then slip them into heavy-duty freezer bags and keep frozen until you're ready to use them.

Lemon juice, but only 100 percent pure. I like Minute Maid brand unsweetened juice, which has saved me on the many occasions I forgot to buy lemons or didn't have time to squeeze them (which is most of the time). Look for it near the frozen concentrated juices.

Nuts – walnuts, almonds, and pecans – are stashed in my freezer at all times. And when I come across unsalted macadamias and skinned hazelnuts,

I stock up on them as well. In my opinion, the freezer is the only place to store nuts, and they keep well for up to a month. The deep freeze keeps them from going "bad" (that's when the nut oil turns rancid).

Frozen puff pastry is a baker's secret ingredient for quick tarts. Trust me, there's no shame in it. Pepperidge Farm is one brand I find locally. But brands like Voila and Dufour are also wonderful if you can find them.

The Weekend Baker's Equipment

Like the pantry list on pages 20–27, this is a checklist of essentials, large and small, for Weekend Bakers.

Shop around when looking for equipment. You don't need to spend a fortune. Tag sales are a great place to pick up smaller items. I cherish my collection of old-time Pyrex mixing bowls in all sorts of sizes, shapes, and colors, and I scour the sales for them. Sure, they're fun to look at, but they're also incredibly efficient, and I use them all the time. I've also found wonderful plates and custard cups at neighborhood sales.

When it comes to purchasing large equipment, be price conscious and do your research. While specialty cookware stores will have it all, restaurant-supply shops are a superb resource, and don't overlook the many Web sites that feature great deals. Also, if you're timing is right, bulk discounters like Costco often stock well-made, name-brand baking equipment at reasonable prices.

large appliances

Many of the recipes in this book can be made without the following appliances, but if you're in the market to buy one, here's my two cents. Though I've been called fanatic about many things, I'm not an equipment junkie. I've been using the same power tools for years. My blender (Hamilton Beach in avocado green) is the one my husband had in college. I've been putting my food processor (Cuisinart, possibly the original model) through its paces for 30 years now, and it still works like a champ. My Braun handheld mixer is the newest member of the family, at only 10 years old. And my KitchenAid stand mixer, my first big-ticket purchase after returning to the States from my cooking-school days in Paris in the early 1980s, is still going strong. It's my most trusted kitchen companion.

Blender: A hardware store version is fine, although if you like to make frozen drinks, you might want to make sure you buy one that does a good job crushing ice.

Hand mixer: You don't need to buy one with a lot of speeds, but you want one with enough strength to churn through thick cookie dough and not burn out. I've also used the KitchenAid 5-speed and if I were to buy a new one today, I'd choose this one.

Food processor: I use my machine for tasks like chopping nuts, pulverizing cookies, and making pie dough, so I don't need one with an extra-large capacity work bowl. An 11-cup model is perfect for all the recipes in the book. Both KitchenAid and Cuisinart make 11-cup versions that will probably last a generation or two, but other, less-expensive brands like Oster and Hamilton Beach also make processors worth investigating.

Stand mixer: I know these machines tend to be on the expensive side, but if it's any consolation, I've had my KitchenAid for more than 20 years. Buy one and it's money well spent, and you'll probably even be able to pass it along to your grandchildren. I can't even count how many double and triple batches of the Ginger Crackles (page 136) I've made in it, a job that would have burned out my handheld mixer. And while I learned to make bread by hand, my KitchenAid makes bread making faster, cleaner, and easier.

I would be remiss if I didn't mention the Sunbeam stand mixer as well. Not only is its retro look as appealing as its more modest price, this machine mixes up cookie, cake, and even bread batters quickly and evenly. It comes with two mixing bowls – small and large – and is ideal for beginning bakers as well as those reluctant to commit to a more expensive model.

pans

The list that follows is a basic one, and for many of the tools included, you'll need to go no farther than your local supermarket or hardware store. Again, tag sales are great places to find baking equipment; just be vigilant and avoid metal pans that are warped or rusted. I've found handsome casseroles, mixing bowls, and serving dishes and some unique fluted tube pans.

Tart Pans

French pastry chefs use straight-sided tart rings with no bottom, but here in the States, shallow, fluted pans are de rigueur for home bakers. They create tarts that look as if they could be displayed in a pastry-shop window. They're about an inch deep, have a removable bottom, and come in several sizes. If you buy only one, choose a pan about 9 1/2 inches (24cm) in diameter. Select aluminum or light-colored pans and avoid the darker ones (these create problems with even baking). Don't confuse a fluted tart pan with a quiche pan, which also has a removable bottom, but is deeper (2 to 3 inches/5 to 7.5cm deep) and has more pronounced fluting.

Pie Plates

I've been advocating 9-inch (22.75cm) Pyrex pie plates for as long as I've been baking pies, and I recommend them for much more than just pies, as you'll see. While there are many other types of pie pans and plates (metal and ceramic), I find they vary too widely in depth and capacity, affecting baking times and results.

Loaf, Round, and Square Pans

Buy at least two 9-inch (22.75cm) round cake pans with 2-inch (5cm) straight sides. I like Doughmakers or Parrish. Treat them well – no scouring pads or dishwashers – and they'll last a lifetime.

As for loaves, squares, and rectangles, Pyrex makes baking dishes in many sizes and they're just fine. They do have rounded corners, though, so if you're particular about that, you might want to seek out metal pans by Parrish or Doughmakers, which are heavy duty and straight sided with sharp corners.

Cookie Sheets

Buy at least two rimless cookie sheets with a raised edge. The raised edge makes sliding a sheet full of cookies from a hot oven safe and easy. Be sure the sheets are heavy-duty aluminum and won't wobble when you try to wiggle them (the flimsy ones will warp in the oven and burn the bottom of your cookies). I have Doughmakers and Cushionaire brands, among others, in my arsenal.

Half Sheet Pans

Buy at least one heavy-duty aluminum rimmed sheet pan measuring 11 3/4 by 16 3/4 inches (29.75 by 42.5cm; measured on the bottom). Professional cooks rely on these for almost everything, and so will you. Most specialty shops carry them, or check the Yellow Pages for restaurant-supply stores, which is where you can often find the best prices.

Springform Pans

These two-piece aluminum pans need to be stored in a safe place, because if they warp or ding (develop little bumps and bruises from being banged around in a cabinet), they'll leak. A 9-inch (22.75cm) pan with 3-inch (7.75cm) sides is the only one you'll need for the recipes in this book.

Saucepans

Small, medium, and large saucepans are important to have on hand, and for more than just baking. Make sure that you buy a heavy-duty variety (mine are stainless steel) so your custards and sauces won't scorch.

Cooling Racks

Racks are essential for bakers. Without racks, what would I do with my hot cookie sheets or cake pans when they come out of the oven? I recommend having several large racks on hand to hold a batch of cookies or a sheet cake. A few small, round or square ones are also handy for 9-inch (22.75cm) cake layers.

measuring tools

Scale

If I could afford to buy every baker a scale, I would. I can't emphasize the importance of weighing enough. Weighing instead of measuring ingredients (especially flour) is the best way to ensure perfect results every time. After the first few times you've weighed your ingredients, measuring will become second nature. My Cuisinart scale has a flat surface to set a bowl or plate on, weighs up to 6 1/2 pounds of ingredients in 1/4-ounce increments, slips right into my tote bag (for when I'm on the road teaching or giving cooking demonstrations), and slides into my kitchen drawer. It's the best $25 I've ever spent. Another good alternative is the Salter scale. It can weigh up to 11 pounds of ingredients at 1/8-ounce increments (about $40).

Measuring Cups and Spoons

For liquid measuring, Pyrex cups are ideal. Invest in 1-cup, 2-cup, 4-cup, and 8-cup sizes (this may seem excessive, but having the discrete sizes makes it easier to measure large quantities more accurately). For dry measuring, buy heavy-duty stainless-steel cups. You will also need measuring spoons for small amounts of liquid and dry ingredients. Avoid decorative measuring spoons and cups. They're not as accurate as the stainless-steel, heavy-duty kind.

hand tools

Whether you already own them or not, these are all useful for baking, and for savory cooking, too.

Ruler

As you know from reading about scales, I'm a stickler for recipe accuracy (the only way to get successful results every time). I tuck a few inexpensive rulers in my kitchen drawer so they are at the ready to measure the thickness of cookie or pie dough, the depth of a baking dish, or the diameter of a tart pan. I like the plastic kind because they are easy to clean.

Microplane Grater

No other tool grates citrus zest or fresh ginger more finely.

Knives

A paring knife (for cutting fruit or trimming doughs), an 8-inch and a 10-inch knife (for chopping nuts or cutting slices), and a serrated knife (for slicing bread or cutting cakes into layers).

Whisks

A medium-sized rounded whisk (for whisking wet and dry ingredients), and small and large elongated whisks (for stirring custards and ganache).

Peeler

The U-shaped peelers are my favorite. They are shaped like the slingshots my brothers used to play with. With the cutting blade set horizontally at the top of the *U,* I achieve great control and positioning, and I peel apples (potatoes and carrots too) that way.

Angled Wooden Spatulas

For stirring sauces, custards, and puddings. Rather than the traditional rounded spoon, this spatula has a flat, angled edge that evenly scrapes the bottom and reaches into the corners of a saucepan.

Offset Spatulas

The metal portion of this spatula juts out from the handle at about a 45-degree angle, keeping your hand free and clear of the batter or frosting. Have at least one long and one short offset spatula in your arsenal. No tool is better for icing cakes and spreading batters. I also couldn't do without my small, squared-off spatula. It's perfect for lifting up small bars or serving cake squares straight from the pan. The spatula (at the base) is about 2 1/2 inches (6.5cm) long and 2 1/4 (5.75cm) inches wide.

Bench Scraper

A wide, straight-sided metal spatula with a plastic or wooden handle. The flat (but dull) edge is great for portioning yeast doughs, cutting lemon bars or brownies into squares, and scraping the crumbs off the counter.

Heatproof Spatulas

You can use the silicone version in place of any rubber spatula but, as it is heatproof, it also can be used to stir custards while they thicken and to stir nuts into brittles.

Nonstick Baking Sheet Liners

Use these to line cookie sheets or half sheet pans. This way, cookies will never stick, cleanup can be a breeze, and the liners can be washed and reused. I use Silpat brand.

Parchment

For lining cake pans, cookie sheets, and half sheet pans. You'll find rolls of this silicone-coated paper at many grocery or specialty shops. I prefer to pick up a big box of large sheets, which are much simpler to manage because they lay flat and are easy to cut into different sizes. I put mine in the drawer underneath my ovens, but a shelf in the basement or the top shelf of a closet will work fine. The box will last a lifetime, and the paper can substitute for tracing paper for a school project or be pressed into service as gift wrap. If you think you won't use the whole box, chip in with a few friends.

Instant-Read Thermometer

For checking the temperature of liquids when making yeast-risen breads.

Large Spoons

Use these for stirring batters and sauces. I keep a few (wooden and stainless steel) in my drawer.

Nonstick Cooking Spray

I don't know how I could bake without it. I use the original Pam (not the ones with olive oil, butter flavor, or flour). It makes quick and even work of greasing pans before flouring and of greasing bowls for rising yeast doughs.

Ice-Cream Scoops

Indispensable for serving ice cream, but I use them to scoop up cookie dough and cupcake batters as well. This way, every cookie or cupcake has that "bakery store" look. Make sure to buy the sturdy, stainless-steel ones. There are no standard sizes, so I measure the diameter of the scoop. I own several sizes, but the two I use most often measure 2 2/3 inches (6.75cm) and 1 2/3 inches (4.25cm) in diameter.

Rolling Pin

I'm partial to the French rolling pin: a sleek, round cylinder without handles. I prefer one without tapered ends. When rolling cookie or pie doughs, I have more control with my hands positioned on the pin and directly over the dough.

Top 10 Tips for Weekend Bakers

Here's my list of most valuable tips for great baking results, not listed in any particular order. They are all important.

1.
read the recipe. reread it. read it again.

I know this mantra sounds a little like "lather, rinse, repeat," but trust me on this. A first read through of a recipe will tell you what the recipe requires as far as time and technical involvement. A second read through will help you identify the ingredients and equipment you'll need, and what, if anything, you need to shop for. With more elaborate recipes like those in the Productions section, a third read through will help you start to visualize what you'll be doing. These additional readings make baking a lot more fun and guarantee a fabulous outcome.

2.
weigh your ingredients.

A cup of flour can vary by as much as an ounce. That doesn't sound like a lot, but it can make a huge difference in a finished cake. For instance, on my scale, one cup of all-purpose flour, which I measure by the spoon-and-sweep method, weighs 4 1/2 ounces, but some folks prefer the dip-and-sweep method, which yields a cup that weighs significantly more. The right amount of flour makes the difference between supple pie dough and a hard-to-handle mess that's on its way to baking into a tough crust. If you refuse to give in and buy a scale, at least promise to use the spoon-and-sweep method: give the flour a good stir, gently spoon into the appropriate-sized metal measuring cup (don't pack it in or tap the cup on the counter), and level off the excess flour with a flat-edged spatula or knife.

3.

trust your senses. follow your instincts.

A recipe can take you only so far. You're the one who will decide if the peaches in the crisp are tender enough or the cake is fully baked. How can you do this? By trusting your senses and instincts. The recipes in this book specify both a baking time and a doneness test. The baking time given is never definitive. It's simply a time window to help keep you organized and focused. The doneness tests (phrases like "until a toothpick or cake tester comes out clean" or "until golden brown") are sensory clues to guide you. Trust your nose, too. You'll begin to smell when your nuts are toasted or your sugar has caramelized by the aroma filling your kitchen. After all, your peaches might be a tad riper than those I bought, or your oven might bake hotter than mine.

4.

have everything set to go.

Pull out all the equipment you'll need and measure all the ingredients beforehand. If you've ever made a stir-fry, you know exactly what I'm talking about. *Mise en place*, French for "put in place," is the fail-safe procedure of any skilled, organized cook and baker, professional or home. I can't emphasize it enough. *Mise en place* will help you become a more efficient baker.

5.

get to know your oven.

Each oven is different and each has its quirks. So, for dependable baking, it's important to get to know your oven. Yours may be hotter than what you've set it to. Or it may have hot spots, places that are actually hotter than the rest of the oven. You might learn that it bakes unevenly and that you need to rotate cookie sheets halfway through baking, or that "bake until golden, 10 to 12 minutes" means that you need to start checking the color of cookies or cakes at 8 minutes.

6.
when mixing, scrape down the bowl.

Whether you're using a KitchenAid or a handheld mixer, every time you mix something in a bowl, some batter splatters to the side or clumps on the beaters. To ensure your batter or dough is mixed thoroughly and evenly, stop the mixer several times during mixing to scrape down the beaters and the sides of the bowl.

7.
when adding flour, mix gently.

Unless otherwise stated, use a light hand (or low speed, if using a mixer) to incorporate flour into a dough or batter. Overmixing can cause a cake, pie crust, cookie, or biscuit to turn out tough and heavy. It can also produce large holes or tunnels in a cake or muffin.

8.
bake one sheet of cookies at a time.

My personal cookie-baking strategy is to bake one sheet of cookies at a time (unless you have a convection oven). Many ovens can be unreliable and even erratic, but this way you are more likely to achieve consistent results every time.

Of course, emergencies arise and then I need to speed things along. In that case, I bake two sheets at a time. I position one oven rack in the top third of the oven and the second in the bottom third. About halfway through the baking time, I rotate and switch the position of the sheets: I turn the top sheet around so that the front is now in the back of the oven and switch its position with the bottom sheet. I rotate the bottom sheet in the same way and slide it into the top spot. This goes quickly, and again, it's important for consistent results.

9.
follow the recipe.

Baking is a science, and recipes are a getting-acquainted process. So, here's where I become a stickler. Unless you're a very experienced baker, follow the recipe exactly as written: use the same ingredients, the same baking pan, and so on. If you've done exactly that and are satisfied with the results, then you can tinker. But again, know that baking is a science – and it can be a darn quirky one when you start monkeying with the recipe.

While this sounds ridiculously basic, you'd be astonished by the volume of calls and comments I've gotten from former students, friends, and readers complaining that a particular recipe didn't work. And nearly every time, once we reconstructed the way they made the recipe, it turned out that a crucial step hadn't been followed, an ingredient had been omitted, or an incorrect substitution had been made.

10.
don't peek.

If your oven doesn't have a window (and even if it does), it will be oh-so-tempting to open the door and steal a glance at how the baking is progressing. *Don't*. Unless you're near the end of the allotted baking time and you need to start checking, refrain from opening the oven door. You can lower the temperature by as much as 50 degrees with just one peek, which will throw off your timing.

5 Indispensable Weekend Baker Techniques

1.
toasting nuts and coconut

Heat the oven to 350 degrees (180°C) and spread the nuts or coconut on a rimmed baking sheet in a single layer. Toast, shaking the pan occasionally to ensure even browning, until the nuts or coconut are fragrant and lightly browned. Depending on the type and quantity of nuts or coconut, this takes at least 8 minutes. Immediately transfer the nuts or coconut to a plate to cool (they'll keep browning after you've removed them from the oven).

To toast nuts on the stovetop, put them in a dry skillet in a single layer and toast over medium heat, shaking the pan frequently to ensure even browning, until the nuts are fragrant and lightly browned, 8 to 12 minutes. Immediately transfer the nuts to a plate to cool.

2.
perfectly whipped egg whites

Egg whites need to be whipped in a very clean bowl with very clean beaters. The slightest bit of grease will inhibit the egg whites from developing volume and air. Before adding the whites, swirl about 1 tablespoon distilled white vinegar in the bowl, coating the sides and bottom, and discard. This will eliminate any greasy residue and won't impart any vinegary flavor.

Whipped egg whites have reached the soft peak stage when you lift the beater and the peak falls back on itself. At this point, you can begin gradually adding the sugar; the whites will start to become thick and shiny as you beat them. They have reached the stiff peak stage when you lift the beater and the peak keeps its shape, rather than falling back.

3.

frosting a cake

Here are a few tricks of the trade to help you frost a cake neatly and smoothly. Using your hands, gently brush away any loose crumbs from the top and sides of the cake layer. Center the cake on its serving plate. To protect the plate from smears during frosting, slide strips of parchment, foil, or waxed paper, overlapping them slightly, under the cake to cover the plate. Spread the frosting on top of the first layer. Brush the crumbs from the top and sides of the second layer, position it on top of the frosted first layer, and press gently on the layer. Next, apply a thin layer of frosting over the top and sides of the cake. This is called a crumb coat, and it keeps stray crumbs from sticking to the final layer of frosting. Set the cake aside for five minutes (chill in the fridge, if possible). Finally, frost the cake, then gently pull away the protective strips.

4.

preparing cake pans

To ensure that your cake comes out easily from its baking pan, it is essential to prepare it as directed in the recipe. Begin with a clean pan. Any dried, crusty pieces left over from its previous use will make it harder to remove the finished cake. In some recipes I recommend that you line the bottom with parchment paper. To make the lining, set the pan on parchment and trace the bottom. Using scissors, cut out the paper shape and set aside. Next, grease the pan with either softened (not melted, unless directed) unsalted butter or a nonstick cooking spray (such as unflavored Pam). Use a paper towel or a pastry brush to apply a thin, even layer of butter over the bottom and sides of the pan, or spray the bottom and sides with an even coating of the spray. Fit the paper into the bottom of the pan. Grease the paper, if directed in the recipe. Sprinkle 2 or 3 tablespoons of all-purpose flour into the pan. Tilt and turn the pan clockwise and then counterclockwise to cover the sides and bottom. Working over the sink or wastebasket, turn the pan over and gently tap it against the surface to remove the excess flour without dislodging the paper. Place the prepared pan upside down on the counter until you are ready to fill it.

5.

making chocolate shavings and curls

Chocolate shavings are an easy garnish and can be made from a thick 10- to 12-ounce block of bittersweet, semisweet, milk, or white chocolate. The chocolate will need to be warmed slightly. Rub it with your palm or use a microwave for short bursts of about 5 seconds each (one or two should do it). Have some parchment or waxed paper ready to catch the shavings. Applying pressure, drag a vegetable peeler across the edge of the block, letting the shavings fall onto the paper. Scoop up the shavings with a soup spoon and scatter them over the top or sides of the cake, pudding, or mousse.

To make curls, use the same technique as for shavings, but the chocolate needs to be a bit warmer. Rub it with your palm or use a microwave for short bursts of about 5 seconds each (two should do it) until it feels just slightly warm; white chocolate will need less time. Press harder on the vegetable peeler. If the chocolate still won't produce big curls, it isn't warm enough, so heat it again for 5 seconds. If the chocolate melts against the peeler, let it cool a bit, and then try again. For wider curls, shave the side. Let the curls fall in an even, single layer on the paper until they cover it. Refrigerate them until firm.

Weekend Baker Go-Withs

A sauce or a topping is a welcome addition to most desserts. They offer complementary and contrasting flavors, textures, and colors. The following six recipes will "go-with" most Weekend Baker desserts.

red berry sauce

MAKES 1 1/3 CUPS

3 half-pints (12 ounces/340 grams) mixed red berries (strawberries and raspberries or blackberries), rinsed and well dried

1/2 cup (4 ounces/113 grams) granulated sugar

2 tablespoons lemon juice

Pinch of table salt

1 teaspoon finely grated lemon zest

Combine the berries, sugar, lemon juice, and salt in a food processor. Process until smooth. To remove the seeds (optional), pour the sauce through a strainer set over a bowl, pressing on the seeds to extract all the juice and pulp. Discard the seeds. Stir the lemon zest into the sauce. Serve immediately, or cover and refrigerate for up to 1 week or freeze for up to 1 month.

emergency strawberry sauce

MAKES 1 1/2 CUPS

14 (about 6 ounces/170 grams) unsweetened whole frozen strawberries

3 tablespoons granulated sugar

1/3 cup (2 1/2 fl ounces/73 ml) boiling water

Put the frozen berries and sugar in a food processor and pour the boiling water over them. Process until smooth, 2 to 3 minutes. Serve immediately, or cool, cover, and refrigerate for up to 1 week or freeze for up to 1 month.

bittersweet chocolate sauce

MAKES 1 1/3 CUPS

6 ounces (170 grams) bittersweet chocolate, finely chopped
1/2 cup (4 fl ounces/117 ml) heavy cream

2 tablespoons water
Pinch of table salt
2 tablespoons (1 ounce/28 grams) unsalted butter

In a medium saucepan, combine the chocolate, cream, water, and salt. Set the pan over medium heat and heat, whisking constantly, until the chocolate is melted and the mixture is smooth. Slide the pan from the heat, add the butter, and whisk until melted and smooth. Serve immediately, or cool, cover, and refrigerate for up to 2 weeks.

caramel sauce

MAKES 1 CUP

3/4 cup (6 ounces/170 grams) granulated sugar
3 tablespoons water
1/3 cup (2 1/2 fl ounces/73 ml) heavy cream

4 tablespoons (2 ounces/57 grams) unsalted butter, cut into 4 pieces
1/4 teaspoon pure vanilla extract
Pinch of table salt

In a medium saucepan, combine the sugar and water and stir until blended. Set over low heat and heat, stirring frequently, until the sugar has completely dissolved, about 4 minutes. Increase the heat to medium-high and bring to a boil without stirring. Continue to boil, without stirring, until the mixture takes on a deep amber color, about 5 minutes. As the mixture darkens, swirl the pan over the heat (do not stir) for even coloring. Slide the pan from the heat and add the cream and butter. The caramel will bubble up and produce very hot steam, so work carefully. Whisk until smooth. Add the vanilla and salt and whisk until smooth. Serve immediately, or cool, cover, and refrigerate for up to 2 weeks. Warm in a small saucepan over low heat or in the microwave before serving.

blueberry sauce

MAKES 2 CUPS

3 pints (12 ounces/340 grams) blueberries, rinsed and well dried

2/3 cup (5 1/4 ounces/149 grams) firmly packed light brown sugar

2 teaspoons lemon juice

1/2 teaspoon finely grated lemon zest

Pinch of table salt

In a medium saucepan, combine 2 cups (8 ounces/227 grams) of the blueberries, the brown sugar, lemon juice, lemon zest, and salt. Set the pan over medium heat and bring to a boil, stirring frequently. Reduce the heat to low and simmer, stirring constantly, until the berries are soft and the liquid is syrupy, about 3 minutes. Slide the pan from the heat, add the remaining 1 cup (4 ounces/113 grams) of berries, and gently press them against the side of the pan with the back of a spoon until lightly crushed. Serve immediately, or cool, cover, and refrigerate for up to 1 week or freeze for up to 1 month.

sweetened whipped cream

MAKES 2 CUPS

1 cup (8 fl ounces/233 ml)
   heavy cream
2 tablespoons granulated sugar

1/2 teaspoon pure vanilla extract
Pinch of table salt

Chill the bowl and beaters if your kitchen is hot. In a medium bowl, combine the cream, sugar, vanilla, and salt. Beat with an electric mixer (a handheld is the right size) on medium-high speed or with a hand whisk until medium-firm peaks form. Serve immediately, or cover and refrigerate for up to 2 hours. *Do Ahead tip:* The ingredients can be combined in the bowl, covered, and refrigerated up to 3 days before beating and serving.

baker's express

Hectic with occasional insanity – does that describe your life? It does mine. Between managing my family (just the immediate one includes four humans and two dogs), keeping up with the house (my kitchen sees some heavy traffic), volunteer work, and work-work, it feels as if there is little time for me to breathe . . . let alone bake. But I love to bake, and I refuse to give it up.

I've designed the Baker's Express section for people with active lives. These recipes can be on your table, on a weekday or weekend, in an hour or less. Baker's Express recipes are trimmed down to only the most important ingredients. Easy-to-follow techniques and shortcuts will produce baked goods that look and taste as if you spent hours in the kitchen.

But just because you need a homemade dessert in a hurry doesn't mean you need to sacrifice quality. Because Baker's Express recipes are made with only a few ingredients, the quality of what goes into them makes all the difference in the finished dessert. You don't need to spend a fortune, but you do need to choose carefully, and stock your pantry, freezer, and fridge with products that are reliably good. For a detailed list, see Pantry Essentials, page 20.

I turn to this section in time-pressed situations when an instant dessert is what's needed. When my son, Alex, has his friends over for an afternoon, I mix up a batch of One-Pot Chocolate Chip Cookies (page 62). In fewer than 30 minutes, they're ready to be devoured by a pack of hungry teenagers. When I've forgotten a promised dessert for a friend's dinner party, the 10-Minute Mocha Pots de Crème (page 98) have saved me. As the title promises, these puddings whiz up in a blender in 10 minutes when I am practically on my way out the door to the party, and chill in the hostess's fridge during dinner. And, for those long winter days when the snow continues to pile up, I cook a batch of Stovetop Double-Chocolate Pudding (page 105).

Top 10 Tips for Express Bakers

Over the years, I've fine-tuned these recipes to reflect the changes in my own lifestyle. And I've developed them further as a result of conversations and letters from readers and home bakers across the country. The recipes in this section take into consideration the baking needs, flavor preferences, and most of all, time challenges of busy people. Here are my guidelines for the quickest and best Express desserts.

1.
bake in shallow pans.

Instead of traditional loaf pans, I choose pie plates and square baking dishes to bake things up in about half the time. I use pie plates for recipes like Jalapeño Corn Bread Wedges (page 89), Pie-Plate Butterscotch Congos (page 60), and Chocolate-Nut Wedges (page 68) and square baking dishes for Lemon–Poppy Seed Squares (page 91) or Pecan-Crusted Pumpkin Squares (page 96). Batter poured into these shallow dishes bakes faster. Serving a wedge or a square of something is playful, and both shapes are easy to pick up and eat with your hands.

2.
bake in small batches.

Most of the recipes in this section yield, say, 8 scones or a dozen brownies, rather than the usual 5 dozen cookies or a cake that serves 16. If you want to bake more than what the recipe yields, the recipes can easily be doubled.

3.
bake individual items.

Muffins, biscuits, cookies, and scones cook in much less time than layer cakes, and they don't require a final assembly. Make layer cakes, Bundt cakes, upside-down cakes, and even sheet cakes when you have enough time to fuss a little. Instead, make smaller individual pies like the Half-Moon Pie Pockets (page 117), rich with the taste of pumpkin and spice, that bake up in 20 minutes. Muffins, another express item that bakes up quickly, are simply a fast variation on longer-cooking traditional quick breads. Take the Supermoist Banana-Nut Muffins (page 81) for example: they bake up in a third of the time banana bread does. To trim off even more oven time, that same batter can be used for mini-muffins or even muffin tops (page 83).

4.
a well-stocked pantry speeds things along.

Tucking away a few store-bought items in your pantry is another time-saver for last-minute desserts. A bag of lightly sweetened granola can do double duty as a morning breakfast and as an almost-instant crunchy topping for the Stovetop Apple-Cranberry Crumble (page 124). Store-bought gingersnaps or amaretti cookies can be crushed to make layers in the Very Berry Lemon Parfaits (page 102), and graham cracker crumbs provide a quick tart crust (page 112). These items enhance quick desserts with little effort. And your pantry can extend beyond the cupboard into the freezer. Frozen puff pastry and frozen 100 percent pure lemon juice are valuable time-savers and still deliver delectable outcomes. I also stash a variety of already chopped nuts in my freezer. They keep for up to one month and add elegance and crunch to toppings, crusts, cakes, and cookies. For a more extensive list, see Pantry Essentials (page 20).

5.
time is everything.

Most desserts require different baking or chilling times, but rest assured, all the Baker's Express recipes are quick and easy. Most of the mixing is done in the time it takes to heat the oven (about 15 minutes), and any baking or chilling that's needed is totally hands off, so you're free to pay the bills, make dinner, spend time with the kids, or get in a little exercise.

6.
break the rules (well, some of them).

Many baking books say that all ingredients should be at room temperature for the best results.

Though this conventional wisdom has its merits, especially for delicate layer cakes and temperamental cookie doughs, I often don't have the time or haven't thought far enough ahead to pull everything out of the fridge in advance. With that in mind, I developed and tested all the recipes in this section with ingredients straight from the fridge, and the results were great (please don't tell my pals from cooking school.)

The only exception is butter. Unless otherwise stated in the recipe, butter really does need to be at room temperature (at least soft enough to leave a dent when pressed gently) for proper mixing. If you need soft butter in a hurry, borrow a technique from the French: they whack cold butter with a rolling pin until it's softened, a handy option if you don't have a microwave.

7.
if you own a microwave, use it.

Speaking of microwaves – and of butter – I'm partial to using mine to soften or melt butter. As long as you keep watch, giving the butter a brief zap will do the job. Remember, only a few seconds or so, depending on your microwave, or you'll end up with a messy, unusable puddle.

The same holds true for melting chocolate. Though the traditional double-boiler (see What Is It? on page 74) method works well, I prefer to use the microwave. As with butter, judicious use of its power is important. Overmelted chocolate will quickly scorch and become grainy. Start with finely chopped chocolate and use a few short bursts (about 15 seconds apiece) of microwave power, stirring in between, to melt the chocolate.

8.

use the stovetop for quickest baking.

You can "bake" on the top of the stove, too. Yes, you read that correctly. A stovetop doesn't need preheating, and cooking on a burner is faster than cooking in the oven. The Stovetop Apple-Cranberry Crumble (page 124) is ready in 17 minutes, compared to the 50 minutes or more a traditional apple pie needs in the oven, plus the 15 minutes or so needed to heat up the oven. So, if you want a dessert in a hurry, turn to the 10-Minute Mocha Pots de Crème (page 98) or the Stovetop Double-Chocolate Pudding (page 105).

9.

want it even faster? try a no-bake dessert.

Did unexpected guests drop in, or did you leave too little time to make the final course for a dinner party? For instant gratification, turn to the Minted Mango Fool with Lime (page 100) or the Very Berry Lemon Parfaits (page 102). Both recipes have a sophisticated presentation and taste that belie the lightning-fast preparation.

10.

got a few extra minutes? use them.

I've streamlined the recipes down to the essential ingredients – remember, this is the express lane. And each recipe delivers a delicious result as is. But sometimes you'll see a Got Extra Time? option or a Go-Withs option. If you have the luxury of a few extra minutes, I've provided ideas for adding ingredients like chopped nuts (toasted if time permits) to an already terrific cookie (page 62) or muffin (page 81), a strawberry sauce to Chocolate-Nut Wedges (page 68), or a lemon glaze to Lemon–Poppy Seed Squares (page

91). These additions take only a little more time and will enhance the dessert, but are definitely optional.

Whether you're new to baking or a dyed-in-the-wool veteran who still wants to fit it into your frenzied life, this is the section for you, so have fun with it. Head to the kitchen, bring out the flour and sugar, and get baking. I know you'll be delighted with the results.

Cookies and Bars

• • •

toasted almond cookies

MAKES 20 COOKIES

my brothers – I have three, all older – and I are all passionate ice cream fans, a trait we picked up from our dad. As kids, in Brooklyn Heights and Connecticut, the sound of the Good Humor ice cream truck's ringing bells was music to our ears. We were all certain of our choices – I was (and still am) a chocolate chip girl, Steve was a Creamsicle guy, Darv's usual was the Chocolate Eclair bar, and Tim adored the Toasted Almond bar. This cookie is my tribute to Tim's favorite Good Humor ice-cream bar. Almond scented, buttery, and made with a generous amount of crunchy almonds, this cookie tastes even better than the ice-cream bar that inspired it.

12 tablespoons (6 ounces/170 grams) unsalted butter, at room temperature

1/2 cup (4 ounces/113 grams) granulated sugar

Pinch of table salt

1 yolk from large egg

3/4 teaspoon pure vanilla extract

1/8 teaspoon pure almond extract

1 1/2 cups (6 3/4 ounces/191 grams) all-purpose flour

1/2 cup (2 ounces/57 grams) slivered almonds, toasted (see page 40)

1. Position an oven rack on the middle rung. Heat the oven to 350 degrees (180°C). Line 2 cookie sheets with parchment paper or nonstick baking liners (I like the Silpat).

2. In a large bowl, combine the butter, sugar, and salt. Beat with an electric mixer (stand mixer fitted with the paddle attachment or handheld mixer) on medium speed until well blended. Add the egg yolk and vanilla and almond extracts and beat until combined. Pour in the flour and toasted almonds and beat on low speed until the dough begins to clump together. The nuts will break up a bit, but that's okay.

3. Using a small ice-cream scoop (about 1 2/3 inches/4.25cm in diameter) or 2 tablespoons, shape rounded mounds of about 2 tablespoons dough (they will be about 1 1/2 inches/4cm in diameter) on the prepared cookie sheets, spacing them about 1 1/2 inches/4cm apart. Using your fingers, press down on each mound to flatten slightly.

4. Bake 1 sheet at a time (make sure to use a cooled sheet for the second batch) until the cookies look dry on top and the edges are golden brown, about 17 minutes. Transfer the cookie sheet to a rack to cool for about 10 minutes. Using a spatula, lift the cookies from the sheet onto a rack and let cool completely.

storage: Layer the baked and cooled cookies between parchment or waxed paper in an airtight container. They can be stored at room temperature for up to 1 week or in the freezer for up to 3 months.

big-time peanut butter cookies

MAKES 20 COOKIES

i've given this classic cookie big-time peanut flavor by making peanut butter the only fat in the recipe. With PB as the key component, the cookies turn out so creamy and moist you won't believe there's no butter. And, with only five other ingredients, the dough comes together in the time it takes to heat up the oven. Can't get much faster than that. If you want a bit of crunch, use peanut butter with chunks.

1 1/3 cups (10 ounces/284 grams) smooth or crunchy peanut butter, at room temperature

3/4 cup (6 ounces/170 grams) firmly packed light brown sugar

1 large egg

1 teaspoon pure vanilla extract

1/4 cup (1 ounce/28 grams) all-purpose flour

1 cup (6 ounces/170 grams) mini candy-coated chocolates (I use mini M&M's), optional

1. Position an oven rack on the middle rung. Heat the oven to 350 degrees (180°C). Line 2 cookie sheets with parchment or nonstick baking liners (I like the Silpat).

2. In a large bowl, combine the peanut butter and brown sugar. Beat with an electric mixer (stand mixer fitted with the paddle attachment or handheld mixer) on medium speed until well blended. Add the egg and vanilla and beat just until blended. Pour in the flour and beat on low speed just until blended. Stir in the chocolate candies, if using (the batter is quite thick and an electric mixer would pulverize the candies).

3. Using a small ice-cream scoop (about 1 2/3 inches/4.25cm in diameter) or 2 tablespoons, scoop up rounded tablespoonfuls of the dough and, using your hands, shape into balls (about 1 1/2 inches/4cm in diameter). Arrange on the prepared cookie sheets, spacing them about 2 inches (5cm)

apart. Using the tines of a fork, press on each ball to flatten slightly. If necessary, lightly coat the tines in flour to prevent them from sticking to the dough.

4. Bake 1 sheet at a time (make sure to use a cooled sheet for the second batch) until the cookies look dry on top, about 12 minutes. Transfer the cookie sheet to a rack to cool for about 10 minutes. Using a spatula, lift the cookies from the sheet onto the rack and let cool completely.

storage: Layer the baked and cooled cookies between parchment or waxed paper in an airtight container. They can be stored at room temperature for up to 1 week or in the freezer for up to 3 months.

got extra time?

Before serving, drizzle a little chocolate glaze (page 313) over the tops of the cooled cookies. To do this, position the cooled cookies on a wire rack set over a large piece of parchment or foil. Using a small spoon, drizzle the cooled glaze over the cookies in a zigzag pattern. Let the chocolate harden, about 10 minutes, before serving. Cover and store the remaining glaze in the fridge. It makes an excellent sauce for cake or ice cream.

prescription-strength fudge brownies

MAKES 1 DOZEN 2-INCH (5CM) BROWNIES

One bite of this superfudgy, chewy brownie and you'll never want to make another brownie recipe. The intense chocolate flavor explodes in your mouth, and the texture attains the perfect balance between fudge and cookie. For extra flavor and texture, you can scatter chopped nuts, peppermint candies, or chocolate or peanut butter chips on top of the batter before baking. And, for a brownie extravaganza, mix 1/2 cup (3 ounces/85 grams) chocolate or peanut butter chips into the batter and then sprinkle 1/2 cup (2 ounces/57 grams) walnuts or pecans over the batter.

Cocoa powder is one of my secret weapons. It imparts just as much – if not more – chocolate flavor as melted chocolate, and you'll have fewer pots to wash come cleanup time. As for cocoa powders, natural or Dutch-process type will work well.

12 tablespoons (6 ounces/170 grams) unsalted butter, cut into 6 pieces

3/4 cup (2 1/4 ounces/64 grams) unsweetened cocoa powder (natural or Dutch process), sifted if lumpy

1 1/2 cups (12 ounces/340 grams) granulated sugar

1/4 teaspoon table salt

2 large eggs

1 1/2 teaspoons pure vanilla extract

3/4 cup (3 1/2 ounces/99 grams) all-purpose flour

1/2 cup topping (choose from semisweet, peanut butter, or white chocolate chips; coarsely chopped walnuts or pecans (no need to toast); or chopped hard peppermint candies), optional

1. Position an oven rack on the middle rung. Heat the oven to 350 degrees (180°C). Lightly grease the bottom and sides of an 8-inch (20cm) square baking dish.

2. Put the butter in a medium saucepan and set over medium heat, stirring occasionally, until the butter is melted. Slide the pan from the heat and add the cocoa powder. Whisk until the mixture is smooth. Add the sugar and salt and whisk until blended. Add the eggs one at a time, whisking after each addition just until blended. Whisk in the vanilla with the second egg. Sprinkle the flour over the chocolate mixture and stir with a rubber spatula just until blended.

3. Scrape the batter into the prepared baking dish and spread evenly. Scatter the topping evenly over the batter, if using. Bake until a toothpick or cake tester inserted in the center comes out with small, gooey clumps of brownie sticking to it, about 32 minutes. Don't overbake or the brownies won't be fudgy. Transfer the baking dish to a rack to cool.

4. Using a bench scraper or a knife, cut the cooled brownie into 3 equal strips, and then cut each strip into 4 equal pieces. If the brownie is still warm, it will be hard to cut it cleanly. But even if these fudgy cookies are completely cool, some sticky crumbs will be left on the knife.

storage: Once the uncut brownie has cooled for about 20 minutes in the baking dish, it can be frozen. Invert the brownie onto a rack, let cool completely, and, still uncut, wrap tightly and freeze for up to 1 month.

pie-plate butterscotch congos

MAKES ONE 9-INCH (22.75CM) "PIE," OR 8 WEDGES

this is probably one of the most versatile desserts in my repertoire. The dough mixes up in no time, and the butterscotch wedges can be tucked into a lunchbox or presented on china plates. For dinner parties, add drama and elegance by serving the wedges warm (15 minutes in a 300-degree /150°C oven does the job) with some Sweetened Whipped Cream (page 46) and a scattering of raspberries or sliced kiwifruits or strawberries.

In the summer, our family loves to pack picnic dinners and head to the beach near our house to catch the last hours of sunlight and take in the breezes from Long Island Sound. These outings are strictly no-frills events, and the congo wedges please all ages. I bring the whole pie plate (sometimes straight from the oven) and wait until after dinner to cut them.

1 1/4 cups (5 1/2 ounces/156 grams) all-purpose flour

1 1/2 teaspoons baking powder

1/4 teaspoon table salt

8 tablespoons (4 ounces/113 grams) unsalted butter, at room temperature

1 cup (8 ounces/227 grams) firmly packed light brown sugar

1 large egg

1 teaspoon pure vanilla extract

1/2 cup (3 ounces/85 grams) butterscotch chips

1/3 cup (1 1/2 ounces/43 grams) medium-fine chopped walnuts (no need to toast)

1/4 cup (3/4 ounce/21 grams) sweetened shredded dried coconut

1. Position an oven rack on the middle rung. Heat the oven to 350 degrees (180°C). Lightly grease the bottom and sides of a 9-inch (22.75cm) pie plate (I use Pyrex).

2. In a small bowl, combine the flour, baking powder, and salt. Whisk until well blended. In a large bowl, combine the butter and brown sugar.

Beat with an electric mixer (stand mixer fitted with the paddle attachment or handheld mixer) on medium speed until well blended. Add the egg and vanilla and beat just until blended. Pour in the flour mixture and beat on low speed just until incorporated. Pour in the butterscotch chips, nuts, and coconut and beat just until combined.

3. Scrape the dough into the prepared pie plate and spread evenly. Bake until a toothpick or cake tester inserted in the center comes out almost clean (it should still have a few moist crumbs clinging to it), 30 to 32 minutes. Transfer the pie plate to a rack to cool.

4. Using a knife or pie server, cut the pie into 8 equal wedges and serve warm or at room temperature.

storage: Once the uncut congo has cooled for about 20 minutes in the pie plate, it can be frozen. Invert the congo onto a rack, let cool completely, and, still uncut, wrap tightly and freeze for up to 1 month.

one-pot chocolate chip cookies

MAKES 26 COOKIES

these cookies have a chewy, chocolaty inside and a sugary, slightly crisp outside. To guarantee their special texture, I use the same technique that keeps my fudge brownies moist: melting the butter in a saucepan. And there's only one pot to clean up.

Friends of my children beg them to bring along these cookies whenever they head out on a road trip. They have been to Girl Scout campouts, ski weekends, family reunions, and even went along on an eighth-grade field trip to Washington, D.C. They really get around.

See the Big Cookie variation at the end of the recipe.

8 tablespoons (4 ounces/113 grams) unsalted butter, cut into 4 pieces

1/2 cup (4 ounces/113 grams) firmly packed light brown sugar

1/3 cup (2 1/2 ounces/71 grams) granulated sugar

1 1/2 cups (6 3/4 ounces/191 grams) all-purpose flour

1 teaspoon baking powder

1/4 teaspoon table salt

1 large egg

1 teaspoon pure vanilla extract

1 cup (6 ounces/170 grams) semisweet chocolate chips (feel free to substitute white chocolate or bittersweet chocolate chips)

1/2 cup (2 ounces/57 grams) coarsely chopped nuts (walnuts or pecans are my favorite – no need to toast), optional

1. Position an oven rack on the middle rung. Heat the oven to 350 degrees (180°C). Line 2 cookie sheets with parchment or nonstick baking liners (I like the Silpat).

2. Put the butter in a medium saucepan and set over medium heat, stirring occasionally, until the butter is melted. Slide the pan from the heat and add the brown sugar and granulated sugar. Whisk until no lumps remain. Set aside to let cool, about 5 minutes.

3. In a medium bowl, combine the flour, baking powder, and salt. Whisk until well blended. Once the butter mixture has cooled, add the egg and vanilla and whisk until blended. Pour in the flour mixture and stir with a rubber spatula until blended. Stir in the chocolate chips and the nuts, if using.

4. Using a small ice-cream scoop (about 1 2/3 inches/4.25cm in diameter) or 2 tablespoons, drop scant 2-tablespoon mounds of the dough onto the prepared cookie sheets, arranging them about 1 1/2 inches (4cm) apart. (At this point, the loaded cookie sheets can be slipped into the freezer until the cookies are frozen, about 1 hour. Then transfer the cookies to heavy-duty freezer bags and freeze for up to 3 months. To bake, remove from the freezer, arrange on lined cookie sheets, and leave on the counter to thaw slightly while the oven heats.)

5. Bake 1 sheet at a time (make sure to use a cooled sheet for the second batch) until the cookies are light golden around the edges and puffed, about 12 minutes. If these cookies are overbaked, they won't come out chewy. Transfer the cookie sheet to a rack to cool for about 10 minutes. Using a spatula, lift the cookies from the sheet onto a rack and let cool completely.

storage: Layer the baked and cooled cookies between parchment or waxed paper in an airtight container. They can be stored at room temperature for up to 5 days or in the freezer for up to 3 months. You don't even need to thaw them completely. They're just as delicious cold.

Big Cookie Variation: In general, my children Alex and Tierney like their cookies on the big side. To appease their ever-growing appetites, I scoop up 1/4-cup portions of this cookie dough, arrange them about 3 inches (7.75cm) apart on the prepared cookie sheets, and flatten the mounds slightly with lightly floured fingertips. Bake 1 sheet at a time until the cookies are light golden around the edges and puffed, about 13 minutes. Remove from the oven and let cool as directed for the regular-sized cookies. Makes 10 cookies.

nutty cinnamon elephant ears

MAKES 22 COOKIES

i have Americanized the classic French cookies known as *palmiers*, or "palm leaves," by adding cinnamon and nuts and keeping their whimsical name. The pastry bakes up as two attached spirals reminiscent of an elephant's ears. With each bite of this pastry cookie, the cinnamon sugar–filled layers shatter into a thousand buttery pieces and dissolve almost instantaneously in your mouth.

While puff pastry is fun to make, I can't remember the last time I made it. It's time-consuming and takes some work. This is why frozen puff pastry is a big exception in my book when it comes to frozen baking items. It's almost as good as what you make from scratch.

1 sheet frozen puff pastry, 9 1/2 inches square (I like Pepperidge Farm brand)

3 tablespoons (1 1/2 ounces/43 grams) unsalted butter, cut into 2 pieces

1/2 teaspoon pure vanilla extract

3/4 cup (6 ounces/170 grams) granulated sugar

1/2 cup (2 ounces/57 grams) confectioners' sugar

1 teaspoon ground cinnamon

1/3 cup (1 1/2 ounces/43 grams) finely chopped walnuts or pecans (no need to toast)

1. Remove 1 sheet of frozen puff pastry from the box, set it on a lightly floured surface, and cover it with plastic wrap so that it doesn't dry out. Do *not* unfold it at this point. Wrap the remaining sheet in plastic wrap and return it to the freezer for another use. Let the covered puff pastry sit on the countertop until thawed and just pliable, about 20 minutes.

2. Meanwhile, position an oven rack on the middle rung. Heat the oven to 375 degrees (190°C). Line 2 cookie sheets with parchment or nonstick baking liners (I like the Silpat).

3. Melt the butter in a small saucepan or in the microwave. Stir in the vanilla and set aside to cool slightly. In a small bowl, combine the granulated sugar, confectioners' sugar, and cinnamon. Stir until well blended. Measure out about 2/3 cup (5 1/4 ounces/149 grams) of the sugar mixture into a small bowl, and stir the chopped nuts into it; set aside.

4. Sprinkle some of the remaining sugar mixture on a work surface. Unfold the thawed puff pastry on top of the sugar mixture. Generously sprinkle some of the sugar mixture on top of the puff pastry, and spread it with your hand to cover the dough to the edges. Using a rolling pin, roll out the dough, sprinkling the top and bottom with more of the sugar mixture to prevent the dough from sticking to the work surface, into a 10-by-18-inch (25-by-45cm) rectangle.

5. Brush the cooled melted butter evenly over the top surface of the dough. Sprinkle the reserved nut-sugar mixture (and any sugar mixture remaining from rolling) over the dough. Spread the sugar with your hand to cover the dough evenly. Starting at a narrow end, roll up the dough, jelly-roll style, to the center. Then, starting at the opposite edge, roll up the dough so that the 2 rolls meet in the center. Turn the roll upside down so that the scrolls face down. (At this point, the rolled dough can be wrapped in plastic wrap and frozen for up to 3 months. Thaw overnight in the fridge, or on a countertop for about 1 hour, before continuing with the recipe.)

6. Using a sharp knife, cut the roll into slices 2/3 inch (1.75cm) thick. Arrange the slices about 2 inches (5cm) apart on the prepared cookie sheets. Bake 1 sheet at a time (make sure to use a cooled sheet for the second batch) until the cookies are golden brown, about 15 minutes. Transfer the sheet to a rack to cool for about 10 minutes. Using a spatula, lift the cookies from the sheet onto a rack and let cool completely.

storage: Layer the baked and cooled cookies between parchment or waxed paper in an airtight container. They can be stored at room temperature for up to 1 week.

Cakes – Small and Large
• • •

maple sugar scones
MAKES 8 SCONES

Unlike most scones, these have two lives. Fresh out of the oven, they are moist, cakelike, and full of the flavor of maple. The next morning, they take on a more traditional crumbly scone texture and a heightened maple taste. They are scrumptious when reheated or toasted and spread with a bit of butter.

3 cups (13 1/2 ounces/383 grams) all-purpose flour

2/3 cup (3 ounces/85 grams) granulated maple sugar (see What Is It? below)

8 tablespoons (4 ounces/113 grams) very cold unsalted butter, cut into 8 pieces

1 teaspoon baking powder

1/2 teaspoon baking soda

1/2 teaspoon table salt

1/2 cup (2 ounces/57 grams) medium-fine chopped pecans, toasted (see page 40), optional

2/3 cup (5 fl ounces/146 ml) buttermilk

2 tablespoons pure maple syrup

1 large egg

for the topping:

2 tablespoons pure maple syrup

2 teaspoons granulated maple sugar

1. Position an oven rack on the middle rung. Heat the oven to 400 degrees (200°C). Line 1 cookie sheet with parchment or a nonstick baking liner (I like the Silpat).

2. In a large bowl, combine the flour, maple sugar, baking powder, baking soda, and salt. Whisk until well blended. Add the butter pieces. Using a pastry blender or 2 table knives, cut the butter into the flour mixture until the butter pieces are no larger than peas. Or combine the dry ingredients and the butter in a food processor and pulse until the butter is incorporated correctly, then dump the mixture into a bowl. Add the nuts, if using, and mix briefly into the butter-flour mixture. Mix together the buttermilk, maple syrup, and egg with a fork just until blended. (I like to measure the buttermilk in a 2-cup Pyrex measuring cup and then mix the syrup and egg with a fork right in the same cup. It saves dirtying a bowl.) Drizzle the liquid over the flour mixture and toss with a rubber spatula just until the dough comes together in moist clumps.

3. Dump the shaggy dough onto a lightly floured work surface. Briefly knead the dough to combine, and then shape it into a 7-inch (17.75cm) round. Using a lightly floured knife, cut the dough into 8 equal wedges. Arrange the wedges on the prepared cookie sheet, spacing them about 2 inches (5cm) apart. Brush the tops of the wedges liberally with the maple syrup and sprinkle evenly with the maple sugar.

4. Bake until puffed and a toothpick or cake tester inserted in the center of 1 scone comes out clean, about 18 minutes. Transfer the cookie sheet to a rack to cool for about 15 minutes. Using a spatula, lift the scones from the sheet to a rack to cool. Serve warm or at room temperature.

storage: Layer the baked and cooled scones between parchment or waxed paper in an airtight container. They can be stored at room temperature for up to 4 days or in the freezer for up to 3 months.

what is it? (pure maple sugar)

Pure maple sugar is made by boiling maple sap or syrup until almost no moisture remains. The end result is a naturally sweet granulated sugar with intense maple flavor. I order mine from King Arthur Flour (www.kingarthur flour.com/800-827-6836), but in a pinch I have substituted the same amount of firmly packed light brown sugar with good results.

chocolate-nut wedges

MAKES ONE 9-INCH (23CM) "PIE," OR 8 WEDGES

these nut-topped wedges deliver the same big chocolate flavor as brownies, but have a slightly more refined, cakelike texture. Adding canola oil rather than butter to the batter makes the texture especially moist, and the hint of cinnamon offers a bit of Mexican complexity. If you are in need of a quickie birthday cake, stick a few candles into the uncut pie and serve it straight from the plate. It's fun, fast, and travels beautifully.

3/4 cup (3 1/2 ounces/99 grams) all-purpose flour

3/4 cup (6 ounces/170 grams) granulated sugar

1/3 cup (2 ounces/57 grams) semi-sweet chocolate chips

1/2 cup (1 1/2 ounces/43 grams) unsweetened cocoa powder (natural or Dutch process), sifted if lumpy

1/4 teaspoon ground cinnamon

1/4 teaspoon baking powder

1/4 teaspoon table salt

1/3 cup (2 1/2 fl ounces/73 ml) canola or corn oil

2 large eggs

1/2 cup (2 ounces/57 grams) coarsely chopped nuts (hazelnuts, walnuts, or pecans), no need to toast

go-withs: Sweetened Whipped Cream (page 46), Emergency Strawberry Sauce (page 43), Summer Jumbled Fruit (page 75), or ice cream (optional).

1. Position an oven rack on the middle rung. Heat the oven to 350 degrees (180°C). Lightly grease the bottom and sides of a 9-inch (22.75cm) pie plate (I use Pyrex).

2. In a medium bowl, combine the flour, sugar, chocolate chips, cocoa powder, cinnamon, baking powder, and salt. Whisk until well blended. Mix together the oil and eggs with a fork just until blended. (I like to measure the oil in a 2-cup Pyrex measure and then mix the egg right in the same cup. It saves dirtying a bowl.) Pour the liquid over the flour mixture and mix with a rubber spatula until blended. Scrape into the prepared pie plate and spread evenly. Scatter the chopped nuts evenly over the top.

3. Bake until a toothpick or cake tester inserted in the center comes out with only a few gooey pieces clinging to it, about 20 minutes. Transfer the baking dish to a rack and let cool. Cut the pie into 8 wedges. Serve with one of the Go-Withs, if desired.

storage: Cover the cooled wedges in the pie plate with plastic wrap and store at room temperature for up to 3 days. To freeze, allow the uncut pie to cool for about 20 minutes in the pie plate, then invert the pie onto a rack, let cool completely, and, still uncut, wrap tightly and freeze for up to 1 month.

warm cinnamon-spiced blueberry cake

MAKES ONE 9-INCH (22.75CM) CAKE, OR 8 TO 10 SERVINGS

the blueberry topping here is added partway through baking so that some of it can sink into the cake to provide a moist filling. Claire Van de Berghe, my trusted recipe tester, reports that her family would like more blueberries in the topping. I like it just the way it is, but if you're crazy for blueberries, like everyone in the Van de Berghe family, add another 1/4 cup (1 1/4 ounces/35 grams), no more. This cake takes a bit longer than an hour from start to finish, but the result is well worth the extra 10 minutes.

1 1/3 cups (6 ounces/170 grams) all-purpose flour

3/4 teaspoon baking powder

1/4 teaspoon baking soda

3/4 teaspoon ground cinnamon

1/4 teaspoon table salt

6 tablespoons (3 ounces/85 grams) unsalted butter, at room temperature

1 cup (8 ounces/227 grams) granulated sugar

2 large eggs

1 teaspoon pure vanilla extract

2/3 cup (5 1/2 ounces/156 grams) sour cream

for the topping:

3/4 cup (3 ounces/85 grams) blueberries, rinsed and well dried

3 tablespoons granulated sugar

1 tablespoon all-purpose flour

1/2 teaspoon ground cinnamon

1. Position an oven rack on the middle rung. Heat the oven to 350 degrees (180°C). Lightly grease and flour the bottom and sides of a 9-by-2-inch (22.75cm-by-5cm) round cake pan, tapping out the excess flour.

2. In a medium bowl, combine the flour, baking powder, baking soda, cinnamon, and salt. Whisk until well blended. In a large bowl, combine the butter and sugar. Beat with an electric mixer (stand mixer fitted with the paddle attachment or handheld mixer) on medium speed until well blended. Add the eggs one at a time and beat just until blended. Add the vanilla with the second egg. Using a rubber spatula, fold the dry ingredients into the butter mixture in 3 batches alternately with the sour cream, beginning and ending with the dry ingredients. Scrape the batter into the prepared pan and spread evenly. Bake for 10 minutes.

3. As soon as you put the cake in the oven, make the topping. In a small bowl, combine the blueberries, sugar, flour, and cinnamon. Mix the ingredients together with a fork, lightly crushing the blueberries.

4. After the cake has baked for 10 minutes, sprinkle the topping evenly over the top of the cake. Continue baking until a toothpick or cake tester inserted in the center of the cake comes out clean, about 30 minutes longer.

5. Transfer the cake to a rack to cool for 10 minutes. Run a knife around the inside edge of the pan to loosen the cake. Using a thick, dry dish towel to protect your hands, invert a large, flat plate on top of the cake pan and, holding both the pan and the plate, invert them together. Lift the pan off the cake. Invert a flat serving plate on the bottom of the cake and invert the cake one more time so that the blueberries are on top. Serve warm or at room temperature.

storage: Cover the cooled cake in plastic wrap and store at room temperature for up to 5 days.

emergency blender cupcakes

MAKES 1 DOZEN FROSTED CUPCAKES

My friends have conscripted me as their dessert coach, and one of my tasks is to help them out of baking crises. An emergency call came late one evening from Craig Umanoff, father of Charlotte and husband to my friend Martha Holmberg (publisher of *Fine Cooking* magazine). Martha was traveling, and Charlotte announced late in the evening that it was her turn to bring cupcakes to school the next morning. Well, Craig is quite a renaissance man and wasn't about to succumb to a boxed cake mix, even at 10:15 p.m., so he was desperate for an easy and quick recipe. We spent a few minutes on the phone and pieced one together. I'm not sure how the cupcakes turned out (Craig likes to improvise), but his predicament did inspire me to develop my own emergency cupcake recipe.

The following cupcakes and frosting are dedicated to all of us who have been caught by surprise and need a few homemade frosted cupcakes a.s.a.p. The frosting is based on one of my mom's old standby recipes, and is very fudgy. The cupcake batter comes together in minutes with the help of a blender, but I've also given directions for whisking it in a bowl – it's almost as quick.

for the cupcakes:

1 cup (4 1/2 ounces/128 grams) all-purpose flour

1/2 cup (1 1/2 ounces/43 grams) unsweetened natural cocoa powder (not Dutch process), sifted if lumpy

1 cup (8 ounces/227 grams) granulated sugar

1/2 teaspoon baking soda

1/4 teaspoon table salt

3/4 cup (6 fl ounces/175 ml) hot water

1/2 cup (4 fl ounces/117 ml) canola or corn oil

1 large egg

1 1/2 teaspoons pure vanilla extract

for the fudgy frosting:

8 ounces (227 grams) bittersweet
    chocolate, finely chopped
8 tablespoons (4 ounces/113 grams)
    unsalted butter, cut into 4 pieces
1 cup (8 fl ounces/233 ml)
    sweetened condensed milk
    (not evaporated)

1/4 cup (2 fl ounces/58 ml) light
    corn syrup
1 teaspoon pure vanilla extract
Pinch of table salt

go-withs: colored sprinkles for garnish (optional)

1. TO MAKE THE CUPCAKES

Position an oven rack on the middle rung. Heat the oven to 375 degrees (190°C). Line 12 regular-sized muffin cups with paper or foil liners.

2.

Combine the flour, cocoa, sugar, baking soda, and salt in a blender. Cover with the lid and blend on medium speed until blended. Pour in the water, oil, egg, and vanilla. Cover with the lid and blend on medium-high speed until smooth and well blended, stopping to scrape down the sides once or twice. Alternatively, combine the flour, cocoa, sugar, baking soda, and salt in a medium bowl. Whisk until well blended. Pour in the water, oil, and vanilla. Add the egg and whisk until blended, about 1 minute.

3.

Pour into the lined muffin cups, dividing evenly. Bake until a toothpick or cake tester inserted in the center of 1 cupcake comes out clean, 17 to 19 minutes. Transfer the muffin pan to a rack to cool for about 10 minutes, and then carefully remove the cupcakes from the pan and set them on the rack to cool completely. (At this point, the unfrosted cupcakes can be covered in plastic and stored at room temperature for up to 3 days or frozen for up to 1 month.)

4. TO MAKE THE FROSTING

While the cupcakes are baking, melt the chocolate and butter in a double boiler (see What Is It? below) or in the microwave (see page 51). Add the condensed milk, corn syrup, vanilla, and salt. Whisk until well blended. Set aside at room temperature, whisking frequently. It will continue to thick as it cools. When the frosting is completely cool, cover the bowl with plastic wrap until the cupcakes are completely cool and ready to frost. No need to refrigerate. (At this point, the cooled frosting can be covered with plastic wrap and stowed at room temperature for up to 1 day or in the refrigerator for up to 2 weeks. Bring the frosting to room temperature before using it.)

5. Using a small spatula or a table knife, spread 2 to 3 tablespoons frosting on top of each cupcake, then dust with colored sprinkles, if desired. (I like my frosting piled high, so I use about 3 tablespoons per cupcake. If you're not as much of a frosting fan, use less and store the unused frosting in the fridge. It will last for about 3 weeks. It can be used as a frosting, or it can be warmed to make a silky fudge sauce.)

storage: Cover the frosted cupcakes with plastic wrap and store at room temperature for up to 4 days.

what is it? (double boiler)

A double boiler provides the gentle heat you need when melting chocolate or cooking custards or other egg-based mixtures. These mixtures are more likely to scorch or curdle over the direct heat of a stove burner. You can buy a double boiler, but it's easy to construct one with a saucepan and a stainless-steel bowl that will rest securely in the top of the pan. Fill the saucepan with about 2 inches (5cm) of water and place the bowl on top. Check the water level before positioning the bowl. The water must not touch the bottom of the bowl. Set the pan and bowl over medium-high heat and bring the water to a boil. Reduce the heat to low and proceed as directed.

gingered shortcakes with jumbled fruit

MAKES 6 SERVINGS

Shortcakes are much-loved American classics, and they're a staple in almost every baker's repertoire. In my ginger version the spice intermingles with the buttery richness of the little cake, adding just enough zing without being aggressive. I buck tradition and cut my shortcakes into squares, rather than circles. I think squares are less fussy, easier to shape, and just as attractive, and there's no waste.

When it comes to the jumbled fruit, I take advantage of the best of my market's offerings, so I've included a summer and a winter variation. In the warmer months, toss together plums, berries, and kiwifruits. It's a heavenly combination and a snap to assemble. My cool-weather version of dried fruits simmered in fresh orange juice complements the ginger and warms the soul. To both, I add a hit of crystallized ginger. It releases the fragrance and flavor of the fruits.

for the shortcakes:

1 2/3 cups (7 1/2 ounces/213 grams) all-purpose flour

3 tablespoons granulated sugar

1 tablespoon baking powder

1/2 teaspoon ground ginger

3/4 teaspoon table salt

8 tablespoons (4 ounces/113 grams) very cold unsalted butter, cut into 8 pieces

3/4 cup (6 fl ounces/175 ml) buttermilk

1/2 teaspoon pure vanilla extract

for the summer jumbled fruit:

3 tablespoons honey

1 tablespoon lime juice

1/2 teaspoon finely grated fresh ginger

1/2 teaspoon finely grated lime zest

Pinch of salt

2 firm but ripe plums, pitted and cut into 1/2-inch-thick wedges

2 ripe kiwifruits, peeled and cut into 1/4-inch-thick wedges

1/2 pint (5 ounces/142 grams/about 1 cup) blueberries or raspberries, rinsed and well dried

2 teaspoons finely chopped crystallized ginger

for the winter jumbled fruit:

1 cup (8 ounces/227 grams) packed dried apricots

1 cup (8 ounces/227 grams) dried figs (I like Calimyrnas)

1 3/4 cup (14 fl ounces/408 ml) orange juice

1/3 cup (2 1/2 ounces/71 grams) firmly packed light brown sugar

3/4 cup (3 3/4 ounces/106 grams) dried tart cherries

1/2 cup (2 1/2 ounces/71 grams) golden raisins

1 teaspoon finely grated fresh ginger

2 teaspoons finely chopped crystallized ginger

go-with: Sweetened Whipped Cream (page 46)

1. TO MAKE THE SHORTCAKES

Position an oven rack on the middle rung. Heat the oven to 400 degrees (200°C). Line 1 cookie sheet with parchment or a nonstick baking liner (I like the Silpat).

2. In a medium bowl, combine the flour, sugar, baking powder, ground ginger, and salt. Whisk until well blended. Using a pastry blender or 2 table knives, cut the butter into the flour mixture until the butter pieces are no larger than peas. Or combine the dry ingredients and the butter in a food processor and pulse until the butter is incorporated correctly, then dump

the mixture into a bowl. Add the buttermilk and vanilla and gently toss with a rubber spatula just until the dough comes together in moist clumps.

3. Dump the shaggy dough onto a work surface – no need to flour the surface. Gently press the dough into a thick rectangle about 6 by 4 inches (15.25cm by 10cm). If the dough is sticky, lightly flour your fingers. (If you want very neat squares, use a sharp knife to trim off a bit of the edges. Personally, I don't bother trimming. I prefer the rustic look of the untrimmed squares.) Using a large, sharp knife or bench scraper, cut the dough into 6 equal squares. Arrange the squares on the prepared cookie sheet, spacing them about 3 inches (7.75cm) apart.

4. Bake until puffed and light brown, about 18 minutes. Transfer the cookie sheet to a rack to cool for about 10 minutes. Using a spatula, slide the shortcakes onto a rack to cool for at least 10 minutes. Serve warm (my preference) or at room temperature.

5. TO MAKE SUMMER JUMBLED FRUIT

In a small saucepan, combine the honey, lime juice, ginger, lime zest, and salt. Set the pan over medium-high heat and stir frequently until the mixture boils and is smooth and syrupy, about 3 minutes. Set aside to cool slightly. (At this point, the syrup can be cooled completely, covered, and stored in the fridge for up to 2 days. To use, reheat on the stovetop or pour the syrup into a 1-cup Pyrex measure and reheat in the microwave before tossing it with the fruit.) Dump the plums, kiwifruits, and berries into a large bowl. Drizzle the warm honey dressing over the fruit, sprinkle with the crystallized ginger, and gently toss to coat the fruit. Serve immediately, or cover with plastic and refrigerate for up to 24 hours. Proceed as directed in step 6.

5. TO MAKE WINTER JUMBLED FRUIT

Using kitchen shears, snip the dried apricots into small pieces and cut the dried figs in halves or quarters, depending on their size. In a medium saucepan, combine the orange juice and brown sugar. Set over medium heat and stir frequently until the sugar is dissolved. Increase the heat to high and bring the liquid to a boil. Reduce the heat to medium and add the apricots and figs. Cook until the juice is reduced slightly and the fruit is just tender, about 4 minutes. Add the dried cherries, golden raisins, and fresh ginger. Simmer until the fruit is tender and the liquid is thick and syrupy, about 4 minutes longer. Remove from the heat and set aside until ready to serve (or let it cool, cover, and refrigerate for up to 4 days, then reheat on the stovetop or in the microwave.) Just before serving, warm the fruit, if necessary, and stir in the crystallized ginger. Proceed as directed in step 6.

6. TO SERVE THE SHORTCAKES

Using a serrated knife, split the shortcakes in half horizonally. Place the bottom halves, cut side up, on serving plates. Spoon some of the fruit, including the juices, over the shortcake bottoms and top with a dollop of the whipped cream. Add a little more of the fruit and top with the shortcake lids, cut side down. Serve immediately.

storage: Wrap the shortcakes in plastic wrap and store at room temperature for up to 24 hours or in the freezer for up to 1 month. Before serving, refresh the shortcakes by warming them in a 300-degree (150°C) oven for about 15 minutes.

uncomplicated fruit-topped yellow cake

MAKES ONE 9-INCH (22.75CM) CAKE, OR 8 SERVINGS

This cake is so simple to mix up that your biggest challenge will be deciding what fruit to put on top. May all your challenges be this easy and delicious. Over the years, I've covered this moist cake with almost every type of fruit. The possibilities are limited only by your market's inventory. Plump raspberries or sliced ripe and juicy apricots or plums are three spectacular choices for summer. In the fall and winter months, try sweet pear or tart apple slices spiked with a hint of ground nutmeg.

1 1/2 cups (6 3/4 ounces/191 grams) all-purpose flour

1 1/2 teaspoons baking powder

1/2 teaspoon table salt

8 tablespoons (4 ounces/113 grams) unsalted butter, at room temperature

1 cup (8 ounces/227 grams) plus 2 teaspoons granulated sugar

1 teaspoon pure vanilla extract

2 large eggs, at room temperature

2/3 cup (5 fl ounces/146 ml) whole milk

for the topping options (choose one):

1/2 pint (5 ounces/142 grams/about 1 cup) berries (blueberries or raspberries are particularly good), rinsed and well dried

or

1 medium (5 ounces/142 grams) ripe plum, peach, apricot, or nectarine, pitted and thinly sliced

or

1 medium (6 ounces/170 grams) ripe pear or apple, peeled, thinly sliced, and tossed with 1/4 teaspoon ground nutmeg or cinnamon

1. Position an oven rack on the middle rung. Heat the oven to 350 degrees (180°C). Lightly grease the bottom and sides of a 9-by-2-inch

(22.75cm-by-5cm) round cake pan and line the bottom with parchment. Lightly grease and flour the parchment and flour the sides, tapping out the excess.

2. In a medium bowl, combine the flour, baking powder, and salt. Whisk until well blended. In a large bowl, beat the butter with an electric mixer (stand mixer fitted with the paddle attachment or handheld mixer) on medium-high speed until smooth. Add 1 cup of the sugar and beat until well combined. Beat in the vanilla. Add the eggs one at a time, beating well after each addition. Add half of the flour mixture and mix on low speed just until blended. Add the milk and mix just until blended. Add the remaining flour mixture and mix just until blended.

3. Scrape the batter into the prepared pan and spread evenly. Choose one of the topping options and arrange the fruit on the top of the batter. Sprinkle with the remaining 2 teaspoons sugar. Bake until a toothpick or cake tester inserted in the middle of the cake comes out clean, about 40 minutes. Transfer the cake pan to a rack to cool for 15 minutes.

4. Run a knife around the inside edge of the pan to loosen the cake. Using a thick, dry dish towel to protect your hands, invert a large flat plate on top of the cake pan and, holding both the pan and the plate, invert them together. Lift the pan off the cake. Invert a flat serving plate on the bottom of the cake and flip the cake one more time so that the fruit is on top. Serve warm or at room temperature.

storage: Cover the cooled cake in plastic wrap and store at room temperature for up to 24 hours.

supermoist banana-nut muffins

MAKES 1 DOZEN MUFFINS

the Dodge clan harbors a major passion for any and all banana-based breads or cakes, and this is the recipe we go to whenever we need to satisfy a craving quickly. Two ingredients make these muffins unusually delicious – vegetable oil (specifically canola or corn), to keep them supermoist, and super-ripe bananas. In fact, for the best banana flavor, the banana peels need to be completely black. Yup, that's right – completely overripe bananas are the only way to give breads, muffins, or cakes the fullest banana flavor possible. They should be so black that you might be tempted to throw them out – don't! Make a batch of these muffins instead.

If you're not in a banana mood when your bananas are beautifully black, just tuck them, peel and all, into a heavy-duty freezer bag and freeze them (up to 3 months) so they're ready when you get a hankering for banana muffins. A partial thaw is all they need (about 5 minutes on the counter should do it), then peel them and drop them into the bowl and proceed with the recipe.

At the end of this recipe, I've included instructions on other ways to use the batter. If you've got extra time, bake the batter in a loaf pan for traditional banana bread. If you're as partial to muffin tops as I am (I always pull the top off and eat it first), bake the batter in a special muffin-top pan. Finally, if you're fond of mini-muffins, this recipe makes three dozen, and they bake in 11 minutes.

1 3/4 cups (8 ounces/227 grams)
    all-purpose flour
2 teaspoons baking powder
1/4 teaspoon baking soda
1/2 teaspoon table salt
3 medium very, very ripe bananas
    (about 14 ounces/397 grams
    total, including peels), peeled
3/4 cup (6 ounces/170 grams)
    firmly packed light brown sugar

1/3 cup (2 1/2 fl ounces/73 ml)
    canola or corn oil
2 large eggs
1 teaspoon pure vanilla extract
2/3 cup (2 1/2 ounces/71 grams)
    coarsely chopped walnuts,
    toasted (see page 40), optional.

1. Position an oven rack on the middle rung. Heat the oven to 375 degrees (190°C). Line 12 regular-sized muffin cups with foil or paper liners.

2. In a medium bowl, combine the flour, baking powder, baking soda, and salt. Whisk until well blended. In a large bowl, combine the bananas, brown sugar, oil, eggs, and vanilla. Beat with an electric mixer (stand mixer fitted with the paddle attachment or handheld mixer) on medium speed until well blended with only small bits of banana visible. Pour in the dry ingredients and gently stir with a rubber spatula just until blended. If using the nuts, add them when the flour is almost blended and stir to incorporate.

3. Scoop the batter into the lined muffin cups, dividing evenly. They will be almost full. Gently tap the pan on the countertop to settle the batter. Bake until the tops are golden brown and a toothpick or cake tester inserted in the center of 1 muffin comes out clean, about 18 minutes. Transfer the muffin pan to a rack to cool for 10 minutes, and then carefully remove the muffins from the pan and set them on the rack to cool. Serve warm or at room temperature.

storage: Cover the cooled muffins with plastic wrap and store at room temperature for up to 3 days.

more baking ideas for the supermoist banana-nut muffin batter

for a banana loaf: Heat the oven to 350 degrees (180°C), not 375 degrees (190°C) as for the muffins. Prepare the batter as directed. Scrape into a lightly greased and floured 8 1/2-by-4 1/2 inch (21.5cm-by-11.5cm) loaf pan and smooth the top. Bake until the top is golden brown and a toothpick or cake tester inserted in the center comes out clean, 55 to 60 minutes. Transfer the pan to a rack to cool for 15 minutes. Using a thin knife, gently loosen the cake from the pan sides and slip it out of the pan. Tip the loaf on its side and let cool on the rack until warm or at room temperature.

for mini-muffins: Prepare the batter as directed. Scoop into 36 lined mini-muffin cups, dividing evenly. They will be almost full. Gently tap the pan on the countertop to settle the batter. Bake until the tops are golden brown and a toothpick or cake tester inserted in the center of 1 muffin comes out clean, about 11 minutes. Transfer the pan to a rack to cool for 5 minutes, and then carefully remove the muffins from the pan and set them on the rack to cool. Serve warm or at room temperature.

for muffin tops: Prepare the batter as directed. Scoop into 10 lightly greased and floured muffin-top cups, dividing evenly. They will be almost full. Gently tap the pan on the countertop to settle the batter. Bake until the tops are golden brown and a toothpick or cake tester inserted in the center of 1 muffin top comes out clean, about 11 minutes. Transfer the pan to a rack to cool for 5 minutes, and then carefully remove the muffin tops from the pan and set them on the rack to cool. Serve warm or at room temperature.

Flavor Variation: My kids would never forgive me if I didn't share one of their favorite versions of these muffins. On occasion, I substitute an equal amount of semisweet chocolate chips (1/2 cup/3 ounces/85 grams mini-chips for the mini-muffins and muffin tops) for the chopped walnuts. They love the combination of banana and chocolate.

multitalented mini-muffins

not only does this buttery yellow muffin come together quickly and bake in 12 minutes, but it can also easily accommodate a variety of flavors suitable for any occasion. I can't tell you how often I pull out this recipe. In fact, I'm pretty sure I can make it in my sleep. I've served the jelly-filled minis to my daughter Tierney's Girl Scout troop (strawberry is her favorite, mine is apricot), the double ginger to the Dress for Success Mid-Fairfield County board, and the chocolate chip ones to the neighbors at our holiday parties. I've even topped the original vanilla muffins with frosting – fudgy (see Emergency Blender Cupcakes, page 72) and Tangy Vanilla (page 174) are crowd-pleasers – and served them up as birthday treats for friends. Whether the recipients are young or old, the setting formal or informal, no one has guessed that they all use the same batter.

for the muffins (original vanilla):

1 cup plus 2 tablespoons (5 ounces/142 grams) all-purpose flour

1 teaspoon baking powder

1/4 teaspoon table salt

6 tablespoons (3 ounces/85 grams) unsalted butter, at room temperature

2/3 cup (5 1/4 ounces/149 grams) granulated sugar, plus 1 tablespoon for sprinkling

1 teaspoon pure vanilla extract

2 large eggs

1/4 cup (2 fl ounces/58 ml) whole milk

for the flavor options (choose one):

Double Ginger: Add 1/2 teaspoon ground ginger and 2 tablespoons finely chopped crystallized ginger to the flour mixture

or

Chocolate Chip: Add 1/3 cup (2 ounces/57 grams) mini chocolate chips with the flour mixture *or*

Jelly Filled: Add 1/2 teaspoon ground cinnamon to the flour mixture and divide 2 tablespoons of your favorite jelly among the muffins.

1. Position an oven rack on the middle rung. Heat the oven to 375 degrees (190°C). Line 24 mini-muffin cups with foil or paper liners.

2. In a medium bowl, combine the flour, baking powder, and salt. If making the double ginger, add both gingers now, and toss so the crystallized ginger doesn't clump together. If making the jelly filled, add the cinnamon now. Whisk until well blended. In a large bowl, beat the butter with an electric mixer (a handheld mixer works best for this small amount) on medium speed until smooth. Add the sugar and beat until well combined. Beat in the vanilla. Add the eggs one at a time, beating well after each addition. Add the milk and beat just until blended. Pour in the flour mixture and stir gently just until blended. If making the chocolate chip, stir the chips in now.

3. Scoop the batter into the lined muffin cups, dividing evenly. They should be very full. Gently tap the pan on the countertop to settle the contents. If making the jelly filled, use a 1/4 teaspoon measuring spoon or a zipper-top plastic bag (see Technique Tip, page 86) to divide the jelly evenly among the muffins. Sprinkle the tops evenly with the remaining 1 tablespoon granulated sugar.

4. Bake until the tops are golden brown and a toothpick or cake tester inserted in the center of 1 muffin comes out clean, about 12 minutes. Transfer the muffin pan to a rack to cool for 5 minutes, and then carefully remove the muffins from the pan and set them on the rack to cool. Serve warm or at room temperature.

technique tip for jelly-filled muffins

Spoon the jelly into a small zipper-top plastic bag. Press out all the air, zip the bag closed, and snip off a small piece from one bottom corner. Position the tip of the bag nearly touching the top of the batter in one muffin cup and gently squeeze out about 1/4 teaspoon jelly. Repeat with the remaining jelly and muffin batter. Do not overdo the amount of jelly – a mini-muffin needs only a smidgen.

Breads

• • •

buttermilk biscuits with savory variations

MAKES 6 BISCUITS

i'll confess that I am sometimes tempted by the "popping fresh" store-bought biscuit. Even now, with years of baking under my belt, the idea of smacking a shiny cardboard cylinder against the counter until it bursts forth with a loud POP still appeals to me. But that's where the attraction ends. Ready-to-bake biscuits never taste as buttery or bake up as crumbly as home-made, no matter what the manufacturer claims. So, while I can't offer you a smack and a loud pop, I can show you how to make the best biscuits ever, along with a couple of flavor variations. They're the real deal – loads of butter flavor, with a tender, slightly crumbly texture. They are perfect slathered with butter or drenched in the sauce from your favorite braise or stew.

1 2/3 cups (7 1/2 ounces/213 grams) all-purpose flour
1 tablespoon granulated sugar
1 tablespoon baking powder
1 teaspoon table salt

8 tablespoons (4 ounces/113 grams) very cold unsalted butter, cut into 8 pieces
3/4 cup (6 fl ounces/175 ml) butter-milk

for the optional flavor additions (choose one):

1/3 cup (1 1/2 ounces/43 grams) finely chopped fresh herbs (I like a combination of basil, chives, and parsley)

or

1/3 cup (1 1/4 ounces/35 grams) finely grated Parmesan cheese

1. Position an oven rack on the middle rung. Heat the oven to 400 degrees (200°C). Line 1 cookie sheet with parchment or a nonstick baking liner (I like the Silpat).

2. In a medium bowl, combine the flour, sugar, baking powder, salt, and one of the optional ingredients, if using. Whisk until well blended. With a pastry blender or 2 table knives, cut the butter into the flour mixture until the butter pieces are no larger than peas. Or combine the dry ingredients and the butter in a food processor and pulse until the butter is incorporated correctly, then dump the mixture into a bowl. Add the buttermilk and gently toss with a rubber spatula just until the dough comes together in moist clumps.

3. Dump the shaggy dough onto a work surface – no need to flour the surface. Gently press the dough into a thick rectangle about 6 by 4 inches (15.25 by 10cm). If the dough is sticky, lightly flour your fingers. (If you want very neat squares, use a sharp knife to trim off a bit of the edges. Personally, I don't bother trimming. I prefer the rustic look of the untrimmed squares.) Using a large, sharp knife or bench scraper, cut the dough into 6 equal squares. Arrange the squares on the prepared cookie sheet, spacing them about 3 inches (7.75cm) apart.

4. Bake until puffed and light brown, about 18 minutes. Transfer the cookie sheet to a rack to cool for about 10 minutes. Using a spatula, lift the biscuits onto a rack to cool. Serve warm or at room temperature.

storage: Wrap the cooled biscuits in plastic wrap and store at room temperature for up to 1 day or in the freezer for up to 1 month. Before serving, refresh the biscuits by warming them in a 300-degree (150°C) oven for about 15 minutes.

jalapeño corn bread wedges

MAKES ONE 9-INCH (22.75CM) PIE, OR 8 WEDGES

most corn breads are too dry and crumbly for my taste. I prefer the moist, slightly sweet kind made with buttermilk and an extra spoonful or two of sugar. For this recipe, I've included the heat of a jalapeño, which contrasts against the bread's sweetness. (If you're not a chile fan, just omit it.) You'll also see that, once again, a pie plate is the baking pan of choice, because the bread bakes more quickly in it, and I like the fun of serving wedges.

This corn bread is a staple on our Thanksgiving table, and I always double or even triple the recipe to guarantee leftovers. My nephew, Clayton Johnson, wraps up as much as he can to take home to Williamstown, Massachusetts. (I wonder how much actually makes it back.) In the Dodge house, leftover corn bread (the nonjalapeño variety) is served for breakfast. My children, Alex and Tierney – and myself – like to heat a wedge up, split it in half, and drizzle on maple syrup.

6 tablespoons (3 ounces/85 grams) unsalted butter, cut into 3 pieces

1 cup (4 1/2 ounces/128 grams) finely ground yellow cornmeal

1 cup (4 1/2 ounces/128 grams) all-purpose flour

1/3 cup (2 1/2 ounces/71 grams) granulated sugar

2 1/2 teaspoons baking powder

1/2 teaspoon table salt

1 cup (8 fl ounces/233 ml) buttermilk

1 large egg

1 jalapeño chile, stemmed, seeded, and minced (see What Is It? below), optional

1. Position an oven rack on the middle rung. Heat the oven to 375 degrees (190°C). Lightly grease the bottom and sides of a 9-inch (22.75cm) pie plate (I use Pyrex).

2. Melt the butter in a small saucepan or the microwave; set aside to cool. In a medium bowl, combine the cornmeal, flour, sugar, baking powder, and salt. Whisk until well blended. Mix together the buttermilk and egg with a fork just until blended. I like to measure the buttermilk in a 2-cup Pyrex measure and then mix the egg right in the same cup. (You can prepare the dry ingredients and wet ingredients, except the butter, up to 1 day ahead. Cover the dry ingredients and keep at room temperature, and cover the wet ingredients and keep in the fridge. Melt the butter just before continuing with the recipe. Pour the buttermilk mixture and the cooled butter over the dry ingredients and add the minced jalapeño, if using. Stir with a rubber spatula just until blended.

3. Scrape into the prepared pie plate and spread evenly. Bake until a toothpick or cake tester inserted in the center comes out clean, about 25 minutes. Transfer the pie plate to a rack to cool for at least 15 minutes. Serve warm or at room temperature, cut into 8 wedges.

storage: Cover the corn bread with plastic wrap and store at room temperature for up to 2 days.

what is it? (jalapeños)

Nowadays, jalapeños are readily available in most grocery stores; however, they vary greatly in heat and intensity. Because of this discrepancy, I buy a few more than I need for a recipe to ensure that I get a nice hot one. To test a chile's intensity, I cut off the stem end along with a little of the jalapeño and cautiously touch the cut edge to the tip of my tongue. A good jalapeño will bite my tongue a bit, a weak one will leave me without the slightest twinge. If your chile tastes bland, try another.

For those who don't like to handle chiles, slide your hands into small plastic bags before working with the jalapeños. This way you can remove the seeds with little worry about the chiles burning your hands. This method is never foolproof, so always wash your hands thoroughly after handling all chiles.

lemon–poppy seed squares

MAKES NINE 2-INCH (5CM) SQUARES

t he lemony flavor of this quick bread comes from pure lemon extract (make sure not to use the imitation type) and, if you have extra time, you can intensify the lemon flavor by making the sweet-tart lemon glaze. You spoon it over the bread, still hot in the pan, so the sweet lemon syrup can seep in. I bake this in a square pan to speed up baking time.

2 tablespoons poppy seeds (see What Is It? below)

1/2 cup (4 fl ounces/117 ml) buttermilk

1 2/3 cups (7 1/2 ounces/213 grams) all-purpose flour

3/4 teaspoon baking powder

1/4 teaspoon baking soda

1/4 teaspoon table salt

6 tablespoons (3 ounces/85 grams) unsalted butter, at room temperature

1 cup (8 ounces/227 grams) granulated sugar

3/4 teaspoon pure lemon extract

1/2 teaspoon pure vanilla extract

2 large eggs

1. Position an oven rack on the middle rung. Heat the oven to 350 degrees (180°C). Lightly grease the bottom and sides of an 8-inch (20cm) square baking dish (I use Pyrex). Stir the poppy seeds into the buttermilk and set aside to soften.

2. In a medium bowl, combine the flour, baking powder, baking soda, and salt. Whisk until well blended. In a large bowl, combine the butter, sugar, and the lemon and vanilla extracts. Beat with an electric mixer (stand mixer fitted with the paddle attachment or handheld mixer) on medium speed until well blended. Add the eggs one at a time, beating well after each addition. Using a rubber spatula, fold in half of the flour mixture just until blended. Gently stir in the buttermilk and poppy seeds. Add the remaining flour and fold just until blended.

3. Scrape the batter into the prepared baking dish and spread it evenly. Bake until a toothpick or cake tester inserted in the center comes out clean, 30 to 33 minutes. Transfer the baking dish to a rack to cool. Serve warm or at room temperature, cut into 2-inch (5cm) squares.

storage: Wrap the uncut, cooled squares (glazed or unglazed) in plastic wrap and store at room temperature for up to 3 days or in the freezer for up to 1 month.

got extra time?

Make a lemon glaze:
While the bread is baking, stir 1/4 cup (2 fl ounces/58 ml) lemon juice and 1/4 cup (1 ounce/22 grams) confectioners' sugar together in a small bowl or 1-cup Pyrex measure. Set aside, stirring occasionally, until the sugar is dissolved. When the bread is just out of the oven, using a toothpick or cake tester, poke about 50 holes all the way through the bread, spacing them evenly. (There's no need to count. Just make sure there are many holes so the cake absorbs the glaze evenly.) Spoon the glaze over the hot bread and let cool for at least 15 minutes.

what is it? (poppy seeds)

Although poppy seeds come from the poppy plant, they have no narcotic effect when added to baked goods. Soaking or crushing the seeds before adding them to a dough or batter is the best way to unleash their full flavor. Because they turn rancid quickly, I buy only small quantities at a time and store them in the fridge for up to 3 months.

classic popovers

MAKES 1 DOZEN (IN A MUFFIN PAN) OR 10 (IN STANDARD POPOVER PANS)

popovers actually pop up, not over, but why argue with an age-old wording? The only magic to making popovers that truly do pop up is heating the pan and moving quickly.

Although popovers are traditional morning food (spread with a thick smear of strawberry jam), I serve the savory variations (see below) as an accompaniment to a dinner of roast beef tenderloin or chicken. They're a quick and effortless alternative to side dishes like rice or potatoes.

1 1/2 cups (12 fl ounces/350 ml) whole milk or half-and-half	1 tablespoon Dijon mustard
4 tablespoons (2 ounces/57 grams) unsalted butter, cut into 4 pieces	1 1/3 cups (6 ounces/170 grams) all-purpose flour
4 large eggs	3/4 teaspoon table salt
	1/8 teaspoon cayenne pepper

1. Position an oven rack on the middle rung and slide a nonstick standard 12-cup muffin pan (4 fl ounces/177 ml per cup) or 2 nonstick popover pans (six 6-fl ounce/175-ml cups per pan) onto the oven rack. Heat the oven to 450 degrees (230°C).

2. In a small saucepan, heat the milk or half-and-half until just warm. Remove from the heat and add the butter. (I measure the milk in a 2-cup Pyrex measure, heat it in the microwave, and add the butter directly to the measuring cup.) Stir until the butter is melted and the milk is cooled to lukewarm. Pour this mixture into a blender and add the eggs and mustard. Cover with the lid and process until blended, about 10 seconds. Add the flour, salt, and cayenne and process just until blended, about 10 seconds longer, stopping to scrape down the sides if necessary. Set aside while the oven continues to heat. (At this point, you can cover the batter and stow it in the fridge – blender and all – for up to 24 hours. Let the batter come to room temperature while the oven heats. It's one less last-minute thing to do before a meal, either dinner or breakfast, and the texture and flavor don't suffer a bit.)

3. When the oven is heated and you're ready to bake the popovers, you need to move quickly. Carefully remove the pan or pans from the oven and *very* lightly coat the cups with nonstick cooking spray. Pour the batter into the heated pans, dividing it evenly. If you're using popover pans, you'll have 1 empty cup per tray. Immediately slide the pan(s) back into the oven.

4. Bake without opening the oven door until the popovers are puffed and well browned, about 25 minutes. Resist the urge to open the oven, especially during the first 20 minutes of baking, or you'll likely to have pancakes instead of popovers. (If you like a drier popover, turn the oven off and leave them in there for another few minutes.) Remove from the oven. Tip the pan(s) onto a rack and let the popovers tumble out. Pierce each popover with the tip of a knife to allow the steam to escape. This will keep the exterior crusty and the insides moist. Serve immediately.

storage: Wrap leftovers in plastic and store at room temperature for up to 1 day. To reheat, loosely wrap in foil and place in a 300-degree oven until warmed, about 15 minutes. They won't retain their puffiness or the crisp exterior, but they'll still be delicious.

flavor variations

Parmesan: Add 1/2 cup (2 ounces/57 grams) finely grated Parmesan cheese and 1 teaspoon coarsely ground black pepper with the flour in step 2 and proceed as directed.

Herb: Add 1/3 cup (1 1/2 ounces/43 grams) lightly packed chopped fresh herbs (I recommend equal parts chives and basil, but any combination will do) to the blender with the milk mixture in step 2 and proceed as directed.

Goat cheese: Add 1/3 cup (2 ounces/57 grams) crumbled fresh goat cheese to the blender with the milk mixture in step 2 and process until smooth. Proceed as directed.

pecan-crusted pumpkin squares

MAKES NINE 2-INCH (5CM) SQUARES

this dense, moist, rustic bread mixes together in minutes, travels well, and is delicious served warm from the oven. It's just as good a day or two after baking, when the flavors have deepened. In the fall and winter months, this bread is ideal comfort food. When I need a hostess gift or a present for a teacher, I often double this recipe, and wrap the breads in plastic, festive-colored cellophane, and a big bow.

Make sure to smell jarred spices before you use them. The aroma should be strong and full. Most spices have a six-month shelf life, after which they begin losing flavor. Thankfully, for anyone who is not a frequent spice user, some companies (McCormick is the brand available here in Connecticut) are packaging spices in small containers. I'm sure they cost slightly more than the larger jars, but I'd prefer to spend a bit more to ensure the most potent flavor.

3/4 cup (3 ounces/85 grams) finely chopped pecans (no need to toast)

1 3/4 cups (8 ounces/227 grams) all-purpose flour

2 teaspoons baking powder

1/4 teaspoon baking soda

1 1/2 teaspoons ground cinnamon

1/4 teaspoon ground nutmeg

1/2 teaspoon table salt

1/8 teaspoon ground cloves

1 cup (8 ounces/227 grams) firmly packed dark brown sugar

1 cup (8 ounces/227 grams) canned solid-pack pumpkin (not seasoned pumpkin pie filling)

1/2 cup (4 fl ounces/117 ml) canola or corn oil

2 large eggs

1 teaspoon pure vanilla extract

1. Position an oven rack on the middle rung. Heat the oven to 350 degrees (180°C). Generously butter – be generous or the nuts won't stick – the bottom and sides of an 8-inch (20cm) square baking dish (I use Pyrex).

Add the nuts and tilt the pan to coat the bottom and sides evenly. Carefully spill out and save the excess nuts for the top.

2. In a medium bowl, combine the flour, baking powder, baking soda, cinnamon, nutmeg, salt, and cloves. Whisk until well blended. In a large bowl, combine the sugar, pumpkin, oil, eggs, and vanilla. Whisk until smooth. (You can prepare the dry ingredients and wet ingredients up to 1 day ahead. Cover the dry ingredients and keep at room temperature, and cover the wet ingredients and keep in the fridge.) Add the flour mixture to the wet ingredients and gently stir just until blended.

3. Scrape the batter into the prepared pan and spread evenly. Scatter the reserved nuts evenly over the batter. Bake until a toothpick or cake tester inserted in the center comes out with moist crumbs clinging to it, about 30 minutes. Transfer the pan to a rack to cool for about 15 minutes. Serve warm or at room temperature, cut into 2-inch (5cm) squares.

storage: Wrap the uncut, cooled square in plastic wrap and store at room temperature for up to 5 days or in the freezer for up to 1 month.

Mousses, Custards, and Puddings
• • •

10-minute mocha pots de crème
MAKES FOUR 1/2 CUP SERVINGS

p̲ot de crème is the French answer to American pudding. And this *no-bake* version whips up in minutes – literally – with the help of a trusty blender.

My friend Sarah is a fabulous cook, but she maintains that when it comes to a dinner party, the only thing that matters is the dessert. One evening, Sarah served these "petits pots" for dessert, and I found their velvety texture addictive. For those fearful of eating uncooked egg yolks, this recipe doesn't use them, and the texture doesn't suffer as a result.

Chocolate and rum provide the key flavors in this pudding. Sarah pairs Mount Gay rum with Ghirardelli bittersweet chocolate (available in my grocery store). Sometimes I splurge and buy Valrhona bittersweet and Myers's dark rum, a combination that always receives raves.

1 cup (8 fl ounces/233 ml) heavy cream

4 ounces (113 grams) bittersweet chocolate, finely chopped

3 tablespoons granulated sugar

1/2 teaspoon instant espresso powder or instant coffee granules (any type, even decaf, will do)

2 tablespoons coffee-flavored liqueur

1 teaspoon pure vanilla extract

go-withs: Sweetened Whipped Cream (page 46) and chocolate shavings (see page 42) for garnish (optional)

1. Have ready 4 small ramekins or classic pot de crème pots (those are the little cups with the lids) just slightly larger than 1/2 cup each. (The vessels do not need to be ovenproof, as this is a *no*-bake recipe. You can even use teacups, so use your prettiest options.)

2. In a small saucepan or the microwave, heat the cream just until boiling. Meanwhile, dump the chopped chocolate, sugar, and espresso powder or coffee granules into a blender. When the cream is just boiling, pour it into the blender. Pop the lid on and blend on medium-high speed until the chocolate is melted and the mixture is frothy and smooth. Add the liqueur and vanilla and process until blended, about 10 seconds.

3. Using a spoon, skim off the foam from the top of the custard and discard. Pour the chocolate cream into the cups or ramekins, dividing it evenly. Top with lids (if you're using proper porcelain pots de crème pots) or cover with plastic wrap and refrigerate for at least 45 minutes. Serve with a dollop of whipped cream and a few chocolate shavings, if desired.

storage: Cover the cups with plastic wrap (no need to press the plastic directly onto the pudding; they won't form a skin) or lids and refrigerate for up to 3 days.

flavor variations

Substitute an equal amount of bourbon or dark rum for the coffee liqueur. You can also substitute a licorice-, orange-, or raspberry-flavored liqueur, but make sure to omit the instant espresso powder or coffee granules when you use these.

minted mango fool with lime

MAKES FOUR 3/4-CUP SERVINGS

there are many theories as to how this easy little dessert got its name. Maybe it's called a fool because you'd be a fool *not* to make it. The fool is a simple dessert consisting of lightly sweetened, puréed fruit folded into whipped cream that comes together in fewer than 20 minutes. This particular fool can be served on its own, layered with fresh mango slices in chilled wineglasses, or used as a filling for shortcakes in place of the traditional whipped cream.

2 medium, ripe mangos (about 14 ounces/397 grams each)

1/3 cup (2 1/2 ounces/71 grams) granulated sugar

2 tablespoons lime juice

Pinch of table salt

Tiny pinch of cayenne pepper

1 tablespoon finely chopped fresh mint

1 cup (8 fl ounces/233 ml) chilled heavy cream

Fresh mango slices for garnish (optional)

1. Peel and pit the mangoes: Stand 1 mango on a work surface, balancing it on one of its narrow sides. Position a large knife just off the center of the mango and cut straight down to release one half. If you meet resistance, you've hit the flat pit that runs through the center of the fruit. Simply move your knife slightly farther from the center. Repeat with the other side. Using a paring knife, cut the mango flesh in 1-inch (2.5cm) crosshatch, taking care not to pierce the skin. Using both hands, push up on the skin side so that the mango flesh pops upward (it looks a bit like a porcupine with squared-off quills). Cut across the bottom of the cubes to free them, and discard the skin. Repeat with remaining mango.

2. Combine the mango cubes, sugar, lime juice, salt, and cayenne in a food processor. Pulse until the mixture is smooth. Add the mint and process briefly. You'll have about 1 1/2 cups purée. Taste and add a little more sugar or salt, if needed. (At this point, the mango purée can be covered and refrigerated for up to 2 days. Alternatively, scrape the purée into a heavy-duty freezer bag and freeze for up to 3 months.) Pop the purée into the refrigerator and stir occasionally while you prepare the whipped cream.

3. In a medium bowl, whip the cream until firm peaks form. Pour about 1 cup of the purée into the whipped cream and fold gently but thoroughly until well blended. Gently stir in the remaining purée, keeping streaks of the purée visible. Spoon into serving bowls alone or layered with the fresh mango slices.

storage: Cover the fool with plastic wrap and refrigerate for up to 1 day.

flavor variations

It's my experience that most puréed fruit (berries, papaya, and banana are excellent candidates) can be folded into whipped cream to create a luscious, flavorful fool. As a rule of thumb, you'll need 1 cup (8 fl ounces/233 ml) seasoned and sweetened purée to fold into 2 cups (16 fl ounces/466 ml) whipped cream – that's about 1 cup (8 fl ounces/233ml) heavy cream before it's whipped up. When seasoning the purée, taste as you add and make sure that the purée is pungent enough to stand up to all that cream. A bland purée will result in a bland fool. A pinch of salt and a squeeze of acid (lime or lemon juice) help bring out the biggest fruit flavor possible.

very berry lemon parfaits

MAKES 4 SERVINGS

Looking for a quick, elegant dessert? Well, this is your recipe. The taste of this subtly flavored lemon cream belies its easy preparation. Here, it is served as a parfait, layered with fresh fruit and crushed amaretti or ginger-snap cookies. It can also be served garnished only with a berry or two. Generally, I serve the parfaits in simple glass dessert cups, but if I'm feeling especially stylish, I'll use wineglasses. They make a chic presentation and their portability makes them just the thing for buffets.

Though a stemmed wineglass presentation is dramatic, some glasses tend to be top heavy and tip over easily, so avoid carrying too many at one time. My daughter, Tierney, and her friend Emmie (both eleven at the time and experienced bakers) learned the hard way. The girls wanted a glamorous presentation and spooned the dessert into several elegant wineglasses. While they were carrying them on a tray to the table, the wineglasses fell to the floor with a crash. The girls considered the cleanup a drag and have since opted for short-stemmed (or, better yet, stemless) glasses.

6 ounces (170 grams) cream cheese, softened

3/4 cup (3 ounces/85 grams) confectioners' sugar

Pinch of table salt

1 cup (8 fl ounces/233 ml) chilled heavy cream

1 1/2 tablespoons lemon juice

1 teaspoon finely grated lemon zest (optional)

1 tablespoon finely chopped fresh mint (optional)

2 pints (20 ounces/568 grams/ about 4 cups) berries (I like a mix of raspberries and blueberries), rinsed and well dried

1 1/3 cups (5 1/4 ounces/149 grams) finely crushed amaretti (see What Is It? on page 111) or gingersnap cookies

4 fresh mint sprigs for garnish (optional)

1. In a medium bowl, combine the softened cream cheese, confectioners' sugar, and salt. Using a handheld electric mixer, beat on low speed until the cream cheese is smooth and the sugar is incorporated. Add the cream and beat until the mixture is smooth. Increase the speed to medium-high and beat until the cream is billowy and holds medium-firm peaks, about 1 minute. Add the lemon juice, lemon zest, and the chopped mint, if using. Stir briefly to blend. (At this point, you can cover the cream and refrigerate it for up to 2 days before assembling the parfaits.)

2. Spoon out 2/3 cup (5 fl ounces/146 ml) of the lemon cream and set aside. Line up 4 parfait glasses or stemmed wineglasses. Beginning and ending with the berries or crushed cookies, evenly layer the berries or cookies and the lemon cream in the glasses, making as many layers as you like. Top each parfait with a dollop of the reserved lemon cream and garnish with a mint sprig, if desired.

storage: Cover the parfaits with plastic wrap and refrigerate for up to 1 day. Garnish just before serving.

flavor variations

Have you ever had the frozen ice cream bars called Creamsicles? If you are a fan of their creamy orange flavor, substitute an equal amount of orange zest and juice for the lemon zest and juice.

Looking for a tropical flavor? Substitute 2 tablespoons of unsweetened coconut milk and 1/3 cup (1 ounce/28 grams) shredded, sweetened dried coconut, lightly toasted, for the lemon zest and juice and the chopped mint. Garnishing each parfait with an additional tablespoon of toasted coconut is an attractive finishing touch.

stovetop double-chocolate pudding

MAKES 4 CUPS, OR 8 SERVINGS

pudding is great comfort food, yet not everyone realizes how easy it is to make from scratch. Let My-T-Fine mix become a thing of the past. This pudding is ready in less than 15 minutes and, served steaming hot or chilled, it's exceptionally rich and smooth.

I give you the option of bittersweet, semisweet, or milk chocolate. When blended with unsweetened natural cocoa powder, any of them will produce a deep chocolate taste. I love all three versions, so try each one and choose your favorite. At the end of the recipe, I've suggested three additional flavoring possibilities: mocha, cinnamon, and orange. Each adds a distinctive taste.

3/4 cup (6 ounces/170 grams) granulated sugar

1/3 cup (1 1/4 ounces/35 grams) cornstarch

1/3 cup (1 ounce/28 grams) unsweetened natural cocoa powder, sifted if lumpy

1/4 teaspoon table salt

3 1/2 cups (28 fl ounces/840 ml) whole milk

4 ounces (113 grams) semisweet, bittersweet, or milk chocolate, chopped

1 teaspoon pure vanilla extract

go-with: Sweetened Whipped Cream (page 46), optional

1. In a medium, heavy saucepan, combine the sugar, cornstarch, cocoa powder, and salt. Whisk until well blended. Pour in about 1/2 cup (4 fl ounces/117 ml) of the milk and whisk until the mixture is smooth. Whisk in the remaining milk.

2. Set the pan over medium-high heat and cook, whisking constantly, until the mixture comes to a full boil. Boil for 1 minute and then remove from the heat. Add the chocolate and vanilla and whisk until the chocolate is melted and the pudding is smooth. Pour into serving bowls. Cover with plastic wrap, pressing it directly onto the surface to prevent a skin from forming. (I don't care for a skin on my chocolate pudding, but if you are one of the millions who *love* a skin, omit this step.) Let cool slightly and serve warm, or refrigerate until room temperature or cold. Garnish with a dollop of whipped cream, if desired.

storage: Cover and refrigerate the cooled pudding for up to 4 days.

flavor variations

Mocha: Mix 1 teaspoon instant coffee granules or espresso powder into the sugar mixture and proceed as directed.

Cinnamon: Mix 1 teaspoon ground cinnamon into the sugar mixture and proceed as directed.

Orange: Mix 2 tablespoons finely grated orange zest into the sugar mixture and proceed as directed.

classic vanilla rice pudding

MAKES ABOUT 3 1/2 CUPS AND, AS FAR I'M CONCERNED,

THAT'S A SINGLE SERVING (BUT, SERIOUSLY, IT MAKES

ABOUT 4 SERVINGS)

nothing takes the chill off of a frosty Connecticut day better than a bowl of smooth, creamy vanilla-scented rice pudding served steaming hot. The pudding is also good served cold.

Simmering, but not boiling, is the key to the silky texture of this pudding. If it's cooked too quickly, the milk will reduce too much before the rice is completely tender, and you'll end up with a lumpy, overly firm pudding.

I've included a few flavor variations. The coconut and coffee versions are just as satisfying as the classic, and add-ins like dried fruit, chocolate, or nuts can be stirred into all three.

4 cups (32 fl ounces/933 ml) whole
    milk
1/2 cup (3 1/2 ounces/99 grams)
    medium-grain white rice (see
    What Is It? below)
Pinch of table salt

1 vanilla bean, split lengthwise, or
    1 1/2 teaspoons pure vanilla
    extract
2 egg yolks from large eggs
1/3 cup (2 1/2 ounces/71 grams)
    granulated sugar

go-withs: Sweetened Whipped Cream (page 46), Emergency Strawberry Sauce (page 43), Summer Jumbled Fruit (page 75), or toasted chopped nuts (see page 40)

1. In a large, heavy saucepan, combine the milk, rice, salt, and split vanilla bean (if using extract, stir it in after the pudding is cooked). Bring to a boil over high heat, stirring constantly. Reduce the heat to low, cover the pan, and simmer, stirring occasionally with a wooden spoon (I like to use my angled wooden spatula; see equipment, page 34) for 15 minutes. Uncover and continue simmering, stirring frequently, until the rice is tender and the pudding is reduced to about 3 1/2 cups, about 10 minutes. (The first few times you make this, I encourage you to pull out a 4-cup Pyrex measure and actually measure the pudding. With more experience, you'll know when the desired density is reached.) You'll need to stir constantly toward the end to avoid scorching. Remember to simmer, not boil, the pudding.

2. In a medium bowl, combine the egg yolks, sugar, and the vanilla extract, if using. Whisk until well blended. Slowly add the cooked rice, whisking constantly so the eggs don't curdle. Pour the mixture back into the saucepan, making sure to scrape the bowl. Set the pan over medium-low heat and cook, stirring constantly with a wooden spoon, until the mixture has thickened and coats the back of the spoon, about 1 minute. Don't let the pudding boil. Remove the pan from the heat and fish out the vanilla bean, if using. Using the dull edge of a small knife, scrape out the seeds and add them to the pudding. Stir in one of the Add-ins (below), if using. Give the pudding one last stir to incorporate the seeds, and then scrape the pudding into a serving bowl or individual dishes and serve hot, warm, room temperature, or chilled. Top with a Go-With, if desired.

storage: Cover the pudding with plastic wrap, pressing it directly on the surface to prevent a skin from forming, and refrigerate for up to 3 days.

what is it? (medium-grain rice)

Medium-grain rice is preferable for the smoothest rice pudding (I like Goya brand). I've tested this recipe with long-grain (basmati) and short-grain (Arborio) rice and the results were not as good. Long-grain rice is too fragile – it breaks down while it simmers – and the short-grain variety throws off too much starch, making for a sticky, rather than creamy, pudding.

Flavor Variations

Fruit, Chocolate, or Nut: Add 3/4 cup (about 4 ounces/113 grams) raisins or other dried fruit (chopped if large), chopped chocolate (any kind), or toasted chopped nuts (see page 40) to the cooled pudding.

Coconut: Substitute 1 can (14 fl ounces/408 ml) coconut milk for 2 cups (16 ounces/466 ml) of the milk and 1/4 teaspoon coconut extract and 1/2 teaspoon pure vanilla extract for the vanilla bean and vanilla extract.

Coffee: Add 2 teaspoons instant espresso powder or instant coffee granules to the bowl at the beginning of step 2.

white chocolate cream with crushed amaretti

t his cream is for all the white chocolate fans out there. It's a cross between a mousse and sweetened whipped cream. It's as light and smooth as whipped cream, but the flavor is more complex. I like pairing it with crushed crisp amaretti cookies (see What Is It? below). The almond flavor and crispy, crunchy texture of the Italian cookies are perfect foils for the smooth cream.

White chocolate is also a natural accompaniment to fruit. In fact, when my kids were little, I'd spoon some of this cream into a small bowl and serve it with sliced fruit or berries, and they happily devoured it.

3 ounces (85 grams) cream cheese, softened

1/4 cup (2 ounces/57 grams) granu-lated sugar

1/2 teaspoon pure vanilla extract

1/4 teaspoon table salt

1 1/2 cups (12 fl ounces/350 ml) heavy cream

6 ounces (170 grams) white choco-late, melted and kept hot

25 amaretti cookies (see What Is It? below), finely crushed (about 1 1/2 cups/6 ounces/170 grams)

go-withs: strawberries, raspberries, or apricot wedges for garnish (optional)

1. In a medium bowl, combine the cream cheese, sugar, vanilla, and salt. Beat with an electric mixer (a handheld mixer works well) on low speed until the cream cheese is completely smooth and the sugar is incorporated. Add the cream and beat on low speed until smooth. Add the hot white chocolate, increase the speed to medium-high, and beat until the cream is billowy and holds firm peaks, about 2 minutes.

2. Line up 6 small dessert cups or stemmed wineglasses on a work surface. Put about 2 tablespoons of the crushed cookies into each glass. Divide the cream evenly among the glasses, and top with the remaining crushed cookies, dividing them evenly. Garnish each with a strawberry, a few raspberries, or an apricot wedge, if desired.

storage: Prepare the cream as directed in step 1, cover, and refrigerate for up to 2 days. Assemble the cream and crushed cookies up to 4 hours before serving (any longer and the cookies won't be crunchy). Refrigerate until serving.

what is it? (amaretti cookies)

Amaretti cookies are small, crisp cookies flavored with almond. While I'm sure that many companies make a similar cookie, the brand I prefer is Amaretti di Saronno Lazzaroni. Most specialty or Italian grocery shops stock them year-round. They come wrapped in tissue in pairs and are easily crushed. Simply unwrap and place the cookies into a heavy-duty zipper-top bag. Zip partially closed, press out the air, and then seal. Use a rolling pin or heavy pan (I like to use my handheld mixer – without the beaters, of course) to crush the cookies gently.

Pies and Tarts, Cobblers and Crisps
• • •

alex's key lime tart
MAKES ONE 9 1/2-INCH (24CM) TART, OR 8 SERVINGS

my son, Alex, is a big fan of Key lime pie. He loves this dessert so much that he developed his own version. Luckily for me – and you – he has allowed me to print it here. The filling mixes up in no time and bakes in only 15 minutes. Alex suggests cooling the tart for at least 45 minutes before serving. Whether he serves it warm, chilled, or thawed slightly from the freezer, Alex insists on topping each slice with a hefty dollop of whipped cream.

You'll notice that Alex doesn't use freshly squeezed Key limes for his tart filling. Initially, he was all in favor of squeezing his own, so I picked up a few bags of the little fruits when I saw them in the grocery store. Alex was thrilled and assured me that the task wasn't too daunting. Well, weeks went by with no Key lime tart cooling on the counter. Not surprisingly, Alex now calls for good-quality bottled Key lime juice.

The pecans in the crust are my small contribution to Alex's creation.

for the crust:

3/4 cup plus 2 tablespoons (3 3/4 ounces/106 grams) graham cracker crumbs

1/3 cup (1 1/4 ounces/35 grams) finely chopped pecans (no need to toast)

2 tablespoons granulated sugar

1/4 teaspoon ground cinnamon

Pinch of table salt

3 tablespoons (1 1/2 ounces/43 grams) unsalted butter, melted and cooled slightly

for the filling:

1 can (14 ounces/408 ml) sweet-
    ened condensed milk (not evapo-
    rated)
2/3 cup (5 fl ounces/146 ml) bottled
    Key lime juice

2 large eggs
1 teaspoon finely grated lime zest
    (optional)
1/2 teaspoon pure vanilla extract
Pinch of table salt

go-withs: Sweetened Whipped Cream (page 46) or Emergency Strawberry Sauce (page 43), optional.

1. Position the oven rack on the middle rung. Heat the oven to 350 degrees (180°C). Have ready a 9 1/2-inch (24cm) tart pan with a removable bottom.

2. TO MAKE THE CRUST
In a medium bowl, combine the graham cracker crumbs, pecans, sugar, cinnamon, and salt. Stir until well blended. Drizzle the melted butter over the crumbs and mix with a fork until evenly moistened and well blended.

3. Dump the crumbs into the tart pan and cover with a large piece of plastic wrap. Place your hands on the plastic wrap and spread the crumbs to coat the bottom of the pan evenly. (The plastic wrap will keep the crumbs from sticking to your hands.) Once the crumbs are in place, and with the plastic wrap still in place, use your fingers to pinch and press some of the crumbs around the inside edge of the pan to cover the sides evenly and completely. Redistribute the remaining crumbs evenly over the bottom of the pan and firmly press down to make a compact layer. I like to use a metal measuring cup with straight sides and a flat bottom for this task.

4. Bake the crust until it smells nutty and is slightly darker, about 10 minutes. Meanwhile, prepare the filling. If the crust is baked before the filling is ready, slide the tart pan onto a rack. Leave the oven set at 350 degrees (180°C).

5. TO MAKE THE FILLING

In a medium bowl, combine the condensed milk, Key lime juice, eggs, lime zest (if using), vanilla, and salt. Whisk until well blended.

6. Scrape the filling into the baked crust. Return the tart to the oven and bake until the filling just barely jiggles when the pan is nudged, about 15 minutes. Transfer the tart pan to a rack and let cool for at least 45 minutes before serving. To remove the tart from the pan, place the pan on a widemouthed can and allow the outside ring to fall away. If it's a bit stubborn, gently grip the ring with your fingers to coax its release. Once the ring is removed, move the tart to a flat surface. Slide a long, thin metal spatula between the pan bottom and the crust to separate the two. Using a spatula or two, transfer the tart to a flat serving plate. No matter what temperature you serve the tart – warm or cool – consider serving it with a dollop of whipped cream or a drizzle of strawberry sauce.

storage: Cover the cooled tart with plastic wrap and refrigerate for up to 2 days or freeze for up to 1 month.

got extra time?

Squeeze your own juice from fresh Key limes. The juice can be used immediately or frozen for up to 3 months.

honey-glazed peach tart

MAKES ONE 9 1/2-INCH (24CM) TART, OR 8 SERVINGS

Up the street from my house is Haydu's, a family-run farm stand. In the summer months, I visit it at least three or four afternoons a week. The vegetables have just been picked (the fresh corn is the best in the area), but I look forward to the peaches all year long. If the kids are with me (and they often are), I always have them take a big sniff to remind them that all fruit should be fragrant – a peach should, quite simply, smell like a peach.

Ripe peaches don't need much dressing up. A puff-pastry base, gorgeous fruit dabbed with a touch of butter, sugar, a hint of cinnamon, and a honey drizzle are all it takes to make this dessert. The chopped pistachios scattered over the baked tart add a splash of color and crunch.

1 sheet frozen puff pastry, 9 1/2 inches square (I like Pepperidge Farm brand)

2 tablespoons firmly packed light brown sugar

1 tablespoon (1/2 ounce/14 grams) unsalted butter, at room temperature

1/2 teaspoon ground cinnamon

2 large, ripe peaches (about 7 ounces/198 grams each) or equivalent weight of ripe plums, apricots or nectarines

2 tablespoons honey

1/4 cup (1 ounce/28 grams) finely chopped unsalted pistachios (no need to toast)

1. Remove 1 sheet of frozen puff pastry from the box, set it on a lightly floured surface, and cover with plastic wrap. Do *not* unfold at this point. Wrap the remaining puff pastry sheet in plastic wrap and return to the freezer. Let the covered puff pastry sit on the countertop until thawed and just pliable, about 20 minutes.

2. Meanwhile, position an oven rack on the middle rung. Heat the oven to 425 degrees (220°C). Line a half sheet pan with parchment or a nonstick liner (I like the Silpat). In a small bowl, mash the brown sugar, butter, and cinnamon together with a fork until blended. Cut the peaches (or other fruits) in half and remove the pits. Thinly slice the halves.

3. On a lightly floured work surface, carefully unfold the puff pastry. Dust the top of the dough with a little flour. Roll out the dough, lightly dusting with flour as needed to prevent the dough from sticking to the rolling pin and work surface, into a 14-inch (35cm) round. Trim off any ragged edges with the tip of a paring knife. Drape the dough loosely around the pin and transfer it to the baking sheet. Using the tines of a fork, prick the dough all over. Arrange the peach (or other fruit) slices, overlapping slightly, in even and concentric circles, leaving a 2-inch (5cm) border uncovered. Scatter bits of the butter mixture evenly over the peaches. Fold the border up and over the outer ring of peaches, pleating the dough as you go, to shape into a circle. (At this point, the tart can be covered with plastic wrap and refrigerated for up to 8 hours before proceeding with the recipe.)

4. Drizzle the honey over the peaches. Bake until the pastry is browned and the peaches are tender and slightly browned on their edges, about 25 minutes. Transfer the baking sheet to a rack and immediately sprinkle the pistachios evenly over the peaches. Serve warm.

storage: You can prepare the tart up to 4 hours ahead and reheat it in a 300-degree (150°C) oven until warm, about 15 minutes.

half-moon pie pockets

MAKES 18 POCKETS

these flaky three-bite pockets burst with flavor, and I've provided four different fillings, courtesy of my trusted colleague Katherine Seeley. The chocolate-nut filling is as close as you can get to the classic French croissant without all the work. The strawberry filling delivers bright, clean flavor, perfect for summer. Lou, Katherine's husband, calls the pumpkin-spice version "pumpkin pie in a pocket." And for something a little different, try filling the pocket with dried fruit stewed in orange juice or apple cider.

2 sheets frozen puff pastry, 9 1/2 inches square each

1 large egg, lightly beaten
2 tablespoons granulated sugar

for the dried-fruit filling:

3/4 cup (7 1/2 ounces/213 grams) finely chopped mixed dried fruits (apricots, figs, and cranberries are a good combination)
1 cup (8 fl ounces/233 ml) orange juice or apple cider

1 tablespoon firmly packed light brown sugar
3/4 teaspoon ground nutmeg

for the chocolate-nut filling:

1 cup (4 1/2 ounces/128 grams) chopped bittersweet chocolate or semisweet chocolate chips

1/3 cup (1/2 ounce/43 grams) chopped nuts (pecans, walnuts, and hazelnuts all work well), toasted if desired (see page 40)

for the strawberry filling:

3 cups (about 20 ounces/567
   grams) chopped strawberries
   (from about 2 pints)
1/4 cup (2 ounces/57 grams)
   granulated sugar

3 tablespoons all-purpose flour
1 1/2 teaspoons pure vanilla extract
Pinch of table salt

for the pumpkin-spice filling:

1 cup plus 2 tablespoons (9
   ounces/255 grams) canned solid-
   pack pumpkin (not seasoned
   pumpkin pie filling)
3 tablespoons firmly packed light
   brown sugar

2 tablespoons all-purpose flour
3/4 teaspoon ground cinnamon
1/2 teaspoon ground ginger
1/2 teaspoon ground nutmeg

1. If you've chosen the dried-fruit filling, prepare it now. Combine the dried fruits in a shallow bowl or dish. Bring the orange juice or cider to a boil in a small saucepan or in the microwave. Pour the boiling liquid over the dried fruits and let sit until they are soft and plumped, 15 to 20 minutes. Drain off and discard the liquid. Add the sugar and nutmeg to the fruits and stir until blended. Set aside to cool completely.

2. Remove both sheets of frozen puff pastry from the box, set them on a lightly floured surface, and cover with plastic wrap. Do *not* unfold at this point. Let the covered puff pastry sit on the countertop until thawed and just pliable, about 20 minutes.

3. Meanwhile, position the oven rack on the middle rung. Heat the oven to 425 degrees (220°C). Line 2 half sheet pans with parchment or a nonstick liner (I like the Silpat). Have ready the beaten egg and the 2 tablespoons granulated sugar.

4. On a lightly floured work surface, carefully unfold the puff pastry. Dust the top of the pastry with a little flour. Roll out each sheet, lightly dusting with flour as needed to prevent the dough from sticking to the rolling pin and work surface, into a 12-inch (30.5cm) square. Using a 4-inch (10cm) round cookie cutter (or the bottom of a 29-ounce tomato can as a guide), cut out 18 circles. Peel away the scraps and cover the rounds with plastic wrap while preparing the filling.

5. For the chocolate-nut, strawberry, or pumpkin-spice filling, combine the ingredients in a medium bowl and stir until well blended.

6. Place about 1 tablespoon filling on the center of a round. Brush the edge of the dough with the egg. Fold half of the dough over the filling to form a half-moon. Using the tines of a fork, press the curved edge to seal tightly. Repeat with the remaining rounds. (At this point, the pie pockets can be covered with plastic wrap and refrigerated for up to 8 hours or frozen for up to 1 month before proceeding with the recipe.)

7. Arrange the pockets on the prepared sheet pans, spacing them about 2 inches (5cm) apart. Brush the tops with the remaining egg and sprinkle evenly with the granulated sugar. Bake until pastry is puffed and browned, 20 to 25 minutes. Transfer the sheet pans to racks to cool. Serve warm.

storage: You can bake the pie pockets up to 6 hours ahead and reheat them in a 300-degree (150°C) oven until warm, about 15 minutes.

crunchy berry summer crisp

MAKES 8 SERVINGS

as this berry crisp bakes, its intoxicating fragrance floats through your kitchen on the summer breeze. (My kids say that it smells like sunshine.)

My technique for topping a crisp is a bit unusual. I start with softened butter. This way it is much easier to incorporate the other ingredients and to achieve a more even distribution of flavors. Then I tuck the topping into the fridge while I prepare the filling, so it hardens up enough to crumble nicely on top of the berries.

for the topping:

8 tablespoons (4 ounces/113 grams) unsalted butter, at room temperature

1/2 cup (4 ounces/113 grams) firmly packed light brown sugar

1/4 teaspoon ground cinnamon

1/4 teaspoon table salt

2/3 cup (2 ounces/57 grams) old-fashioned rolled oats (not instant)

1/2 cup (2 1/4 ounces/64 grams) all-purpose flour

1/3 cup (1 1/2 ounces/43 grams) coarsely chopped pecans (no need to toast)

for the filling:

2/3 cup (5 1/4 ounces/149 grams) firmly packed light brown sugar

1/4 cup (1 1/4 ounces/35 grams) all-purpose flour

1/4 teaspoon table salt

3 pints (30 ounces/850 grams/about 6 cups) assorted fresh berries, rinsed and well dried

1 teaspoon finely grated lemon zest (optional)

1 teaspoon lemon juice

go-withs: Sweetened Whipped Cream (page 46) or vanilla ice cream.

1. Position the oven rack on the middle rung. Heat the oven to 375 degrees (190°C). Have ready a shallow 10-cup baking dish. (I like to use a ceramic oval.)

2. TO MAKE THE TOPPING

In a medium bowl, combine the butter, brown sugar, cinnamon, and salt. Mix with a spoon until blended. Add the oats, flour, and pecans. Stir until well blended. Refrigerate while preparing the fruit filling. (At this point, the topping can be covered and refrigerated for up to 2 days or frozen for up to 1 month before using.)

3. TO MAKE THE FILLING

In a large bowl, combine the brown sugar, flour, and salt. Stir with a rubber spatula until blended. Add the berries, lemon zest (if using), and lemon juice and toss gently until the fruit is evenly coated. Pile the berry filling into the baking dish and spread evenly.

4. Remove the topping from the refrigerator. Using your fingers, crumble the topping and scatter it evenly over the fruit. Bake until the filling is bubbling and the topping is browned, about 30 minutes. Transfer to a rack and let cool at least 15 minutes. The crisp is best when served warm from the oven. Serve with a dollop of whipped cream or a generous scoop of vanilla ice cream, if desired.

storage: Cover the cooled crisp with plastic wrap and store at room temperature for up to 1 day.

cinnamon-sugar dumplings with strawberry sauce

MAKES 8 SERVINGS

the technical term for this stovetop dessert is "a grunt," but I've never thought the name was appropriate for a scrumptious, homey dessert that's ridiculously easy to prepare. It consists of warm stewed strawberries served with cinnamon-sweetened steamed dumplings to soak up all the juices of the fruit. Almost any tender fruit can be substituted for the strawberries, so, once you're comfortable with the recipe, I encourage you to experiment.

for the dumplings:

1 1/2 cups (6 3/4 ounces/191 grams) all-purpose flour

3 tablespoons granulated sugar

1 teaspoon baking powder

1/2 teaspoon ground cinnamon

1/4 teaspoon baking soda

1/4 teaspoon table salt

1 cup (8 fl ounces/233 ml) buttermilk

4 tablespoons (2 ounces/57 grams) unsalted butter, melted and slightly cooled

1/2 teaspoon pure vanilla extract

for the sauce:

2 quarts (40 ounces/1,134 grams/about 8 cups) strawberries, rinsed and well dried

1/2 cup (4 ounces/113 grams) granulated sugar

2 tablespoons all-purpose flour

1/4 teaspoon table salt

2/3 cup (5 fl ounces/146 ml) water

1/3 cup (2 1/2 fl ounces/73 ml) orange juice

1. TO MAKE THE DUMPLINGS

In a medium bowl, combine the flour, sugar, baking powder, cinnamon, baking soda, and salt. Whisk until well blended. Set aside to finish later.

2. TO MAKE THE SAUCE

Core the strawberries (cut the enormous ones in half) and set them aside. Combine the sugar, flour, and salt in a 10- or 11-inch (25 to 28cm) skillet with 2 1/2-inch (6.5cm) sides (10- to 12-cup capacity) and whisk until blended. Add the water and orange juice and whisk until blended. Set the skillet over medium-high heat and bring to a boil, whisking frequently.

3.

While the liquid is coming to a boil, add the buttermilk, melted butter and vanilla to the dumpling mixture and stir gently with a rubber spatula just until blended. The batter will be thick. When the liquid in the skillet is boiling, stir in the berries and return to a boil. Once boiling, drop the dumpling batter in large spoonfuls (about 8) onto the berries, spacing the spoonfuls evenly. The batter will almost completely cover the berries, and the spoonfuls will merge into one another but still remain somewhat intact. Immediately cover the skillet with a tight-fitting lid or a double layer of foil. Reduce the heat to low and simmer vigorously for 15 minutes. (Don't be tempted to peek, as you might release the trapped steam that cooks the dumplings.)

4.

After 15 minutes, uncover and insert a toothpick or cake tester in the center of one dumpling; it should come out clean. Slide the skillet from the heat and let cool for about 10 minutes for the juices to thicken slightly. Using a large serving spoon, scoop up the dumplings and the warm strawberries into shallow bowls and drizzle with some additional spoonfuls of the sauce. Serve at once.

stovetop apple-cranberry crumble

MAKES 8 SERVINGS

baking an apple pie takes some planning and time, about an hour for the baking alone. Express Bakers need the great apple flavor of a pie, but in less than half the time. This crumble doesn't disappoint. For enhanced color and taste, I've added a few cranberries (another classic American ingredient) to the mix.

Heating the crumble topping in a skillet by itself releases the natural earthy flavors of the granola. A drizzle of maple syrup and a dash of cinnamon are all that are needed before the topping is ready to sprinkle over the cooked apples and cranberries.

While fresh cranberries are available during the winter months, they're scarce in spring and summer. So plan ahead and buy a few extra bags to tuck away in the freezer. They freeze beautifully, so the crumble can be enjoyed out of season.

for the filling:

- 3 tablespoons (1 1/2 ounces/43 grams) unsalted butter, cut into 3 pieces
- 2 pounds (907 grams) apples, peeled, cored, and thinly sliced (I like Golden Delicious, but any firm, medium-tart apple will do.)
- 3/4 cup (2 1/2 ounces/71 grams) fresh or frozen cranberries
- 1/2 cup (4 ounces/113 grams) firmly packed light brown sugar
- 3 tablespoons all-purpose flour
- 1 teaspoon ground cinnamon
- 1/4 teaspoon ground nutmeg
- 1 teaspoon pure vanilla extract
- Pinch of table salt

for the topping:

3 tablespoons (1 1/2 ounces/85 grams) unsalted butter, cut into 3 pieces

1/2 teaspoon ground cinnamon, or more if needed

2 cups crunchy, lightly sweetened granola

3 tablespoons pure maple syrup

go-withs: vanilla or cinnamon ice cream or Sweetened Whipped Cream (page 46) for garnish (optional)

1. TO MAKE THE FILLING

Put the butter in a 10- to 11-inch (25 to 28cm) skillet with 2-inch (5cm) high sides and set over medium-high heat. When the butter is melted, add the apples, cranberries, brown sugar, flour, cinnamon, nutmeg, vanilla, and salt. Toss until well blended. Continue cooking over medium-high heat, shaking the pan or gently stirring the contents with a wooden spoon, until the sugar is melted and the apples just begin to caramelize, about 5 minutes. Cover the skillet with a tight-fitting lid or a double layer of foil and reduce the heat to low. Continue to simmer, shaking the pan often, until the apples are tender when pierced with the tip of a knife, about 12 minutes longer.

2. TO MAKE THE TOPPING

Meanwhile, put the butter in a separate medium skillet and set over medium heat. When the butter is melted, stir in the 1/2 teaspoon cinnamon and add the granola. Cook, stirring constantly, until the granola is hot and evenly coated with the butter and cinnamon. Taste the granola and add more cinnamon if needed. Drizzle the maple syrup over the granola and cook, stirring, until hot and well blended, about 2 minutes. Set aside and keep warm until the filling is ready.

3. When the apples are tender, uncover the pan. If the apples have released a ton of juice (more than about 1 cup/8 fl ounces/233 ml), increase the heat to high and boil briefly to reduce the liquid. Slide the skillet from the heat and scatter the topping over the filling. Serve the crisp straight from the skillet hot, warm, or at room temperature. Accompany with a scoop of vanilla or cinnamon ice cream or a dollop of whipped cream, if desired.

baking in stages

I'm a much happier person (and I function better too) when I know what's going on ahead of time and can make a plan. I know it's not possible to gaze into a crystal ball, see what's ahead, and be ready with the perfect upside-down cake, fruit pie, or creamy pudding, but the more advance notice I have, the better I can cope. Maybe it's the control-freak side of me (I've heard that bakers tend to be control freaks). Or maybe the pleasure I derive from baking begins with being able to consider many different dessert ideas, and then figure out how to make my choice in a logical, systematic, and efficient way. This lets me have my cake without losing my sanity.

So, in the spirit of planning, this section is about approaching dessert making in steps. I think you'll agree that the philosophy of "do some now, do some later" makes baking infinitely more manageable. This not only saves time but also makes the experience less stressful – and a lot more fun. The recipes in this section use time strategies and storage techniques that allow for stress-free baking.

Baking in Stages recipes are based on three cardinal rules:

1.
fit dessert making into your schedule.

I used to think that once I started a recipe, I had to go through the entire process without stopping. I believe this is why most people don't bake – the time commitment seems overwhelming. But you don't have to bake a dessert from start to finish or even in a single day. The recipes in this section are broken down into brief, doable stages. Once you complete the first step, you can run an errand, go to the gym, pick up the kids from school, and then come back for the next step. Or you can stretch the process over several days. Buttery Pull-Apart Dinner Rolls (page 208) provide one excellent example: the dough can be made one day, refrigerated overnight, shaped, and then refrigerated for up to 24 hours before baking. Examine the

warm cinnamon-spiced blueberry cake
page 70

emergency blender cupcakes
with fudgy frosting
page 72

pumpkin-spice half-moon pie pockets
page 117

10-minute mocha pots de crème
page 98

supermoist banana-nut muffin tops
page 83

stovetop apple-cranberry crumble
page 124

three-bite whoopee pies
page 132

toffee chocolate-nut wedges
page 138

Do Ahead steps at the beginning of each recipe to assess how to fit baking into your day – or week.

2.

bake it and store it.

There's nothing I like more than pulling an impressive dessert out of the fridge or freezer. It's my equivalent of an ice skater's triple lutz or a magician's sleight of hand. The bake-and-store approach makes me feel like a miracle-worker, especially when I hear the oohs and aahs from my friends and family.

Certain desserts are prime candidates for freezing. A cheesecake's rich flavors and creamy texture remain unchanged, even after a month in the freezer. Its taste doesn't suffer, and the chocolate and coffee flavors in Mocha Swirl Cheesecake (page 159) don't diminish at all.

Cookies – raw or baked – freeze perfectly, and they thaw quickly too (a lifesaver when you're in a hurry). I like storing a batch of Three-Bite Whoopee Pies (page 132) in the freezer. That way they're just a brief thaw away from satisfying a sudden craving for something sweet. When planning for my girlfriends' holiday cookie swap, I start two months early. Shaping batches of dough for the Ginger Crackles (page 136) and freezing them in advance means that it's easy for me to make the 12 dozen cookies I have promised. That's right, 12 dozen! As the swap date draws near, I carve out 30 minutes or so here and there and begin to bake trays of the cookies. Once cooled, the cookies head straight back into the freezer until the day before the big swap. You too can bake 144 cookies when you plan ahead and make them in stages.

The fridge is a great holding zone. Some desserts, such as Tangy Lemon Squares (page 148), rest there beautifully for up to four days. Others, such as All-Star Custards (page 219) and Bursting with Raspberries Bread Pudding (page 216), taste delicious if refrigerated for up to two days after baking.

And many desserts could simply be left on the kitchen counter (away from the heat) or any other clear surface. Most cookies, for example, keep well at room temperature – some even for weeks, if they're not devoured in the meantime. Chocolate-Macadamia Biscotti (page 142), Apricot-Pistachio Biscotti (page 145), and Toasted-Coconut Meringue Kisses (page 140) are all good keepers. (The kisses are just as crispy and flavorful after two weeks as when they are freshly made.)

Cakes keep well at room temperature too. The Nutty Caramel–Chocolate Upside Downer (page 182) tastes even better the following day. The chocolate flavor deepens and the cake stays incredibly moist and rich. The Southern Molasses Cake (page 176) is divine served warm from the oven, but if you're making it a day or two ahead, it's just as delicious. It stays moist and its spicy flavor only intensifies.

3.
make it now, bake it later.

I'll admit that a few desserts are better served straight from the oven. But I'll let you in on a little secret – my Chocolate-Raspberry Soufflés (page 222), a traditional last-minute dessert, travel from freezer to oven to table without a whisk in sight. These beauties come out of the oven so puffed, light, and chocolaty that you won't believe they have been made ahead and frozen. With no last-minute whites to beat or delicate folding to be done, you're free to converse with your guests at dinner and still serve them a restaurant-quality dessert.

Baking an uncooked pie straight from the freezer produces spectacular results with no thawing required. Whether you use this technique with Crumble-Topped Pear–Rum Raisin Pie (page 250) or Glazed Apricot-Plum Galette (page 228), freeze-ahead pies will be your trump card come holiday time. It makes Thanksgiving entertaining so much easier and enjoyable.

You can choose to make these recipes straight through to the end, or you can make them in stages. Read the Do Aheads at the beginning of each recipe. They'll tell you exactly how to plan ahead. The stages are broken down into their "doability," and each includes appropriate storage instructions.

So, if you're a planner, enjoy this section. It was written just for you. Even if you're not, the recipes that follow might inspire you to start strategizing. Because, oddly enough, sometimes a little planning can make for some truly spontaneous moments. And often, those turn out to be the most wonderful moments of all.

three-bite whoopee pies

MAKES ABOUT 20 PIES

You may know this old-time dessert as moon pies, devil dogs, or whoopee pies. No matter what the name, the pies are moist and tender – halfway between cookie and cake – and they carry an intense chocolate flavor. While vanilla is the traditional filling, I've also included recipes for peanut butter and chocolate.

do aheads

• The chocolate wafers can be prepared through step 3, layered between parchment or waxed paper in an airtight container or a large zipper-top bag, and stored in the fridge for up to 1 week or in the freezer for up to 3 months.

• The filling can be prepared as directed in step 4, scraped into a container with a tight-fitting lid or a large zipper-top bag, and stored in the fridge for up to 1 week or in the freezer for up to 3 months. Bring to room temperature before assembling the pies.

• The whoopee pies can be prepared through step 6. Layer them between parchment or waxed paper in an airtight container or a large zipper-top bag, and store in the fridge for up to 1 week or in the freezer for up to 3 months.

for the chocolate wafers:

2 cups (9 ounces/255 grams) all-purpose flour

2/3 cup (2 ounces/57 grams) unsweetened natural cocoa powder (not Dutch process), sifted if lumpy

1/2 teaspoon baking soda

1/2 teaspoon table salt

12 tablespoons (6 ounces/170 grams) unsalted butter, at room temperature

1 1/2 cups (12 ounces/340 grams) granulated sugar

1 teaspoon pure vanilla extract

1 cup (8 fl ounces/233 ml) buttermilk

for the vanilla filling:

12 tablespoons (6 ounces/170 grams) unsalted butter, at room temperature

1 1/3 cups (6 1/4 ounces/177 grams) Marshmallow Fluff (not crème)

3/4 cup (3 ounces/85 grams) confectioners' sugar

2 ounces (57 grams) cream cheese, at room temperature

1 1/2 teaspoons pure vanilla extract

1/4 teaspoon table salt

for the chocolate filling:

Vanilla filling (above)

3 ounces (85 grams) bittersweet or semisweet chocolate, chopped, melted, and cooled slightly

2 ounces (57 grams) unsweetened chocolate, chopped, melted, and cooled slightly

for the peanut butter filling:

Vanilla filling (above)

1/2 cup (4 ounces/113 grams) smooth or chunky peanut butter

1. TO MAKE THE CHOCOLATE WAFERS

Position an oven rack on the middle rung. Heat the oven to 375 degrees (190°C). Line 3 cookie sheets with parchment or nonstick baking liners (I like the Silpat).

2. In a medium bowl, combine the flour, cocoa, baking soda, and salt. Whisk until well blended. In a large bowl, combine the butter, sugar, and vanilla. Beat with an electric mixer (stand mixer fitted with the paddle attachment or handheld mixer) on medium-high speed until well blended. Pour in about two-thirds of the dry ingredients and mix on low speed just until blended. The mixture will look sandy, with small pebbles of dough. Add the buttermilk and continue mixing just until blended. Pour in the remaining flour mixture and mix just until blended.

3. Using a small ice-cream scoop about 1 2/3 inches (4.25cm) in diameter or 2 tablespoons, drop 2-tablespoon mounds of the dough onto the prepared cookie sheets, spacing them about 2 inches (5cm) apart. Bake 1 sheet at a time (make sure to use a cooled sheet for the next batch) until the mounds are puffed and a toothpick or cake tester inserted in the center of 1 mound comes out clean, about 11 minutes. Transfer the cookie sheet to a rack and let cool for 5 minutes. Using a spatula, lift the cookies from the sheet onto a rack and let cool completely.

4. TO MAKE THE FILLING

While the chocolate wafers are baking, select and prepare the filling. To make the vanilla filling, combine the butter, marshmallow, confectioners' sugar, cream cheese, vanilla, and salt in a medium bowl. Beat with the electric mixer (stand mixer fitted with the whisk attachment or handheld mixer) on medium speed until well blended and smooth. To make the chocolate filling, make the vanilla filling as directed. Scrape the melted chocolates into the bowl and beat until well blended. To make the peanut butter version, make the vanilla filling as directed. Add the peanut butter and beat until well blended.

5. Cover the bowl with plastic wrap and set the filling aside until the chocolate wafers are ready to be assembled. If the filling is very soft, refrigerate it, stirring frequently, until it's firm enough to hold its shape.

6. TO ASSEMBLE THE PIES

Arrange half of the cooled chocolate wafers, flat side up, on a work surface. Mound about 1 1/2 tablespoons filling in the center of each. Top with the remaining wafers, rounded side up, and press gently on top until the filling spreads just to the edges. Refrigerate until the filling is firm, about 1 hour, or until ready to serve. They're delicious straight from the fridge, but I like them best when they are barely chilled, about 1 hour out of the fridge.

ginger crackles

a chewy gingersnap with a soft, moist texture. I call these cookies "crackles" because the tops are ridged with beautiful cracks. If you have a large stand mixer, consider doubling the recipe and storing some of the shaped dough in the freezer. These cookies appear on the cover of the book.

do aheads

• The dough can be made, shaped, and the balls coated with sugar through step 3 and then frozen for up to 2 months before baking. For best results, position the shaped dough snugly on a small cookie sheet and freeze until very firm. Then pile the frozen balls into a heavy-duty freezer bag and store in the freezer. When you're ready to bake, remove only the number of cookies you need, place them on the prepared cookie sheet, and leave them on the counter while the oven heats up. Bake as directed in step 4.

• The cookies can be prepared through step 4. Layer them between sheets of parchment or waxed paper in an airtight container and store in the fridge for up to 1 week or in the freezer for up to 3 months.

2 1/4 cups (10 ounces/284 grams) all-purpose flour

2 teaspoons ground ginger

1 teaspoon baking soda

3/4 teaspoon ground cinnamon

1/2 teaspoon ground cloves

1/4 teaspoon table salt

8 tablespoons (4 ounces/113 grams) unsalted butter, at room temperature

1/4 cup (2 ounces/57 grams) vegetable shortening

1 cup (8 ounces/227 grams) granulated sugar, plus 2/3 cup (5 1/4 ounces/149 grams) for rolling

1 large egg

1/4 cup (2 fl ounces/58 ml) light molasses (see What Is It? below)

1. Position an oven rack on the middle rung. Heat the oven to 350 degrees (180°C). Line 2 large cookie sheets with parchment or nonstick baking liners (I like the Silpat).

2. In a large bowl, combine the flour, ginger, baking soda, cinnamon, cloves, and salt. Whisk until well blended. In another large bowl, combine the butter, shortening, and 1 cup sugar. Beat with an electric mixer (stand mixer fitted with the paddle attachment or handheld mixer) on medium-high speed until well combined. Add the egg and molasses and beat until well blended. Pour in the dry ingredients and mix on low speed until well blended.

3. Pour the remaining 2/3 cup sugar into a shallow bowl. Using a small ice-cream scoop about 1 1/2 inches (4cm) in diameter or your palms, shape the dough into 1-inch (2.5cm) balls. Roll each ball in the sugar and set 2 inches (5cm) apart on the prepared cookie sheets.

4. Bake 1 sheet at a time (make sure to use a cooled sheet for the second batch) until puffed and lightly browned around the edges, about 13 minutes. Transfer the cookie sheet to a rack and let cool for 5 minutes. Using a spatula, lift the cookies from the sheet onto a rack and let cool completely.

what is it? (molasses)

Molasses is a natural by-product of sugar refinement. The first stage of refining produces light molasses, the next stage dark molasses, and the final stage yields blackstrap, which is the thickest and most bitter. Sulfur used to be added to molasses as a clarifying agent, but you'll rarely see sulfured molasses on the grocery shelves today. I always use unsulfured and get great results from Grandma's brand light molasses.

toffee chocolate-nut wedges

MAKES ONE 9 1/2-INCH (24CM) TART, OR 16 WEDGES

bar cookies are the workhorse of the cookie world – they bake up in one pan, yet can be cut up to serve a crowd. Sometimes bars are lacking in the glamour department, so I've jazzed up the look of this particular bar cookie by baking it in a fluted tart pan and covering the top with chocolate and nuts. When finished, they resemble sophisticated scallop-edged fans and have a down-home toffee taste. If you need to bake a slew of cookies, I've included instructions for making 6 dozen. (See Big-Batch Tip, below.)

do aheads

• The wedges can be prepared through step 3. Layer them between sheets of parchment or waxed paper in an airtight container and store in the fridge for up to 1 week or in the freezer for up to 3 months.

8 tablespoons (4 ounces/113 grams) unsalted butter, at room temperature

1/2 cup (4 ounces/113 grams) firmly packed dark brown sugar

1/4 teaspoon table salt

1 yolk from large egg

1/2 teaspoon pure vanilla extract

1 cup (4 1/2 ounces/128 grams) all-purpose flour

5 ounces (142 grams) bittersweet or semisweet chocolate, chopped

3 tablespoons heavy cream

1/2 cup (2 ounces/57 grams) chopped pecans, toasted (see page 40)

1. Position an oven rack on the middle rung. Heat the oven to 350 degrees (180°C). Lightly grease the bottom and sides of a 9 1/2-inch (24cm) tart pan with a removable bottom.

2. In a large bowl, combine the butter, dark brown sugar, and salt. Beat with an electric mixer (stand mixer fitted with the paddle attachment or handheld mixer) on medium speed until well blended. Add the egg yolk and vanilla and beat just until combined. Pour in the flour and beat on low speed until the dough begins to clump together. Scrape the dough into the prepared pan, scattering the pieces evenly. Using your fingertips (lightly floured, if necessary), pat the dough onto the bottom (not up the sides) of the prepared pan to form an even layer. Bake until the top looks dry and the dough begins to pull away from the sides of the pan, 25 to 27 minutes.

3. Meanwhile, melt the chocolate with the cream in a double boiler (see What Is It? on page 74) or in the microwave (see page 51). Stir until smooth. When the crust is baked, transfer the pan to a rack. Pour the warm ganache (the chocolate-cream mixture) over the warm crust and spread evenly to within 1/2 inch (1.25cm) of the edge. (An offset spatula is a great tool for this job.) Scatter the pecans evenly over the ganache and gently press them into the chocolate. Let cool completely until the chocolate is set, about 4 hours at room temperature or about 2 hours in the refrigerator. Remove the outer ring of the tart pan and cut the "cookie tart" into 16 wedges. Serve the wedges chilled or at room temperature.

Big-Batch Tip: Double all the ingredients, following the same directions and timing, and bake in a 9-by-13-inch (22.75-by-33cm) baking pan. (I like to use a straight-sided metal pan for this version, as it makes a cleaner-looking shortbread cookie.) Once cooled, cut into small bars. You'll have about 6 dozen or so.

toasted-coconut meringue kisses

MAKES ABOUT 40 KISSES

the elegant appearance of these kisses belies their ease of preparation. Try them alongside your favorite ice cream or with a mix of fresh fruit. They also benefit from being drizzled with Emergency Strawberry Sauce (page 43) or scattered with fresh berries. These crispy little gems last up to a month.

do aheads

• The meringues can be prepared through step 4. Store in an airtight container at room temperature for up to 1 month.

3/4 cup (3 ounces/85 grams) confectioners' sugar

1/2 cup (3 1/2 ounces/99 grams) superfine sugar (see page 21)

1/4 teaspoon table salt

4 large egg whites (1/2 cup/4 1/2 ounces/128 grams)

1/2 teaspoon cream of tartar

1/4 teaspoon pure vanilla extract

1/3 cup (1 1/2 ounces/43 grams) unsalted pistachios, chopped medium-fine (no need to toast)

1/3 cup (1 ounce/28 grams) shredded sweetened dried coconut, lightly toasted (see page 40)

go-with: 3 tablespoons finely chopped unsalted pistachios for garnish (optional)

1. Position 2 oven racks on the top and bottom third rungs of the oven. Heat the oven to 175 degrees (80°C). Line 2 cookie sheets with parchment paper.

2. Sift together the confectioners' sugar, superfine sugar, and salt. (I like to sift ingredients onto a sturdy, yet flexible, surface. A paper plate or piece of parchment works well. The flexibility allows me to add the sifted ingredients slowly to the bowl without spilling.) In a large bowl, combine the egg whites and cream of tartar. Beat with an electric mixer (stand mixer fitted with the whisk attachment or handheld mixer) on medium-low speed until the whites are frothy. Increase the speed to medium-high and beat until the whites form soft peaks. Continue beating while gradually sprinkling in the sifted sugars. When all the sugar has been added, increase the speed to high and whip until firm, glossy peaks form. Add the vanilla and the 1/3 cup chopped nuts and beat just until blended, about 10 seconds.

3. Spoon about half of the meringue into a large pastry bag fitted with a number 8 (large) star tip. Pipe wavy mounds, about 1 1/2 inches (4cm) wide and 2 inches (5cm) from tip to base, onto the prepared cookie sheets, spacing them about 1/2 inch (1.25cm) apart. They will look like tall, wavy kisses. If the tip gets clogged with a nut, use the back of a small knife or spoon to pry open the points of the star tip slightly and the nut will wiggle out. Sprinkle the toasted coconut evenly over the meringues. Then dust evenly with the 3 tablespoons pistachios, if desired.

4. Place a cookie sheet on each rack and bake until the meringues are dried and crisp but not browned, about 3 hours. Turn off the oven and let the meringues cool in the oven for about 1 hour. Remove from the oven and gently lift the meringues off the parchment.

chocolate-macadamia biscotti

MAKES ABOUT 3 DOZEN BISCOTTI

biscotti, traditional Italian cookies, have become very popular in the United States with the gourmet coffee shop set. While many people bake biscotti until they are crisp, I like to underbake them, preferring a softer, slightly chewy version. Your choice depends on whether you intend to dunk them in coffee or tea or just nibble on them. To appease both the softer and drier camps, I've included baking times for both.

This is one of a handful of recipes for which I strongly recommend using a stand mixer. The handheld type just won't blend the thick batter. If you don't have a stand mixer, use the next best thing, your hands. The dough is sticky and mixing it will be a bit messy, but the finished biscotti are well worth it.

do aheads

• The biscotti can be prepared through step 3. Wrap the dough logs in plastic wrap and refrigerate for up to 2 days before baking. While the oven is heating up, unwrap the dough and proceed with the recipe.

• The biscotti can be prepared through step 4. Loosely cover the cookie sheet with aluminum foil and keep at room temperature for up to 12 hours before proceeding with the final baking.

• The biscotti can be prepared through step 6. Layer them between sheets of parchment or waxed paper in an airtight container and store at room temperature for up to 2 weeks or in the freezer for up to 3 months.

1 cup (5 ounces/142 grams) unsalted macadamia nuts

1 2/3 cups (7 1/2 ounces/213 grams) all-purpose flour

1 cup (8 ounces/227 grams) firmly packed light brown sugar

2/3 cup (2 ounces/57 grams) unsweetened natural cocoa powder (not Dutch process), sifted if lumpy

1 teaspoon ground cinnamon, or 2 teaspoons finely grated orange zest (optional, see the flavoring note, below)

2 teaspoons baking powder

1/4 teaspoon baking soda

1/4 teaspoon table salt

1/2 cup (3 ounces/85 grams) semi-sweet chocolate chips or chopped (1/4-inch pieces) bittersweet chocolate (optional)

2 large eggs

2 tablespoons coffee-flavored liqueur, if using cinnamon, or orange juice, if using orange zest (optional, see the flavoring note, below)

1 teaspoon pure vanilla extract

1. Position an oven rack on the middle rung. Heat the oven to 325 degrees (165°C). Line 1 large cookie sheet with parchment or a nonstick baking liner (I like the Silpat). Cut the macadamia nuts until coarsely chopped. These nuts are tricky to cut. They roll around and can easily get away from you. To avoid ending up with too many tiny pieces, I spread the nuts on a paper plate and cut them with a few swipes of a chef's knife. The paper plate keeps them contained (no rolling), so you'll have more control over their size. Set the nuts aside.

2. In the large bowl of a stand mixer fitted with the paddle attachment or, if mixing by hand, in a large bowl, combine the flour, brown sugar, cocoa powder, cinnamon or orange zest, baking powder, baking soda, and salt. Whisk until well blended. Add the nuts and the chocolate chips, if using, and beat on low speed or stir with a wooden spoon briefly to mix. In a small bowl, lightly whisk together the eggs, liqueur or orange juice (if using), and the vanilla. (I like to use a 1-cup Pyrex measure for this job; the spout makes pouring easier.) With the mixer on low speed or stirring

with the wooden spoon, slowly pour in the egg mixture. Continue beating or mixing with the spoon or your hands until the dough is well blended and forms moist clumps, about 2 minutes.

3. Dump the dough onto an unfloured work surface. Scrape out any dry ingredients from the bowl and gently knead them into the dough, lightly flouring your hands if the dough is too sticky. Divide the dough into 2 equal piles. Shape each pile into a log 8 inches (20cm) long and about 3 inches (7.75cm) in diameter, flouring your hands as needed. Transfer the logs to the prepared cookie sheet, spacing them about 3 1/2 inches (9cm) apart.

4. Bake until the tops are cracked and the dough inside the cracks no longer looks wet, about 32 minutes. Transfer the cookie sheet to a rack and let cool for about 15 minutes. Leave the oven set at 325 degrees (165°C).

5. Cut the logs on the diagonal into slices 1/2 inch (1.25cm) thick. I like to use a serrated (bread) knife to create neat slices. The top layer is the most fragile and most likely to break apart, so I use a gentle sawing motion to cut through the crust. After that, a firm downward push on the knife is all that's needed. Arrange the slices, cut side down, on the cookie sheet. It's all right if they touch, because they don't spread.

6. Bake until the biscotti are dried to your taste, 10 (for soft and chewy) to 20 (dry and crisp) minutes. Transfer the cookie sheet to a rack and let cool completely.

flavoring note: A touch of ground cinnamon and coffee liqueur adds a Mexican edge to the biscotti. If you're not a fan of cinnamon, try the orange zest and juice alternative. Chocolate and orange complement each other well.

apricot-pistachio biscotti

Unlike store-bought varieties, homemade biscotti are intensely flavored and can vary from slightly chewy to quite crisp, depending on your personal preference. And, because of their sturdy nature and long shelf life, biscotti are a perfect gift at any time of the year.

This is one of a handful of recipes for which I strongly recommend using a stand mixer, as the handheld type won't get the job done. If you don't have a stand mixer, use the next best thing, your hands. The dough is sticky and messy, but the finished biscotti are well worth the inconvenience.

do aheads

• The biscotti can be prepared through step 3. Wrap the dough logs in plastic wrap and refrigerate for up to 2 days before baking. While the oven is heating up, unwrap the dough and proceed with the recipe.

• The biscotti can be prepared through step 4. Loosely cover the cookie sheet with aluminum foil and keep at room temperature for up to 12 hours before proceeding with the final baking.

• The biscotti can be prepared through step 6. Layer them between sheets of parchment or waxed paper in an airtight container and store at room temperature for up to 2 weeks or in the freezer for up to 3 months.

2 1/4 cups (10 ounces/284 grams) all-purpose flour

1 cup (8 ounces/227 grams) granulated sugar

2 teaspoons finely grated lemon zest

1 1/2 teaspoons baking powder

1/2 teaspoon table salt

1 cup (5 ounces/142 grams) unsalted pistachio nuts

1/2 cup (4 ounces/113 grams) lightly packed dried apricots, coarsely chopped or snipped

2 large eggs

1 yolk from large egg

1 tablespoon lemon juice

1 teaspoon pure vanilla extract

1. Position an oven rack on the middle rung. Heat the oven to 325 degrees (165°C). Line 1 large cookie sheet with parchment or a nonstick baking liner (I like the Silpat).

2. In the large bowl of a stand mixer fitted with the paddle attachment or, if mixing by hand, in a large bowl, combine the flour, sugar, lemon zest, baking powder, and salt. Whisk until well blended. Add the nuts and apricots and beat on low speed or with a wooden spoon briefly. In a small bowl (I like to use a 1-cup Pyrex measure for this job; the spout makes pouring easier), lightly whisk together the eggs, egg yolk, lemon juice, and vanilla. With the mixer on low speed or stirring with the spoon, slowly pour in the egg mixture. Continue beating or mixing with the spoon or your hands until the dough is well blended and begins to form moist clumps, about 2 minutes.

3. Dump the dough onto the unfloured work surface. Scrape out any dry ingredients from the bowl and gently knead them into the dough, lightly flouring your hands if the dough is too sticky. Divide the dough into 2 equal piles. Shape each pile into a log 10 inches (25cm) long and about 2 inches (5cm) in diameter, flouring your hands as needed. Transfer the logs to the prepared cookie sheet, spacing them about 3 1/2 inches (9cm) apart.

4. Bake until the tops are cracked and the dough inside the cracks no longer looks wet, about 40 minutes. Transfer the cookie sheet to a rack and let cool for about 15 minutes. Leave the oven set at 325 degrees (165°C).

5. Cut the logs on the diagonal into slices 1/2 inch (1.25cm) thick. I like to use a serrated (bread) knife to create neat slices. The top layer is the most fragile and most likely to break apart, so I use a gentle sawing motion to cut through the crust. After that, a firm downward push on the knife is all that's needed. Arrange the slices, cut side down, on the cookie sheet. It's all right if they touch, because they don't spread.

6. Bake until the biscotti are dried to your taste, 10 (for soft and chewy) to 20 minutes (for dry and crisp). Transfer the cookie sheet to a rack and let cool completely.

flavoring note: For a festive winter holiday cookie, substitute dried cranberries (1/2 cup/2 1/2 ounces/71 grams) for the apricots. Cranberries and pistachios are delicious together and also make the most of the season's traditional colors.

tangy lemon squares

MAKES 2 DOZEN SMALL BAR COOKIES

this version of lemon squares is streamlined and straightforward. The simple-to-make crust mixes up quickly and presses into the pan with little fuss. The lemon curd filling is baked in the prepared crust so that there is no need to stir the curd over simmering water on top of the stove. I get the same rich, tangy taste and smooth, luxurious texture in half the time and effort as the classic.

do aheads

• If you're not planning to serve the baked bars within 24 hours, leave them uncut. Let them cool completely, cover the pan with plastic wrap, and refrigerate for up to 4 days before serving. They can also be stored, uncut, for up to 3 months in the freezer.

for the crust:

3/4 cup (3 1/2 ounces/99 grams) all-purpose flour

1/2 cup (2 ounces/57 grams) confectioners' sugar

1/2 teaspoon table salt

8 tablespoons (4 ounces/113 grams) cold unsalted butter, cut into 8 pieces

for the filling:

1 1/2 cups (6 ounces/170 grams) confectioners' sugar

3/4 cup (6 fl ounces/175 ml) lemon juice

1/2 cup (4 fl ounces/117 ml) heavy cream

1 tablespoon finely grated lemon zest

1/4 teaspoon table salt

3 large eggs

1. TO MAKE THE CRUST

Position an oven rack on the middle rung. Heat the oven to 350 degrees (180°C). Lightly grease the bottom and sides of an 8-inch (20cm) square baking dish (I use Pyrex) and line the bottom with parchment.

2.

Combine the flour, sugar, and salt in a food processor. Pulse briefly until blended. Add the butter pieces. Process until the dough forms moist crumbs and sticks together when pinched; there should be no dry bits. Scatter the crumbs in the baking dish and press them evenly into the bottom, lightly flouring your fingertips to prevent sticking if necessary. Bake until golden brown (the edges will be a bit darker), about 25 minutes. Transfer to a rack. Reduce the oven temperature to 300 degrees (150°C).

3. TO MAKE THE FILLING

As soon as the crust goes into the oven, combine the sugar, lemon juice, cream, lemon zest, and salt in a medium bowl. Whisk until well blended and the sugar is dissolved. Add the eggs and whisk just until blended. (Overmixing can aerate the filling too much, causing it to puff and crack in the oven.)

4.

Once the crust is baked and the oven has cooled to 300 degrees (150°C), give the custard a final whisking and pour over the baked crust. Return to the oven and bake until filling jiggles slightly when the baking dish is nudged, about 25 minutes. Transfer the baking dish to a rack and let cool completely. Chill until firm, 2 to 4 hours, then cut into small rectangles (see Technique Tip, page 150). Keep covered in the refrigerator until ready to serve.

technique tip for cutting bar cookies

Cutting bar cookies can be tricky. I've found that I get the neatest edges this way:

1. Before you cut, use a ruler and mark off the lines.
2. Heat a bench scraper (see page 34) under very hot water and towel dry.
3. Using the hot scraper, cut straight down without dragging the blade.
4. Heat and dry the scraper before every cut.

soft chocolate-almond oatmeal cookies

MAKES ABOUT 45 COOKIES

expect a soft, cakelike chocolate cookie that gets its distinct taste from almond extract and crunchy toasted almonds. Thanks to my friend Annie Giamattei, these cookies have been a lunchbox and after-school favorite in the Dodge house for many years.

do aheads

• The cookies can be prepared through step 4. Layer them between sheets of parchment or waxed paper in an airtight container and store in the fridge for up to 1 week or in the freezer for up to 3 months.

2 cups (6 1/2 ounces/184 grams) quick-cooking rolled oats (not instant)

1 1/2 cups (6 3/4 ounces/191 grams) all-purpose flour

1/2 cup (1 1/2 ounces/43 grams) unsweetened natural cocoa powder (not Dutch process), sifted if lumpy

1/2 teaspoon baking soda

1/4 teaspoon table salt

1 1/3 cups (10 3/4 ounces/305 grams) firmly packed light brown sugar

16 tablespoons (8 ounces/227 grams) unsalted butter, at room temperature

1 large egg

1 teaspoon pure vanilla extract

1/2 teaspoon pure almond extract

1/3 cup (2 1/2 fl ounces/73 ml) whole milk

1 cup (4 1/2 ounces/128 grams) slivered almonds, toasted (see page 40)

1. Position an oven rack on the middle rung. Heat the oven to 350 degrees (180°C). Line 3 cookie sheets with parchment or nonstick baking liners (I like the Silpat).

2. In a medium bowl, combine the oats, flour, cocoa, baking soda, and salt. Whisk until well blended. In another large bowl, combine the brown sugar and butter. Beat with an electric mixer (stand mixer fitted with the paddle attachment or handheld mixer) on medium speed until well combined. Add the egg and vanilla and almond extracts and beat until well blended. Pour in half of the dry ingredients and mix on low speed just until blended. Add the milk and mix just until blended. Pour in the remaining flour mixture and mix just until blended. Add the nuts and mix briefly to combine.

3. Using a small ice-cream scoop about 1 2/3 inches (4.25cm) in diameter or your palms, shape the dough into 1 1/2-inch (4cm) balls. Arrange the mounds on the prepared cookie sheets, spacing them about 2 inches (5cm) apart. Lightly dampen your fingertips and press on each mound to flatten slightly so it's about 1/2 inch (1.25cm) thick.

4. Bake 1 sheet at a time (make sure to use a cooled sheet for the next batch) until the cookies are puffed and still moist-looking on top, about 11 minutes. Transfer the cookie sheet to a rack and let cool for about 10 minutes. Using a spatula, lift the cookies from the sheet onto a rack and let cool completely.

big-batch cornmeal shortbread

MAKES 45 COOKIES

Cornmeal adds texture to this shortbread. No matter which flavoring you choose – vanilla, ginger, spice, or nuts – the results will be toasty, buttery, crumbly, and rich. A perfect food for afternoon tea or packed in a tin for a spring picnic, homemade shortbread also makes a welcome holiday gift from your kitchen.

Traditional shortbread is baked in special molds that limit the amount you can bake at one time. This quick and easy Big-Batch version makes 45 professional-looking shortbread rectangles all at once. Using a 9-by-13-inch (22.75-by-33cm) baking pan eliminates the need to shape the shortbreads individually, and you don't need to chill the dough before baking to keep their shape. To make an even bigger batch, double the recipe and press into two 9-by-13-inch (22.75-by-33cm) pans.

do aheads

• The dough can be prepared through step 3 and refrigerated in the baking pan for up to 2 days or frozen for up to 1 month. Be sure the pan is tightly wrapped in plastic to prevent it from picking up any other flavors. If you freeze the dough, thaw it in the fridge for about 12 hours before proceeding.

• The shortbread can be prepared through step 4. Layer the cookies between sheets of parchment or waxed paper in an airtight container. They're best eaten within 4 days if kept at room temperature, or they can be stored in the freezer for up to 3 months.

for the vanilla shortbread:

2 cups (9 ounces/255 grams) all-purpose flour

1 1/4 cups (6 1/4 ounces/177 grams) finely ground yellow corn-meal

1/2 teaspoon table salt

24 tablespoons (12 ounces/340 grams) unsalted butter, at room temperature

1 1/2 cups (6 ounces/170 grams) confectioners' sugar

2 teaspoons pure vanilla extract

for the flavor options (choose one):

Ginger: 1 1/2 teaspoons ground ginger and 3/4 cup (3 ounces/85 grams) minced crystallized ginger

or

Spice: 2 1/2 teaspoons ground cinnamon, 1/2 teaspoon ground nutmeg, and a pinch of ground cloves

or

Nuts: 1 cup (4 ounces/113 grams) finely chopped, toasted nuts (pistachios, hazelnuts, pecans, or walnuts are delicious), see page 40

1. Position an oven rack on the middle rung. Heat the oven to 325 degrees (165°C). Lightly grease the bottom and sides of a 9-by-13-inch (22.75-by-33cm) baking pan (I prefer a straight-sided metal pan for this recipe, as it makes for a cleaner-looking cookie). Line the bottom with parchment.

2. In a medium bowl, combine the flour, cornmeal, and salt. Choose one of the flavoring options and add the ingredients to the bowl. Whisk until well blended. In a large bowl, combine the butter, confectioners' sugar, and vanilla. Beat with an electric mixer (stand mixer fitted with the paddle attachment or handheld mixer) on medium-high speed until smooth and creamy. Add the flour mixture and beat on low speed until the dough begins to form moist clumps.

3. Dump the dough into the prepared pan. Using lightly floured finger-tips, press the dough into the pan to form an even layer. (I use a short, cylindrical wooden block – yes, I swiped it from my kid's block collection! – and roll it over the dough to smooth it.) Using the tip of a knife or a small metal spatula, cut the dough all the way through, forming bars 1 inch (2.5cm) by about 2 1/2 inches (6.5cm) (1 inch/2.5cm across the short side and just a smidgen over 2 1/2 inches/6.5cm on the long side). With the tines of a fork, prick each bar three times all the way through, spacing the holes evenly and on the diagonal. Lightly flour the tines as necessary to prevent sticking.

4. Bake until the tops look dry and the edges are ever so slightly browned, about 40 minutes. Transfer the pan to a rack. Using a sharp knife or a bench scraper (I prefer the bench scraper), cut the shortbread into bars using the lines as a guide. Be sure to do this when the shortbread is just out of the oven (once cooled, it will crumble when cut). Let the bars cool completely before removing them from the pan.

Cakes – Small and Large

• • •

classic crumb cake

MAKES ONE 9-BY-13-INCH (22.75-BY-33CM) CAKE, OR 12 SERVINGS

When I was growing up in Brooklyn Heights, an unbelievably delicious store-bought crumb cake was a special breakfast treat on weekends. I was especially (if not obsessively) partial to the crumb topping, picking off every last bit before discarding the cake and moving on to my next piece. I can't begin to tell you how that irritated my brothers. In this recipe the cake is every bit as delicious as its topping.

The crumb topping is lightly sugared and spiced and is prepared first, so that it has time to cool and will be easy to crumble over the batter. When the cake is fresh from the oven, the crumb topping is slightly crunchy – a lovely contrast to the soft, moist cake. Over the next day or so, the crumbs soften and the cinnamon-nutmeg flavor becomes more pronounced.

do aheads

• The crumb topping can be prepared through step 1 up to 1 day ahead. Cover with plastic wrap and store at room temperature.

• The dry ingredients and the wet ingredients, except the butter, can be prepared as directed in step 3 up to 1 day ahead. Keep the dry ingredients covered and at room temperature and the wet ingredients covered and in the fridge. Melt the butter just before continuing with the recipe.

• The cake can be prepared through step 5, covered with plastic wrap, and stored at room temperature. It holds beautifully for up to 4 days, and I think it tastes better than it does fresh from the oven. This isn't the type of cake that greatly benefits from being served when still warm, so there's no need to wake up at the crack of dawn to bake it.

for the topping:

16 tablespoons (8 ounces/227 grams) unsalted butter, cut into 6 pieces

1/2 cup (4 ounces/113 grams) granulated sugar

3/4 cup (6 ounces/170 grams) firmly packed light brown sugar

1 1/2 teaspoons ground cinnamon

1/4 teaspoon ground nutmeg

Pinch of table salt

2 2/3 cups (12 ounces/340 grams) all-purpose flour

for the cake:

3 cups (13 1/2 ounces/383 grams) all-purpose flour

1 1/4 cups (10 ounces/284 grams) granulated sugar

1 1/2 teaspoons baking powder

1/2 teaspoon table salt

2 large eggs

1 cup (8 fl ounces/233 ml) whole milk

12 tablespoons (6 ounces/170 grams) unsalted butter, melted and cooled slightly

2 teaspoons pure vanilla extract

go-with: confectioners' sugar for dusting (optional)

1. TO MAKE THE TOPPING

In a large saucepan, melt the butter over medium heat. Slide the pan from the heat and add the granulated sugar, brown sugar, cinnamon, nutmeg, and salt. Stir with a rubber spatula, pressing when necessary, until there are no lumps of sugar. Add the flour and mix until well blended and pasty. Set aside.

2. TO MAKE THE CAKE

Position an oven rack on the middle rung. Heat the oven to 350 degrees (180°C). Lightly grease the bottom and sides of a 9-by-13-inch (22.75-by-33cm) baking pan or dish.

3.

In a large bowl, combine the flour, granulated sugar, baking powder, and salt. Whisk until well blended. In a medium bowl, combine the eggs, milk, melted butter, and vanilla. Whisk until well blended.

4.

Pour the wet ingredients over the dry ingredients and gently stir with a rubber spatula just until blended. Scrape the batter into the prepared pan and spread evenly. Break up the topping mixture with your fingers into medium-sized pieces and sprinkle evenly over the cake batter to form a generous layer.

5.

Bake until the cake springs back when lightly pressed in the center and a toothpick or cake tester inserted in the center comes out clean, about 40 minutes. Transfer the pan to a rack to cool. Serve warm or at room temperature. Before serving, sift some confectioners' sugar over the top, if desired.

Shortcut Tip: Melting all the butter you need for the cake and the crumb topping recipe in one pan shaves off a bit of time. Before I use it in the recipes, I give the butter a good stir, and then I pour off the 3/4 cup (6 fl ounces/175 ml) for the cake before continuing with the remainder for the crumb topping.

mocha swirl cheesecake

MAKES ONE 9-INCH (22.75CM) CAKE, OR 16 SERVINGS

every Weekend Baker must have a great cheesecake in his or her repertoire. Not only is a cheesecake one of the easiest desserts to make, it
also freezes beautifully, so it's ready to thaw and serve whenever you need
it. Chocolate and mocha are two of my favorite flavors and in combination
they're to die for.

When Claire Van de Berghe, friend and chief Weekend Baker recipe
tester, made this cake, she was surprised by how easy it was to handle.
Claire initially worried that the cookie crust would crumble when she trans-
ferred the cake to the serving plate and that the cake would be difficult to
slice. Instead, she found the cake unexpectedly sturdy, making it a good
dessert to take on the road to a friend's house.

do aheads

• The cookie crust can be prepared through step 3, covered with plastic
wrap, and stored at room temperature for up to 2 days before proceeding
with the cake.

• The cheesecake can be prepared through step 8. Once cooled, it can be
covered with plastic wrap and refrigerated for up to 3 days. Or it can be
frozen for up to 1 month. Wrap the entire pan tightly in plastic wrap, or
remove the outer ring of the springform pan and loosen the cake from the
bottom as directed in step 9, but don't remove it quite yet. Place the cake
in the freezer until well chilled and the top is firm. (This "prefreeze" pre-
vents the plastic from marring the smooth top of the cake.) Lay out 2 large
pieces of plastic wrap in a cross pattern and slide the cake from its bottom
onto the center of the cross. Wrap well in the plastic. To serve, unwrap the
frozen cake and set it on a flat serving plate. Cover loosely with plastic
wrap and thaw in the refrigerator.

1 1/2 cups (6 ounces/170 grams) chocolate cookie crumbs (from about 30 chocolate wafers – I use Famous Chocolate Wafers by Nabisco)

3 tablespoons granulated sugar

4 tablespoons (2 ounces/57 grams) unsalted butter, melted

for the filling:

8 ounces (227 grams) bittersweet chocolate, finely chopped

1 tablespoon water or dark rum

1 1/2 teaspoons instant coffee granules (any kind, even decaf, will do)

3 packages (8 ounces/227 grams each) cream cheese, at room temperature

1 1/4 cups (10 ounces/284 grams) granulated sugar

1/4 teaspoon table salt

1/2 cup (4 1/2 ounces/128 grams) sour cream

2 teaspoons pure vanilla extract

3 large eggs

1. Position an oven rack on the middle rung. Heat the oven to 400 degrees (200°C). Have ready a 9-inch (22.75cm) springform pan.

2. TO MAKE THE CRUST

In a medium bowl, combine the cookie crumbs and sugar. Stir until well blended. Drizzle the melted butter over the crumbs and mix with a fork until evenly moistened and well blended.

3. Dump the crumbs into the springform pan and cover with a large piece of plastic wrap. Place your hands on the plastic wrap and spread the crumbs to coat the bottom of the pan evenly. (The plastic wrap will keep the crumbs from sticking to your hands.) Once the crumbs are in place, and with the plastic wrap still in place, use your fingers to pinch and press some of the crumbs around the inside edge of the pan to cover the sides evenly and completely. Redistribute the remaining crumbs evenly over the bottom of the pan and firmly press down to make a compact layer. I like to use a metal measuring cup with straight sides and a flat bottom for this task.

4. Bake the crust until it is slightly darker, about 10 minutes. Set aside on a wire rack to cool. Reduce the oven temperature to 300 degrees (150°C).

5. TO MAKE THE FILLING

While the crust is baking, begin to make the filling. Melt the chocolate in a double boiler (see What Is It? on page 74) or in the microwave (see page 51). Stir until smooth and set aside. In a medium bowl, combine the water or rum and coffee granules. Set aside, stirring occasionally until the coffee dissolves.

6. In a large bowl, beat the cream cheese with an electric mixer (stand mixer fitted with the paddle attachment or handheld mixer) on medium-high speed until very smooth and fluffy. Add the sugar and salt and beat until well blended and smooth; there should be no lumps. Add the sour cream and vanilla and beat until well blended, scraping down the sides of the bowl frequently. Reduce the speed to medium and add the eggs one at a time, beating well after each addition. Once the eggs have been added to the batter, it's important to mix thoroughly without overbeating, or the cheesecake will puff and crack during baking. Scoop up about 2 cups of the mixture and transfer it to the bowl with the coffee liquid; stir until blended. Scrape the cooled chocolate into the remaining batter in the large bowl and stir until well blended.

7. Reserve about one-fourth of the mocha batter for the top of the cheesecake. Spread about one-third of the chocolate batter on the cooled crust in the springform pan. Drizzle about one-half of the remaining mocha batter in a circular pattern over the chocolate. Carefully pour about one-half of the remaining chocolate batter over the top. Drizzle with the remaining mocha batter, then pour the remaining chocolate batter into the pan. Drizzle the reserved mocha batter over the top. Using a knife or the wooden end of a rubber spatula, gently swirl the batters together so that they are mixed but not completely blended. There should still be medium streaks of each batter visible. Gently rap the pan against the countertop several times to settle the contents. Don't worry if the batter isn't completely smooth on top. It will even out during baking.

8. Bake until the center of the cheesecake barely jiggles when the pan is nudged, about 1 hour. The edges will puff and develop a few small cracks. Set the pan on a rack and let cool completely. Cover and refrigerate until very cold, at least 6 hours.

9. To serve, release the springform clasp and lift off the ring. Run a long, thin spatula under the bottom crust. Carefully slide the cake onto a flat serving plate. Cut into slices with a thin knife run under hot water and wiped dry, repeating the process for each slice.

rich orange butter cake
with citrus wedges

MAKES ONE 10-INCH (25CM) BUNDT CAKE, OR 12 SERVINGS

this cake is one of the longest keepers in my repertoire. Inherently moist and buttery, it holds up well at room temperature and freezes wonderfully. I bake the cake in a Bundt pan, which is a tube pan with fluted sides. The shape is elegant and the hole in the center is ideally suited for a mixture of seasonal fresh fruits. In winter I like to fill it with orange and grapefruit wedges. The colorful mix of fruit spilling out from the cake makes a sophisticated presentation and a refreshing dessert. Served plain, it is a lovely tea or snack cake.

Just a brief note regarding the orange juice and zest in the recipe: Using freshly squeezed juice and zest is certainly preferred, but I've made this cake without the zest and with store-bought pasteurized fresh juice, and the results have been excellent. I'll leave the decision up to you and your time constraints.

do aheads

• The cake can be prepared through step 3, covered, and stored at room temperature for up to 4 days, or wrapped and frozen for up to 3 months. Thaw at room temperature before serving.

• The citrus wedges can be prepared, covered, and refrigerated for up to 1 day before serving.

for the cake:

3 cups (13 1/2 ounces/383 grams) all-purpose flour

2 1/2 teaspoons baking powder

1/4 teaspoon baking soda

1/4 teaspoon table salt

16 tablespoons (8 ounces/227 grams) unsalted butter, at room temperature

1 1/3 cups (10 1/2 ounces/298 grams) granulated sugar

2 teaspoons finely grated orange zest (optional)

4 large eggs

1 cup (8 fl ounces/233 ml) orange juice

for the glaze:

3/4 cup (6 fl ounces/175 ml) orange juice

3/4 cup (3 ounces/85 grams) confectioners' sugar

go-with: Citrus Wedges (below).

1. TO MAKE THE CAKE

Position an oven rack on the middle rung. Heat the oven to 350 degrees (180°C). Lightly grease and flour the bottom and sides of a 12-cup Bundt pan or other fluted tube pan (see equipment note, page 166), tapping out the excess flour.

2.

In a medium bowl, combine the flour, baking powder, baking soda, and salt. Whisk until well blended. In a large bowl, beat the butter with an electric mixer (stand mixer fitted with the paddle attachment or handheld mixer) on medium-high speed until smooth. Add the sugar and the orange zest, if using, and beat until well combined. Add the eggs one at a time, beating well after each addition. Add half of the flour mixture and mix on low speed just until blended. Add the orange juice and mix just until blended. Add the remaining flour mixture and mix just until blended. Scrape the batter into the prepared pan and spread evenly.

3. Bake until light brown and a toothpick or cake tester inserted in the center comes out with just a few small crumbs attached, 38 to 43 minutes.

4. TO MAKE THE GLAZE

Meanwhile, make the glaze. In a small bowl or a 2-cup Pyrex measure, combine the orange juice and the confectioners' sugar. Stir frequently while the cake is baking until the sugar is dissolved.

5. When the cake is done, transfer the pan to a rack and let cool for about 15 minutes. If necessary, run a thin knife around the pan sides to loosen the cake. Invert the cake onto the rack and lift off the pan. Set the rack over a large plate or pan. Using a wooden skewer or cake tester, poke 30 or 40 holes all the way through the cake, spacing them evenly. Give the glaze a stir and spoon it evenly over the top (the fluted side) of the cake. Let the cake cool completely.

6. Using 2 long metal spatulas or your hands, transfer the cake to a serving plate and pile the citrus wedges in the center. Slice the cake with a serrated knife and accompany each slice with some of the citrus wedges.

Citrus Wedges

4 large white grapefruit

4 large blood oranges

4 large navel oranges

1 tablespoon chopped fresh mint leaves

Using a sharp knife, cut away the ends of 1 grapefruit. Stand it on one end and, using long strokes of the blade, cut away the zest and pith. Hold the skinned fruit over a large bowl and carefully cut the fruit sections from the white inner pith, allowing the wedges and their juices to fall into the bowl. Repeat with remaining fruits. Toss the wedges with the mint. Serve immediately, or cover and refrigerate until serving.

equipment note: I use a heavy Bundt pan made by Nordic Ware, but there are many different types available. Cakes baked in less substantial, thinner-walled tube pans will bake up faster (about 38 minutes), so the first time you make this cake, check for doneness on the earlier side. Once baked, jot the bake time in the margin of your book for future reference.

Flavor Variations: The citrus wedges can be replaced with raspberries and a spoonful of Sweetened Whipped Cream (page 46). You can also use a mix of fresh berries or slices of mango, pineapple, or melon. Or you can substitute already-prepared fruit. My grocery store has several varieties of cut-up fruits available, as well as jars of prepared citrus wedges. Check and see what's to be had in your local store.

big-batch scone mix
a.k.a. scrumptious scones
for hurried people

MAKES 4 BATCHES SCONES (8 SCONES PER BATCH)

i love scones. They're tender, buttery, easy to make, and ever so versatile. I especially like to serve them straight from the oven, although it isn't always possible with my busy schedule. So, as a Weekend Baker, I plan ahead and whisk up a quadruple lot of the dry ingredients. It takes all of 10 minutes (even less if you use a scale) and keeps in the pantry forever (well, for at least 2 months). This way, half of the work is already done and you can rustle up a batch of scones while the oven heats up. To speed things along, measure out a batch of the dry ingredients, cut in the butter, cover, and refrigerate for up to 1 day. When the oven is heated, all that's required is to mix in the flavoring choice and the buttermilk. It couldn't be easier, even on a weekday morning.

If you want to make an individual batch I've included the amounts for 8 scones in the ingredients list. The recipe directions are exactly the same as they are for the Big Batch. Begin with step 2 and, instead of measuring out the dry ingredients from the container, simply whisk together the flour, sugar, baking powder, baking soda, and salt and proceed as directed.

do aheads

• The dough can be prepared through step 3, covered, and refrigerated for up to 1 day before continuing with the recipe.

• The scones can be prepared through step 6, cooled completely, tucked into a heavy-duty freezer bag, and frozen for up to 3 months. To thaw and heat, remove a scone or two from the bag and set in a skillet or on a griddle, cover with foil or a large lid, and heat on low or medium-low until thawed and warmed through. This trick works for reheating room-temperature scones as well, much better than microwaving.

for the Big-Batch dry mix:

9 cups (40 1/2 ounces/1,148 grams) all-purpose flour

1 1/4 cups (10 ounces/284 grams) granulated sugar

2 tablespoons plus 2 teaspoons baking powder

1 teaspoon baking soda

1 1/4 teaspoons table salt

for an individual batch of 8 scones:

2 1/2 cups (12 1/2 ounces/354 grams) dry mix (note that 1 cup of this mixture weighs 5 ounces/142 grams)

8 tablespoons (4 ounces/113 grams) very cold unsalted butter, cut into 6 pieces

Flavor option (below)

3/4 cup (6 fl ounces/175 ml) buttermilk

1 teaspoon pure vanilla extract

for the flavor options (choose one):

3/4 cup (4 ounces/113 grams) chopped bittersweet or semisweet chocolate or 3/4 cup (3 ounces/85 grams) chopped, toasted walnuts or pecans (see page 40

or

1 teaspoon finely grated orange zest and 1/2 cup (2 1/2 ounces/71 grams) dried cranberries or dried currants or 1/2 cup (4 ounces/113 grams) chopped dried apricots

or

1/2 teaspoon ground ginger and 1/4 cup (1 1/4 ounces/35 grams) chopped crystallized ginger

1. TO MAKE THE BIG-BATCH DRY MIX

In a large container with a tight-fitting lid (I like to use a 12-cup Tupperware), combine the flour, sugar, baking powder, baking soda, and salt. Whisk until well blended. Pop the top on the container, label it, and stow it at room temperature until ready to use.

2. TO MAKE A BATCH OF SCONES

Position an oven rack on the middle rung. Heat the oven to 400 degrees (200°C). Line a cookie sheet with parchment or a nonstick baking liner (I like the Silpat).

3.
Open the dry ingredient container and give the ingredients a good whisking. Using a light hand, carefully measure out 2 1/2 cups (12 1/2 ounces/354 grams) and dump into a large bowl. Add the butter pieces. Using a pastry blender (see What Is It? on page 170) or 2 table knives, cut the butter into the flour mixture until the butter pieces are no larger than peas.

4.
Choose a flavor option and add it to the bowl. Toss with a rubber spatula until well dispersed. Drizzle the buttermilk and vanilla over the flour mixture and toss with the spatula just until the dry ingredients are wet and the dough comes together in moist clumps.

5.
Dump the shaggy dough onto a lightly floured work surface. Briefly knead the dough to combine, and then shape it into a 7-inch (17.75cm) round. Using a lightly floured table knife or bench scraper, cut the dough into 8 equal wedges. Arrange the wedges on the prepared cookie sheet, spacing them about 2 inches (5cm) apart.

6.
Bake until the scones are golden brown and a toothpick or cake tester inserted in the center of 1 scone comes out clean, about 18 minutes. Transfer the cookie sheet to a rack to cool for about 15 minutes. Using a spatula, lift the scones from the sheet onto a rack to cool.

for a single batch:

2 1/4 cups (10 ounces/284 grams) all-purpose flour

1/4 cup (2 ounces/57 grams) granulated sugar

2 teaspoons baking powder

1/4 teaspoon baking soda

1/4 teaspoon table salt

8 tablespoons (4 ounces/113 grams) very cold unsalted butter, cut into 6 pieces

3/4 cup (6 fl ounces/175 ml) buttermilk

1 teaspoon pure vanilla extract

what is it? (pastry blender)

A pastry blender is a horseshoe-shaped hand tool with curved tines and a handle. It's an effective way to cut butter into dry ingredients without putting your hands on the butter (which would cause it to melt). If you don't own a pastry blender, 2 table knives are a good stand-in.

banana layer cake with fudgy frosting or tangy vanilla frosting

MAKES ONE 9-INCH (22.75CM) LAYER CAKE, OR 12 SERVINGS

I've spent years perfecting this cake: banana layers coated with fudgy, glossy chocolate frosting. It's a childhood favorite of Chris, my husband, one that he looks forward to every January. In fact, it has established itself as the official Dodge birthday cake, and party guests look forward to it with great anticipation. The layers are rich, moist, full of banana flavor, and sturdy enough for a novice baker to handle easily. The fudgy blender frosting provides an enticing contrast to the banana. For the deepest banana flavor, the peels need to be completely black, so black that you might be tempted to throw the bananas out. Bananas this ripe are the only kind that will give breads, muffins, and cakes the strongest banana flavor.

In the spirit of diversity and to satisfy readers who might want an alternative to chocolate, I developed a vanilla frosting for this cake. Mixing sour cream into a traditional butter–confectioners' sugar frosting refines its overtly sugary nature and adds a subtle tang that balances well against the banana. Much to my surprise, the entire Dodge family (including Chris) liked the Tangy Vanilla Frosting (page 174) as much as its chocolate counterpart.

do aheads

• The cake layers can be prepared through step 3, wrapped in plastic wrap, and stored at room temperature for up to 2 days or in the freezer for up to 3 months. Thaw at room temperature before frosting.

- The cake can be prepared through step 5, covered, and stored in the fridge for up to 3 days.

- The frosting can be prepared as directed in step 4, covered, and refrigerated for up to 1 week. Bring to room temperature before frosting the cake layers.

for the cake:

2 2/3 cups (12 ounces/340 grams) all-purpose flour

1 tablespoon baking powder

1/2 teaspoon table salt

1/4 teaspoon baking soda

16 tablespoons (8 ounces/227 grams) unsalted butter, at room temperature

1 3/4 cups (14 ounces/397 grams) granulated sugar

3 medium, very, very ripe bananas (about 14 ounces/397 grams total weight, including peels), peeled

2 teaspoons pure vanilla extract

4 large eggs

1/2 cup (4 fl ounces/117 ml) butter-milk

3/4 cup (3 ounces/85 grams) chopped, toasted walnuts (see page 40), optional

for the fudgy frosting:

6 ounces (170 grams) unsweetened chocolate, chopped

1 1/3 cups (10 1/2 ounces/298 grams) granulated sugar

1 cup (8 fl ounces/233 ml) evaporated milk (not sweetened condensed)

6 tablespoons (3 ounces/85 grams) unsalted butter, cut into 2 pieces

1 tablespoon pure vanilla extract

1/2 teaspoon table salt

go-withs: toasted shredded unsweetened dried coconut or chopped, toasted walnuts (see page 40) for garnish (optional)

1. TO MAKE THE CAKE

Position an oven rack on the middle rung. Heat the oven to 350 degrees (180°C). Grease and flour the bottom and sides of two 9-by-2-inch (22.75-

by-5cm) round cake pans, tapping out the excess flour. (I like to line the bottoms of the pans with parchment rounds to ensure easy and clean removal, but it's not mandatory for this recipe.)

2. In a medium bowl, combine the flour, baking powder, salt, and baking soda. Whisk until well blended. In a large bowl, beat the butter with an electric mixer (stand mixer fitted with the paddle attachment or handheld mixer) on medium-high speed until smooth. Add the sugar and beat until well combined. Add the bananas and vanilla and beat until well blended and only small bits of banana remain. Add the eggs two at a time, beating well after each addition. The mixture will look curdled and a bit lumpy. Don't worry, it will all come together. Add half of the flour mixture and mix on low speed just until blended. Add the buttermilk and mix just until blended. Add the remaining flour mixture and mix just until blended. Stir in the walnuts, if using. Scrape the batter into the prepared pans, dividing it evenly.

3. Bake until the tops are light brown and a toothpick or cake tester inserted in the center of 1 layer comes out clean, about 30 minutes. Transfer the pans to racks and let cool for about 15 minutes. Run a thin knife around the sides of each pan to loosen the cake. Invert the layers onto the racks, lift off the pans, and let cool completely.

4. TO MAKE THE FUDGY FROSTING
While the cake is baking, make the fudgy frosting. Melt the unsweetened chocolate in a double boiler (see What Is It? on page 74) or in the microwave (see page 51). Meanwhile, combine the sugar, evaporated milk, butter, vanilla, and salt in a blender; there's no need to blend at this point. (For those of us who have small blenders – mine is an ancient Hamilton Beach that Chris used for mixing up margaritas at college – it's impossible to make a full batch of this frosting. If you're not confident of the size and ability of your blender, divide the recipe in half and make 2 batches.) When the chocolate is melted, remove it from the heat or the microwave and give

it a stir. Scrape the hot melted chocolate into the blender. Cover with the lid and blend on high speed until the mixture darkens and is very thick, about 2 minutes. You'll also hear the engine working harder when the frosting is sufficiently thick, and it will appear to be barely moving in the blender. It will not be pourable. Scrape the frosting into a clean bowl and set aside at room temperature. When the frosting is cool, cover the bowl with plastic wrap until the cake is completely cool and ready to frost.

5. TO FROST THE CAKE

Brush away any loose crumbs from the cooled cake layers. Center 1 layer, top side down, on a flat serving plate. To protect the plate from smears during frosting, slide small strips of foil or parchment under the bottom of the cake to cover the plate. Using a metal spatula or the dull edge of a table knife, spread 1 cup of the frosting evenly over the layer. Place the second layer, top side down, on top of the frosting. Be sure the sides are lined up and then press gently on the layer. Apply a very thin layer of frosting over the entire cake to seal in any crumbs. Spread the remaining frosting over the top and sides of the cake. Garnish the top with the coconut or walnuts, if using. The cake is best served at room temperature.

Tangy Vanilla Frosting

16 tablespoons (8 ounces/227 grams) unsalted butter, at room temperature

3 cups (12 ounces/340 grams) confectioners' sugar

1 1/2 teaspoons pure vanilla extract

1/4 teaspoon table salt

1/3 cup (3 ounces/85 grams) sour cream

In a large bowl, beat the butter with an electric mixer (stand mixer fitted with the paddle attachment or handheld mixer) on medium-high speed until very smooth and creamy. Add the confectioners' sugar, vanilla, and salt and beat until blended and fluffy. Add the sour cream and, using a rubber spatula, gently stir just until blended. Cover and set aside at room temperature until the layers are completely cool and ready to be frosted.

southern molasses cake

MAKES ONE 10-INCH (25 CM) BUNDT CAKE, OR 12 SERVINGS

Von Corbett is a friend, and a fabulous baker who serves with me on the board of the charity Dress for Success Mid-Fairfield County. While I was writing this book, Von and I spent some time chatting about old-fashioned recipes for molasses cake and how much we love its deep, spicy flavors. Von described a cake that she had discovered in the recipe files of her grandmother Helene Bradshaw, one that Von fondly remembered from her childhood in Caswell County, North Carolina. Mrs. Bradshaw's molasses cake is made with vegetable oil (for moist texture), molasses, and lots of ginger (for a spicy flavor) and baked in a fluted tube pan (for an elegant presentation). On top of all this, it's amazingly quick and easy to mix. Thanks to Von for letting me include the recipe.

do aheads

• The dry ingredients and the wet ingredients can be prepared as directed in step 2 up to 1 day ahead. Keep the dry ingredients covered and at room temperature and the wet ingredients covered and in the fridge. Bring the water to a boil just before continuing with the recipe.

• The cake can be prepared through step 4, covered, and stored at room temperature for up to 5 days, or wrapped and frozen for up to 3 months. Thaw at room temperature before serving.

- 3 cups (13 1/2 ounces/383 grams) all-purpose flour
- 1 cup (8 ounces/227 grams) granulated sugar
- 2 tablespoons ground ginger
- 2 1/2 teaspoons baking soda
- 2 teaspoons ground cinnamon
- 1/4 teaspoon table salt
- 1 cup (8 fl ounces/233 ml) light molasses
- 1 cup (8 fl ounces/233 ml) canola or corn oil
- 2 large eggs
- 1/4 cup (2 1/4 ounces/78 grams) sour cream
- 2 1/2 teaspoons vanilla extract
- 1 cup (8 fl ounces/233 ml) boiling water

go-withs: Sweetened Whipped Cream (page 46) and/or Caramel Sauce (page 44) for garnish (optional)

1. Position an oven rack on the middle rung. Heat the oven to 350 degrees (180°C). Lightly grease and flour the bottom and sides of a 12-cup fluted Bundt or other fluted tube pan (see equipment note on page 166), tapping out the excess flour.

2. In a large bowl, combine the flour, sugar, ginger, baking soda, cinnamon, and salt. Whisk until well blended. In a medium bowl, combine the molasses, oil, eggs, sour cream, and vanilla. Whisk until well blended.

3. Pour the wet ingredients over the dry ingredients and add the boiling water. Stir with a rubber spatula just until blended. Scrape the batter into the prepared pan and spread evenly.

4. Bake until a toothpick or cake tester inserted in the center comes out with just a few small crumbs attached, 43 to 50 minutes. Transfer the pan to a rack and let cool for about 15 minutes. If necessary, run a thin knife

around the pan sides to loosen the cake. Invert the cake onto the rack and lift off the pan so the fluted side is up. Set aside to cool completely. Using 2 long metal spatulas or your hands, transfer the cake to a flat serving plate. Slice the cake with a serrated knife and serve plain or with Sweetened Whipped Cream (page 46) and/or Caramel Sauce (page 44).

my mom's mile-high vanilla sponge cake

MAKES ONE 10-INCH (25CM) CAKE, OR 12 SERVINGS

this cake was often resting on the kitchen counter during my childhood. It was my mother's "signature" cake. Sometimes Mom flavored it with vanilla, other times she covered it with a chocolate topping (below), and still other times she scented the cake with orange zest and orange juice and served it with fresh fruit. No matter which version, it's a lovely, light cake that's at home at teatime as well as at the dinner table, casual or fancy.

do aheads

• The cake can be prepared through step 5, covered, and stored at room temperature for up to 2 days.

7 large eggs

1 1/2 cups (12 ounces/340 grams) granulated sugar

3 tablespoons warm water

2 teaspoons pure vanilla extract

1/4 teaspoon table salt

1 1/2 cups (6 3/4 ounces/191 grams) all-purpose flour

for orange version: Substitute 3 tablespoons orange juice for the water and add 2 teaspoons finely grated orange zest with the yolks.

go-withs: Blueberry Sauce (page 45), Emergency Strawberry Sauce (page 43), or Creamy Chocolate Topping (below) for garnish (optional)

1. Position an oven rack on the middle rung. Heat the oven to 350 degrees (180°C). Have ready a 10-inch (25cm) tube pan with straight sides and, preferably, a removable bottom. (This is an angel food cake pan.) If yours doesn't have a removable bottom, line the bottom with parchment.

Some tube pans have small "legs" that protrude from the top rim of the pan. These little legs allow the pan to be inverted for the cooling process without crushing the cake. If your pan doesn't have legs, select a slender, long-necked bottle (a vinegar or beer bottle) that will slide easily into the center hole of the tube pan. Once the cake is baked, invert the pan onto the bottle and let cool as directed. Do *not* grease the pan.

2. Separate the egg yolks from the whites, placing each in a large bowl. To the yolks, add 1 cup (8 ounces/227 grams) of the sugar, the warm water, and the vanilla. Beat with an electric mixer (stand mixer fitted with the whisk attachment or handheld mixer) on medium-high speed until the mixture is pale yellow and tripled in volume, about 3 minutes. When the whisk or beaters are lifted, the mixture will fall back into the bowl and form a ribbon; it should linger a bit on the surface.

3. In a medium bowl, using a clean whisk attachment or beaters, beat the whites with the salt on medium-high speed until soft peaks form. Gradually add the remaining 1/2 cup (4 ounces/113 grams) sugar and beat until the whites are glossy and form medium-firm peaks (the peaks will hold their shape but the tips will flop over).

4. Using a rubber spatula, scoop about one-fourth of the beaten whites into the yolk mixture. Gently stir just until combined. Sprinkle the flour over the top and fold until blended. Gently fold in the remaining beaten whites just until blended. Scrape the batter into the prepared pan, spread it evenly, and smooth the top.

5. Bake until the top is golden brown and a toothpick or cake tester inserted in the center comes out clean, about 55 minutes. Remove from the oven and immediately turn the pan upside down and rest it on its legs (or slide it onto the bottle) directly on the counter. Leave the pan upside down until the cake has cooled completely, about 3 hours. When the cake has

cooled, run a long, thin knife around the pan sides and the tube sides to loosen the cake. If using a pan with a removable bottom, remove the outer ring and set the cake on the work surface. Run the knife between the cake and the bottom of the pan and carefully lift and remove the cake from the pan and set on a flat serving plate. If using a pan without a removable bottom, invert the cake onto a rack, lift off the pan, and place the cake upright on a flat serving plate.

6. To serve, cut into slices with a serrated knife. Accompany with a berry sauce or the chocolate topping, if desired.

Creamy Chocolate Topping

1 1/4 cups (10 fl ounces/292 ml) heavy cream
2/3 cup (2 1/2 ounces/71 grams) confectioners' sugar

1/4 cup (3/4 ounce/21 grams) unsweetened Dutch-process cocoa powder, sifted if lumpy
1 teaspoon pure vanilla extract

In a large bowl, combine the cream, confectioners' sugar, cocoa powder, and vanilla. Stir to moisten the cocoa powder. Cover with plastic and refrigerate for at least 2 hours or for up to 3 days. Beat with an electric mixer (stand mixer fitted with the whisk attachment or handheld mixer) on medium-high speed until firm peaks form when the beaters are lifted. Serve each slice with a dollop of the topping or spoon it on top of the cake and spread evenly.

nutty caramel–chocolate upside downer

althoughthis is an upside-down cake, it's unusual because of its caramel-nut topping, rather than the traditional pineapple or other fruit topping. I love fruit upside-down cakes, and I've included one (page 189), but while working on an upside-downer story for *Fine Cooking* magazine, I became obsessed with the idea of a nutty caramel–topped chocolate cake. After some trial and error, I succeeded in developing the perfect combination of tender chocolate cake, nuts, and caramel. The juicy topping of a fruit upside downer comes from the mingling of the sugar and fruit juices while baking. Nuts don't release moisture the way fruit does, so I've added water to the nut topping. The result is a rich, chocolaty cake covered with caramel and nuts.

This cake tastes even better a day or two after it's made. As it sits, it absorbs more of the moisture from the caramel topping, making it even moister, almost fudgy.

do aheads

• The caramel and nuts can be prepared through step 2, covered, and kept at room temperature for up to 1 day before proceeding with the recipe.

• The cake can be prepared through step 4. Let cool completely, cover with plastic wrap, and store at room temperature for up to 3 days.

3/4 cup (6 ounces/170 grams)
firmly packed dark brown sugar

5 tablespoons (2 1/2 ounces/71
grams) unsalted butter

3 tablespoons water

1 1/4 cups (6 ounces/170 grams)
assorted coarsely chopped
unsalted nuts (I like a mixture of
slivered blanched almonds and
chopped walnuts and pecans),
toasted (see page 40)

for the cake:

1 1/3 cups (6 ounces/170 grams)
all-purpose flour

1/2 cup (1 1/2 ounces/43 grams)
unsweetened natural cocoa powder (not Dutch process), sifted if
lumpy

3/4 teaspoon baking powder

1/4 teaspoon baking soda

1/4 teaspoon table salt

10 tablespoons (5 ounces/142
grams) unsalted butter, at room
temperature

1 cup (8 ounces/227 grams) granulated sugar

1 teaspoon pure vanilla extract

1/4 teaspoon pure almond extract
(optional)

3 large eggs

1/2 cup (4 fl ounces/117 ml) buttermilk

1. Position an oven rack on the middle rung. Heat the oven to 350 degrees (180°C). Lightly grease the sides (not the bottom) of a 9-by-2-inch (22.75-by-5cm) round cake pan.

2. TO MAKE THE NUTS AND CARAMEL

In a small saucepan, combine the brown sugar, butter, and water. Set the pan over medium heat and cook, stirring often, until the butter is melted and the mixture is smooth. Bring to a boil and pour into the prepared pan, swirling to coat the bottom evenly. Scatter the toasted nuts evenly over the surface and gently press into the caramel.

3. TO MAKE THE CAKE

In a medium bowl, combine the flour, cocoa, baking powder, baking soda, and salt. Whisk until well blended. In another medium bowl, beat the butter with an electric mixer (stand mixer fitted with the paddle attachment or handheld mixer) on medium-high speed until smooth. Gradually add the sugar and continue beating until fluffy. Beat in the vanilla and almond extracts. Add the eggs one at a time, beating briefly after each addition. Sprinkle half of the flour mixture over the butter and mix on low speed just until the flour disappears. Add the buttermilk and mix just until blended. Add the remaining flour mixture and mix just until blended. Scoop spoonfuls of the batter evenly into the cake pan, taking care not to disturb the nuts. Carefully spread the batter evenly in the pan. Tap the pan gently a few times on the counter to settle the contents.

4.

Bake until a toothpick or cake tester inserted in the center comes out clean, about 45 minutes. Immediately run a thin knife around the sides of the pan to loosen the cake. Using a thick, dry kitchen towel to protect your hands, invert a flat serving plate on top of the pan and, holding both the pan and the plate, invert them together. Leave the pan over the cake for about 3 minutes to allow the caramel to drip onto the cake. Lift off the pan and, using a small metal spatula or knife, scrape out any stubborn caramel clumps stuck to the pan and reposition them on the top of the cake. Serve the cake warm or at room temperature.

old-fashioned berry icebox cake

MAKES ONE 9-INCH (22.75 CM) CAKE, OR 12 SERVINGS

the original icebox cake is one of the simplest, most comforting desserts I know. It's also one of the first desserts my mother taught me to make. The classic consists of crisp chocolate wafers in short stacks, sandwiched with sweetened whipped cream. The stacks are turned on their side, each stack lined up next to the other in more whipped cream. As the cake rests in the fridge, the cookies absorb moisture from the cream, softening them enough so that they slice easily.

I've tinkered with the traditional recipe only slightly, adding fresh berries and mascarpone to the whipped cream, and adopting a round shape. The finished dessert can be topped with more fresh berries and cut into familiar cake wedges. It has an elegant look, but the sumptuous texture is the same as the original.

And because I can never resist anything chocolate, I've also provided a mocha cream version (page 188). Originally intended to serve as an optional topping for My Mom's Mile-High Vanilla Sponge Cake (page 179), I discovered it also made a mean icebox cake. I was testing the icebox cake the same day as the sponge cake. I ended up with a few chocolate wafers and some extra chocolate cream, so I smeared the cream and cookies together for an impromptu Sunday night treat for my family.

do aheads

• The fruit mixture can be prepared as directed in step 1, covered with plastic, and stored in the fridge for up to 3 days, or it can be frozen (I like to use a heavy-duty zipper-top bag) for up to 3 months before thawing and continuing with the recipe.

• The cake can be prepared through step 4, covered, and refrigerated for up to 3 days before serving. Just before serving, tidy up the sides with the extra cream and garnish with the berries and mint.

1 1/2 pints (15 ounces/425 grams/about 3 cups) blackberries, rinsed and well dried

1 cup (8 ounces/227 grams) granulated sugar

2 tablespoons orange juice or orange-flavored liqueur

2 teaspoons finely grated orange zest

Pinch of table salt

12 large strawberries, rinsed, well dried, hulled, and cut into quarters

1/2 pint (5 ounces/142 grams/about 1 cup) raspberries, rinsed and well dried

2 cups (16 fl ounces/467 ml) heavy cream

1 container (8 ounces/227 grams) mascarpone cheese

75 crisp chocolate wafers (about 1 1/2 boxes, 9 ounces/255 grams each, Famous Chocolate Wafers by Nabisco)

go-with: berries and mint leaves for garnish (optional)

1. In a medium saucepan, combine the blackberries, sugar, orange juice or liqueur, orange zest, and salt. Set the pan over medium heat and cook, stirring frequently, until the fruit juices are released and the sugar is dissolved. Set a strainer over a medium bowl and pour the fruit and juices into the strainer. Using the back of a spoon or a rubber spatula, press on the blackberries to force the pulp through the strainer. Remember to scrape the underside of the strainer to free the clinging pulp. Discard the contents of the strainer. Add the strawberries to the hot mixture and, using a fork, press them against the inside of the bowl to crush them. Add the raspberries. This time, instead of crushing the berries, just press them gently against the bowl. Taste and add a little more sugar to sweeten the berries or a pinch more salt to bring out their flavors, if needed. Put the fruit mixture into the refrigerator and stir frequently until well chilled, at least 1 hour. If you're in

a rush, set the bowl into a larger, ice-filled bowl (see What Is It? below) and stir frequently until chilled.

2. Meanwhile, position the ring of a 9-inch (22.75cm) springform pan (don't use the bottom) on a flat serving plate. (Remember to make room in your fridge for the plate and pan.)

3. When the fruit mixture is chilled, pour the cream and mascarpone into a large bowl. Beat with an electric mixer (stand mixer fitted with the whisk attachment or handheld mixer) on medium-high speed until firm peaks form. Pour the fruit into the whipped cream and, using a rubber spatula, fold gently, but thoroughly, until blended. Measure out about 1/2 cup of the cream, cover, and refrigerate. (The extra cream is used to touch up the sides after unmolding.)

4. Spoon about 1 cup of the cream into the prepared pan (springform pan ring and plate) and spread evenly. Beginning with the outer edge, arrange the cookies, flat side down and slightly overlapping, in a spiral pattern. Once the outer row is complete, continue with an inner ring of cookies that slightly overlaps the first row (15 cookies for each layer). Spread another 1 1/3 cups of the cream over the cookie layer. Arrange a second layer of cookies over the cream. Repeat the layering of cookies and cream three more times, finishing with a layer of cream. Cover with plastic wrap and refrigerate for 1 day.

5. Before serving or up to 4 hours ahead of time, run a long, thin knife or metal spatula between the edge of the cake and the ring. Release the springform clasp and lift off the ring. Using a small metal spatula or the dull side of a table knife, spread the reserved cream around the outer edge of the cake. Arrange the berries and mint leaves on top, if using. To serve, cut into slices with a thin knife run under hot water and wiped dry, repeating the process for each slice.

Mocha Cream

3 3/4 cups (30 fl ounces/875 ml) heavy cream

1 container (8 ounces/227 grams) mascarpone cheese

2 cups (8 ounces/227 grams) confectioners' sugar

3/4 cup (2 1/4 ounces/64 grams) unsweetened Dutch-process cocoa powder, sifted if lumpy

2 3/4 teaspoons instant coffee granules (any type, even decaf, will do)

2 teaspoons pure vanilla extract

go-withs: chocolate shavings (see page 42) or Sweetened Whipped Cream (page 46) and chocolate-covered espresso beans for garnish (optional)

In a large bowl, combine the cream, cheese, sugar, cocoa powder, coffee granules, and vanilla. Whisk until well blended. Cover with plastic and refrigerate for at least 2 hours or for up to 2 days. Beat with an electric mixer (stand mixer fitted with the whisk attachment or handheld mixer) on medium-high speed until firm peaks form when the beaters are lifted. Assemble the cake as directed, substituting the mocha cream for the fruit cream. Garnish with chocolate shavings or a small amount of whipped cream and chocolate-covered espresso beans, if desired.

what is it? (ice bath)

An ice bath is used when you want to stop cooking or cool a mixture quickly. To make one, simply combine water and ice in a large bowl. Because you must work fast, always prepare the ice bath in advance of when you need it and have it close by while you're working.

all-season upside-down cornmeal cake

MAKES ONE 9-INCH (22.75CM) CAKE, OR 8 SERVINGS

P ineapple and a soft vanilla cake are the classic upside-down formula, but in reality any fruit can be used – even rehydrated dried fruit – so I've included several options. Depending on how much time you have, the fruit can simply be scattered or arranged as a spiral design.

The texture of cornmeal is perfect for soaking up every last drop of juice from the fruit. Its porousness absorbs the juice, making this cake moist and infusing it with fruit flavor. The good news is that most of the work can be done ahead, and the batter whips up quickly and easily while the oven is heating.

Claire, head recipe tester for *The Weekend Baker*, made the dried-fruit variation and, because she had extra time, created a sunflower shape by arranging cut dried apricots in a ring around the outer rim and scattering the dried cranberries in the center. The results were striking.

While the cake is delicious at room temperature, I like it warm when the sweet juices are still hot and haven't soaked in completely.

do aheads

• You can complete the recipe through step 4, let cool completely, cover the cake pan with plastic wrap, and leave at room temperature for up to 1 day.

for the fruit (choose one):

12 plump dried apricots, 1 cup (8 fl ounces/233 ml) orange juice, pinch of
   ground cinnamon, and 1/3 cup (2 ounces/57 grams) dried tart cherries or
   dried cranberries

or

1 small (14 ounces/377 grams) ripe pineapple

or

2 medium-sized (7 ounces/198 grams) ripe pears

for the caramel:

3/4 cup (6 ounces/170 grams) firmly packed dark brown sugar	4 tablespoons (2 ounces/57 grams) unsalted butter, cut into 3 pieces

for the cake:

1 2/3 cups (7 1/2 ounces/213 grams) all-purpose flour	1/4 teaspoon table salt
1/2 cup (2 1/2 ounces/71 grams) finely ground yellow cornmeal	1 cup (8 fl ounces/233 ml) butter-milk
1/3 cup (2 1/2 ounces/71 grams) granulated sugar	6 tablespoons (3 ounces/85 grams) unsalted butter, melted and cooled
2 1/2 teaspoons baking powder	1 large egg
1/4 teaspoon ground cinnamon	1 teaspoon pure vanilla extract

1. Position an oven rack on the middle rung. Heat the oven to 350 degrees (180°C). Lightly grease the sides of a 9-by-2-inch (22.75-by-5cm) round cake pan.

2. SELECT AND PREPARE THE FRUIT

If using dried apricots, combine the apricots, juice, and cinnamon in a small saucepan. Set over high heat, cover, and bring to a boil. When it reaches a boil, reduce the heat to low and simmer until the apricots are plump and tender, about 10 minutes. Remove the cover, add the dried cherries or cran-berries, and simmer for another 2 minutes. Pour the contents of the pan into a strainer and discard the liquid. (Or reserve 1/4 cup (2 fl ounces/58 ml) of the liquid and substitute it for 1/4 cup of the buttermilk in the cake recipe.) Spread the fruits on paper towels to drain and let cool completely.

Coarsely chop the apricots or, if you've got some extra time, cut each apricot on the diagonal into 3 slices.

If using pineapple, trim away the skin and cut into slices 3/8 inch (9.5mm) thick. Using a small round cookie cutter, cut out the core from each slice and discard. Cut each pineapple ring in half.

If using pears, peel and cut in half lengthwise. Using a small melon baller or a teaspoon, scoop out the core from each half and discard. Cut the pear halves lengthwise into slices 3/8 inch (9.5mm) thick.

3. TO MAKE THE CARAMEL

In a small saucepan, combine the brown sugar and butter. Set over medium heat and cook, stirring often, until the butter is melted and the mixture is smooth. Bring to a boil and pour into the prepared pan. Spread to coat the bottom evenly.

4.
Arrange the prepared fruit, slightly overlapping, in the caramel-coated cake pan.

5. TO MAKE THE CAKE

In a medium bowl, combine the flour, cornmeal, sugar, baking powder, cinnamon, and salt. Whisk until well blended. In a small bowl, combine the buttermilk, melted butter, and egg. Whisk until well blended. Pour the wet ingredients onto the dry ingredients and, using a rubber spatula, gently fold until the batter is just blended. Scoop spoonfuls of the batter evenly into the cake pan, taking care not to disturb the fruit, and carefully spread the batter evenly in the pan. Tap the pan gently a few times on the counter to settle the contents.

6.
Bake until the center feels firm when gently pressed and a toothpick or cake tester inserted in the center comes out clean, about 45 minutes. Immediately run a thin knife around the sides of the pan to loosen the cake. Using a thick, dry dish towel to protect your hands, invert a flat

serving plate on top of the pan and, holding both the pan and the plate, invert them together. Leave the pan over the cake for about 5 minutes to allow the juices and caramel to drip onto the cake. Lift off the pan and, using a small metal spatula or knife, scrape out any stubborn fruit stuck to the pan and reposition them on top of the cake. Serve the cake warm or at room temperature.

banana layer cake with fudgy frosting
page 171

mocha swirl cheesecake
page 159

classic crumb cake
page 156

old-fashioned berry icebox cake
page 185

olive and herb focaccia
page 204

buttery pull-apart dinner rolls
page 208

coconut all-star custards
page 219

bursting with raspberries bread pudding
page 216

fruit-filled marshmallowy meringues

MAKES 10 SERVINGS

d on't be fooled by the crisp exterior of these meringues. Within the thin, crusty shell is a soft, creamy, marshmallow-like center. The high sugar level keeps the crust crunchy, and cornstarch and a touch of vinegar keep the interior supple and soft. The vinegar stabilizes the beaten whites and adds a subtle tang that helps cut through the sugar.

My fruit choices change according to the season. In winter, I top the meringues with sliced mango, sliced star fruit, kiwifruit wedges, and red grapes. My summertime favorites are fresh berries, accented with sprigs of fresh mint.

Some bakers will know this meringue as a Pavlova, named for the famous Russian ballerina, Anna Pavlova. These airy nests are a graceful and elegant presentation worthy of their famous namesake.

do aheads

• The meringues can be prepared through step 2, covered, and refrigerated for up to 4 hours before proceeding with the recipe.

• The baked meringues can be prepared through step 4 and stored in an airtight container at room temperature for up to 1 day.

6 large egg whites (3/4 cup/6 1/4 ounces/177 grams), at room temperature

1/4 teaspoon cream of tartar

1 1/4 cups (8 3/4 ounces/248 grams) superfine sugar (see page 21)

3 tablespoons cornstarch

1/4 teaspoon table salt

1 1/2 teaspoons vinegar (distilled white, champagne, white wine, or balsamic works well)

1 teaspoon pure vanilla extract

4 cups (20 ounces/567 grams) mixed fruits (see above for suggestions)

go-withs: Red Berry Sauce (page 43) or Sweetened Whipped Cream (page 46), optional

1. Position the oven racks on the top and bottom third rungs of the oven. Heat the oven to 350 degrees (180°C). Line 2 large cookie sheets with parchment.

2. In a large bowl, combine the whites and cream of tartar. Beat with an electric mixer (stand mixer fitted with the whisk attachment or handheld mixer) on medium-low speed until the whites are frothy. Increase the speed to medium-high and beat until the whites form soft peaks. Continue beating while gradually sprinkling in the sugar. When all the sugar has been added, increase the speed to high and whip until firm, glossy peaks form. Continue beating and sprinkle in the cornstarch and salt. Add the vinegar and vanilla and beat just until blended. Using a rubber spatula, give the meringue a few gentle folds.

3. Scoop up a heaping 1/2 cup of the whites and place it on the prepared baking sheet, piling it high. Using the back of a large tablespoon, shape a nest by sculpting out the center of the mound, leaving the sides high and the center low. The nest will be 3 or 4 inches (7.75 or 10cm) and about 1 1/2 inches (4cm) high. Resist the urge to make them all look the same. The beauty of the Pavlova comes from its graceful, free-form appearance (think of the puffed-up ballerina costumes in *Swan Lake*). Repeat with the remaining meringue, making 10 nests in all and arranging them about 2 inches (5cm) apart.

4. Reduce the oven temperature to 200 degrees (95°C). Bake until the meringues are tacky but gooey when pressed with a finger, about 1 1/2 hours. They will remain white, but don't worry if a few of the meringue tips become light brown. Turn off the oven and let the meringues cool in the oven for 1 hour. Remove the cookie sheets from the oven, gently lift the meringues off the paper, and set them on a rack to cool completely.

5. Just before serving, arrange the nests on individual plates and pile the centers with fruit. Drizzle with the berry sauce or top with a spoonful of whipped cream, if desired.

Breads – Yeast

• • •

soft white sandwich bread

MAKES 2 LOAVES

fitting bread baking into your busy schedule is no problem with this tasty and easy sandwich bread that mixes up in no time. It can even rise in the fridge, so it's ready to go when you want a loaf of freshly baked bread. As a bonus, the recipe makes two loaves, one for this week's toast or sandwiches and the other to store in the freezer for next week.

do aheads

• The dough can be prepared through step 4 but let rise only until about 1 1/2 times original size (rather than double the size), then refrigerate for up to 24 hours before proceeding with the recipe.

• The loaves can be prepared through step 6 but let rise only until about 1 1/2 times original size (rather than double the size), then refrigerate for up to 8 hours before proceeding with the recipe. Remove from the fridge and leave on the counter while the oven heats.

• The bread can be prepared through step 8 and cooled completely. Consider serving 1 loaf fresh and freezing the second in a heavy-duty freezer bag for up to 2 months.

6 cups (27 ounces/765 grams) all-purpose flour

3 1/2 teaspoons (measured from 2 packets) instant yeast (see page 20)

1/4 cup (2 ounces/57 grams) granulated sugar

2 1/2 teaspoons table salt

2 cups (8 fl ounces/233 ml) whole milk

6 tablespoons (3 ounces/85 grams) unsalted butter, cut into 4 pieces, plus 2 tablespoons, melted, for glazing (optional)

1. TO MIX BY HAND

In a large bowl, combine the flour, yeast, sugar, and salt. Stir with a wooden spoon until blended.

2.

In a small saucepan, combine the milk and the 6 tablespoons butter. Set over medium heat and heat, stirring constantly, until the butter melts and the mixture registers about 120 degrees (49°C) on an instant-read thermometer. Alternatively, combine the milk and butter in a bowl and heat in the microwave. In order for the yeast to grow, the liquid needs to be between 115 and 125 degrees (46 and 52°C). Drizzle the warm liquid over the flour mixture and stir with the wooden spoon until a rough, shaggy dough forms. Lightly dust a work surface with a little flour. Dump the dough onto the surface.

3.

Knead the dough with your hands. It will be sticky at first, but resist the urge to add more flour. First, gather the dough together. Next, using the heel of one hand, push the top part of the dough away from you. Fold that piece over the dough nearest you. Give the dough a quarter turn clockwise and repeat. Keep on kneading until the dough is smooth and no longer sticky, about 10 minutes. Shape the dough into a ball. Proceed as directed in step 4.

1. TO MIX IN A STAND MIXER

In the large bowl of a stand mixer, combine the flour, yeast, sugar, and salt. Whisk until well blended.

2. In a small saucepan, combine the milk and the 6 tablespoons butter. Set over medium heat and heat, stirring constantly, until the butter melts and the liquid registers about 120 degrees (49°C) on an instant-read thermometer. Alternatively, combine the milk and butter in a bowl and heat in the microwave. In order for the yeast to grow, the liquid needs to be between 115 and 125 degrees (46 and 52°C).

3. Fit the mixer with the dough hook. With the mixer on medium-low speed, slowly pour the warm milk mixture into the flour mixture and mix until the flour is completely incorporated. Increase the speed to medium-high and beat until the dough is smooth and pulls away from the bottom and sides of the bowl, about 6 minutes. If the dough climbs up the hook, stop the mixer and scrape the dough back into the bowl. Don't venture too far away while the dough is mixing, as the mixer might dance around on the counter because of the large amount of dough. Proceed as directed in step 4.

4. LET THE DOUGH RISE
Scoop up the dough and shape it into a ball. Lightly grease the bowl and pop the dough back into it. Cover the top securely with plastic wrap. (I like to use a large rubber band to hold the plastic in place.) Let the covered dough rise in a warm spot until doubled in size, about 45 minutes.

5. Lightly grease two 8 1/2-by-4 1/2-inch (21.5-by-11.5cm) loaf pans (I use Pyrex). Turn the dough out onto a clean work surface (there's no need to flour; the dough is soft but not sticky) and press down gently to deflate it. Using a bench scraper or a knife, divide the dough into 2 equal pieces. Work with 1 piece at a time and cover the other with plastic wrap. Press the dough into a 7-by-12-inch (17.75-by-30.5cm) rectangle. Starting at a short side, roll up like a jelly roll. Pinch the bottom and side seams closed. Place the dough on the counter, seam side down and perpendicular to you. Using the outside edge of your slightly curved palms, press gently but firmly on the bottom seam until the dough forms a smooth rectangle 8 inches (20cm) long, with a rounded, taut-skinned top. Place the dough, seam side down, into a prepared pan. Press on the dough to flatten and fill the pan in an even layer. Repeat with the remaining dough.

6. Cover the pans loosely (to allow for rising) but completely with plastic wrap and let the dough rise in a warm spot until doubled in size, about 25 minutes. The center of the dough will rise about 1 inch (2.5cm) above the rims of the pans.

7. When ready to bake, position an oven rack on the middle rung. Heat the oven to 375 degrees (190°C). Remove the plastic and, using the tip of a very sharp knife or razor blade, cut a slit about 1/2 inch deep (1.25cm) down the center of each loaf, traveling its length.

8. Bake until the loaves are puffed and browned, about 40 minutes. Transfer the pans to a rack and brush the top of the loaves with the 2 table-spoons melted butter, if using. (This will keep the top soft and especially buttery.) Tip the baked loaves onto a rack and remove the pans. Set the loaves on their sides and let cool completely.

peasant boule

MAKES 1 ROUND LOAF

I used to make this buttery, soft-crusted round when I was head baker at the Hay Day Country Market in Greenwich, Connecticut. The dough is soft and light, and a bit stickier than many bread doughs, but once it's baked you'll appreciate its moist and chewy texture. This *boule* always sold out first, probably because it's equally tasty sliced and toasted, used for sandwiches, or served beside a winter stew. Come weekends and holidays, we made several batches, and still couldn't keep up with demand. The optional addition of a mixture of fresh herbs adds a unique and flavorful touch.

do aheads

• The dough can be prepared through step 4 but let rise only until about 1 1/2 times original size (rather than double the size), then refrigerate for up to 12 hours before proceeding with the recipe.

• The dough can be prepared through step 6 but let rise only until about 1 1/2 times original size (rather than double the size), then spray the surface with a coating of nonstick cooking spray (save the melted butter coating for just before baking), and cover the loaf loosely but completely with plastic wrap (you can cover the pan with a large bowl or plastic container, if you prefer). Refrigerate for up to 8 hours before proceeding with the recipe. Remove from the fridge and leave on the counter while the oven heats.

• Prepare the bread through step 8 and let cool completely. It can be stored at room temperature for up to 3 days or frozen in a heavy-duty plastic freezer bag for up to 2 months.

3 1/3 cups (15 ounces/425 grams) all-purpose flour

2 1/4 teaspoons (1 packet) instant yeast (see page 20)

2 tablespoons granulated sugar

1 1/2 teaspoons table salt

1 1/2 teaspoons baking powder

1 1/3 cups (10 1/2 fl ounces/306 ml) very warm water (between 115 and 125 degrees/46 and 52°C)

2/3 cup (2 ounces/579 grams) finely chopped mixed fresh herbs (I like a combination of chives, parsley, and basil), optional

2 tablespoons unsalted butter, melted

1. TO MIX BY HAND

In a large bowl, combine the flour, yeast, sugar, salt, and baking powder. Stir with a wooden spoon until blended.

2.
Check the water temperature; it should register about 120 degrees (49°C) on an instant-read thermometer. In order for the yeast to grow, the liquid needs to be between 115 and 125 degrees (46 and 52°C). Drizzle the warm water over the flour mixture and stir with a wooden spoon until a rough, shaggy dough forms. Add the chopped herbs, if using, and stir until incorporated. Lightly dust a work surface with a little flour. Dump the dough onto the surface.

3.
Knead the dough with your hands. It will be sticky at first, but resist the urge to add more flour. First, gather the dough together. Next, using the heel of one hand, push the top part of the dough away from you. Fold that piece over the part of the dough nearest you. Give the dough a quarter turn clockwise and repeat. Keep kneading until the dough is smooth and no longer sticky, about 10 minutes. Shape the dough into a ball. Proceed as directed in step 4.

1. TO MIX IN A STAND MIXER

In the large bowl of a stand mixer, combine the flour, yeast, sugar, salt, and baking powder. Whisk until well blended.

2.

Check the water temperature; it should register about 120 degrees (49°C) on an instant-read thermometer. In order for the yeast to grow, the liquid needs to be between 115 and 125 degrees (46 and 52°C).

3.

Fit the mixer with the dough hook. With the mixer on medium-low speed, slowly pour the warm water into the flour mixture and mix until the flour is completely incorporated. Add the chopped herbs (if using). Increase the speed to medium-high and beat until the dough is smooth and pulls away from the bottom and sides of the bowl, about 6 minutes. If the dough climbs up the hook, stop the mixer and scrape the dough back into the bowl. Don't venture too far away while the dough is mixing, as the mixer might dance around on the counter because of the large amount of dough. Proceed as directed in step 4.

4. LET THE DOUGH RISE

Scoop up the dough and shape it into a ball. Lightly grease the bowl and pop the dough back into it. Cover the top securely with plastic wrap. (I like to use a large rubber band to hold the plastic in place.) Let the covered dough rise in a warm spot until doubled in size, about 45 minutes.

5.

Generously butter an 8-inch (20cm) round cake pan. Turn the dough out onto a clean work surface (there's no need to flour; the dough is soft but not sticky) and press down gently to deflate it. Shape the dough into a round 7 inches (17.75cm) wide and place it, smooth side up, in the prepared pan. Generously brush with some of the melted butter. You may not need all the butter.

6. Let the dough rise (no need to cover it) in a warm spot until doubled in size, about 25 minutes. It will fill the pan and will be light and airy to the touch.

7. Position an oven rack on the middle rung. Heat the oven to 375 degrees (190°C). Brush the dough with the remaining butter.

8. Bake until the *boule* is well browned and sounds hollow when tapped, about 40 minutes. Transfer the pan to a rack, tip the baked bread onto the rack, and remove the pan. Set the loaf right side up and let cool completely.

olive and herb focaccia

MAKES 1 FLATBREAD

When I worked in Paris as a pastry apprentice, there was an Italian bakery down the street from my tiny walk-up apartment. Frequenting an Italian bakery in Paris might seem strange, but this one made heavenly focaccia. At the time, it was the perfect antidote to all the desserts I turned out all day long. This recipe recalls that flatbread.

do aheads

• The dough can be prepared through step 4, but let rise only until about 1 1/2 times original size (rather than double the size), then refrigerate for up to 24 hours before proceeding with the recipe.

• The dough can be prepared through step 5 and covered loosely but completely with plastic wrap, but let rise only until about 1 1/2 times original size (rather than double the size), then refrigerate the loaf for up to 8 hours before proceeding with the recipe. Remove from the fridge and leave on the counter while the oven heats.

3 1/3 cups (15 ounces/425 grams) all-purpose flour

1 tablespoon minced fresh thyme

2 1/4 teaspoons (1 packet) instant yeast (see page 20)

2 teaspoons table salt

1 teaspoon granulated sugar

1 1/4 cups (10 fl ounces/284 ml) water, warmed to between 115 and 125 degrees (46 and 52°C)

1 tablespoon olive oil, plus more for brushing on the dough

for the topping:

20 pitted Kalamata olives, roughly
   chopped
4 tablespoons olive oil

2 teaspoons chopped fresh thyme
1 teaspoon coarse salt

1. TO MIX BY HAND

In a large bowl, combine the flour, thyme, yeast, salt, and sugar. Stir with a wooden spoon until well blended.

2. Check the water temperature; it should register about 120 degrees (49°C) on an instant-read thermometer. In order for the yeast to grow, the liquid needs to be between 115 and 125 degrees (46 and 52°C). Drizzle the warm water and the 1 tablespoon olive oil over the flour mixture and stir with the wooden spoon until a rough, shaggy dough forms. Lightly dust a work surface with a little flour. Dump the dough onto the surface.

3. Knead the dough with your hands. It will be sticky at first, but resist the urge to add more flour. First, gather the dough together. Next, using the heel of one hand, push the top part of the dough away from you. Fold that piece over the dough nearest you. Give the dough a quarter turn clockwise and repeat. Keep on kneading until the dough is smooth and no longer sticky, about 10 minutes. Shape the dough into a ball. Proceed as directed in step 4.

1. TO MIX IN A STAND MIXER

In the large bowl of a stand mixer, combine the flour, thyme, yeast, salt, and sugar. Whisk until well blended.

2. Check the water temperature; it should register about 120 degrees (49°C) on an instant-read thermometer. In order for the yeast to grow, the liquid needs to be between 115 and 125 degrees (46 and 52°C).

3. Fit the mixer with the dough hook. With the mixer on medium-low speed, slowly pour the warm water and the 1 tablespoon oil into the flour mixture and mix until the flour is completely incorporated. Increase the speed to medium-high and beat until the dough is smooth and pulls away from the bottom and sides of the bowl, about 8 minutes. If the dough climbs up the hook, stop the mixer and scrape the dough back into the bowl. Don't venture too far away while the dough is mixing, as the mixer might dance around on the counter because of the large amount of dough. Proceed as directed in step 4.

4. LET THE DOUGH RISE

Scoop up the dough and shape it into a ball. Lightly oil the bowl with some olive oil and pop the dough back into it. Cover the top securely with plastic wrap. (I like to use a large rubber band to hold the plastic in place.) Let the covered dough rise in a warm spot until doubled in size, about 45 minutes.

5. Lightly grease a heavy cookie sheet. Turn the dough out onto it and press down gently to deflate. Using your hands, shape the dough into an oval about 3/4 inch (2cm) thick (the oval will be about 10 inches (25cm) long and 7 inches (17.75cm) at its widest point). Lightly brush the dough with about 1 tablespoon olive oil and loosely cover the surface directly with plastic wrap. Let the dough rise in a warm spot until puffed and almost doubled, about 20 minutes.

6. Position an oven rack on the middle rung and heat the oven to 425 degrees (220°C). Remove the plastic wrap from the dough. Lightly coat your middle 3 fingertips with flour and press into the dough down to (but not through) the bottom. Repeat this dimpling all over the dough (about 2 dozen dimples in all), dipping your fingertips into flour as necessary. To top the dough, scatter the olives over the surface, pressing them into the dimples. Drizzle evenly with 1 1/2 tablespoons of the olive oil and sprinkle with the thyme and coarse salt.

7. Bake until the top of the focaccia is browned, 25 to 30 minutes. Remove the pan from the oven and, using a large metal spatula, transfer the focaccia to a rack. Drizzle with remaining 2 1/2 tablespoons olive oil. Serve warm.

buttery pull-apart dinner rolls

MAKES 16 ROLLS

When organizing parties, a typical conversation revolves around what to serve and who brings what. Most people are hesitant to make bread, so I always volunteer to bring the rolls. Here's the recipe I turn to again and again. This easy-to-handle dough produces soft, fragrant, professional-looking rolls that can be made one day, shaped the next, and baked the next – who could ask for better? The rolls nestle together in the pan as they rise and bake, and easily pull apart after they're baked. Don't overlook the flavor variations. They pair beautifully with any meal.

do aheads

• Prepare the dough through step 4 but let rise only until about 1 1/2 times original size (rather than double the size), then refrigerate for up to 24 hours before proceeding with the recipe.

• Prepare the dough through step 8 but let rise only until about 1 1/2 times original size (rather than double the size), then cover the rolls loosely but completely with plastic wrap. Refrigerate the rolls for up to 12 hours before proceeding with the recipe. Remove from the fridge and leave on the counter while the oven heats.

• Prepare the rolls through step 10 and let cool completely. Freeze the rolls in a heavy-duty freezer bag for up to 2 months. Thaw overnight in the refrigerator or on the counter for about 4 hours.

1 cup (8 fl ounces/233 ml) half-and-half

6 tablespoons (3 ounces/85 grams) unsalted butter, cut into 6 pieces, plus 2 tablespoons, melted, for glazing (optional)

3 2/3 cups (16 1/2 ounces/468 grams) all-purpose flour

2 1/4 teaspoons (1 packet) instant yeast (see page 20)

1/3 cup (2 1/2 ounces/71 grams) granulated sugar

1 teaspoon table salt

3 egg yolks from large eggs

for the flavor variations (choose one):

Poppy Seed: 1 tablespoon plus 1 teaspoon poppy seeds

or

Black Pepper and Cheese: 2 cups (5 ounces/142 grams) loosely packed finely shredded extra-sharp Cheddar cheese and 2 teaspoons coarsely ground black pepper

or

Herb: 3/4 cup (2 ounces/57 grams) chopped mixed fresh herbs (I like 1/2 cup/1 1/2 ounces/43 grams flat-leaf parsley, 1/4 cup/3/4 ounce/20 grams chives, and 1 teaspoon thyme)

1. In a small saucepan, combine the half-and-half and the 6 tablespoons butter. Set over medium heat and heat, stirring constantly, until the butter melts and the liquid registers about 125 degrees (52°C) on an instant-read thermometer. Set aside.

2. TO MIX BY HAND

In a large bowl, combine the flour, yeast, sugar, and salt. (If making the poppy seed version, add 1 tablespoon seeds now.) Stir with a wooden spoon until well blended.

3. Check the temperature of the half-and-half mixture; it should now register about 120 degrees (49°C) on an instant-read thermometer. In order for the yeast to grow, the liquid needs to be between 115 and 125 degrees (46 and

52°C). Drizzle the warm liquid over the flour mixture and add the egg yolks. Stir with the wooden spoon until a rough, shaggy dough forms. Lightly dust a work surface with a little flour. Dump the dough onto the surface.

4. Knead the dough with your hands. It will be sticky at first, but resist the urge to add more flour. (If making the Cheddar version, add the cheese and pepper once all the flour is incorporated.) First, gather the dough together. Next, using the heel of one hand, push the top part of the dough away from you. Fold that piece over the dough nearest you. Give the dough a quarter turn clockwise and repeat. Keep on kneading until the dough is smooth and no longer sticky, about 10 minutes. (If making the herb version, add the herbs now and knead briefly to incorporate.) Shape the dough into a ball. Proceed as directed in step 5.

2. TO MIX IN A STAND MIXER

In the large bowl of a stand mixer, combine the flour, yeast, sugar, and salt. If making the poppy seed version, add 1 tablespoon seeds now. Whisk until well blended.

3. Check the temperature of the half-and-half mixture; it should register about 120 degrees (49°C) on an instant-read thermometer. In order for the yeast to grow, the liquid needs to be between 115 and 125 degrees (46 and 52°C).

4. Fit the mixer with the dough hook. With the mixer on medium-low speed, slowly pour the warm liquid into the flour mixture. Add the egg yolks. Mix until the flour is completely incorporated. If making the Cheddar cheese version, add the cheese and pepper now. Increase the speed to medium-high and beat until the dough is very smooth and pulls away from the bottom of the bowl (a little will stick to the sides), about 5 minutes. If making the herb version, add the herbs now. If the dough climbs up the hook, stop the mixer and scrape the dough back into the bowl. Don't venture too far away while the dough is mixing, as the mixer might dance around on the counter because of the large amount of dough. Proceed as directed in step 5.

5. LET THE DOUGH RISE

Scoop up the dough and shape it into a ball. Lightly grease the bowl and pop the dough back into it. Cover the top securely with plastic. (I like to use a large rubberband to hold the plastic in place.) Let the covered dough rise in a warm spot until doubled in size, 45 to 55 minutes.

6.
Lightly grease a 9-by-13-inch (22.75-by-33cm) baking dish (I use Pyrex). Turn the dough out onto a clean work surface and press down gently to deflate. There's no need to flour the work surface or your hands unless you're making the herb variation, in which case the dough may be sticky. Using a bench scraper or a chef's knife, divide the dough into 16 equal pieces, 2 to 2 1/3 ounces (57 to 71 grams) each. (To be sure of uniform rolls, use a scale to weigh the portions.)

7.
Work with 1 piece of dough at a time, and keep the others covered with plastic wrap or a damp towel. Again, there's no need to flour your hands unless you're making the herb variation. With a cupped palm, press down gently but firmly, rolling the piece in tight circles on the work surface until it forms a smooth-skinned ball with a seam on the bottom. Put the ball, seam side down, in the prepared baking dish, cover loosely with plastic, and repeat with the remaining dough. The dough balls can be arranged in rows or placed randomly; just be sure they're evenly spaced.

8.
Cover the baking dish with plastic wrap and let the balls rise in a warm spot until they're about 1 1/2 times their original size and have risen about three-fourths of the way up the sides of the baking dish (they won't yet fill the dish), 40 to 60 minutes.

9. Position an oven rack on the middle rung. Heat the oven to 375 degrees (190°C). If making the poppy seed version, sprinkle the rolls with the 1 teaspoon of seeds now.

10. Bake until the rolls are puffed and well browned, 20 to 25 minutes. Remove from the oven and brush the tops with the melted butter, if using. Serve warm.

Mousses, Custards, and Puddings
• • •

pumpkin crème brûlée
MAKES 8 SERVINGS

a survey of America's restaurants would probably list crème brûlée among the most popular desserts. I'll admit that I too am a big fan. Because I also love pumpkin pie, I flavor my crème brûlée with pumpkin and spice. The taste is subtler than classic pumpkin pie, and its creamy texture is soothing.

When making crème brûlée at home, I serve it in a large baking dish. I find that it makes caramelizing the top easier, and I get a crisper, more even coating. I've also provided directions in the recipe for making it in ramekins.

do aheads

• The unbaked crème brûlée can be prepared through step 3. Let cool completely and cover with plastic wrap. Refrigerate for up to 1 day before proceeding with the recipe. Please note that the chilled custard will take a few more minutes to bake.

• The baked crème brûlée can be prepared through step 4. Let cool completely and cover with plastic wrap. Refrigerate for up to 3 days.

4 cups (32 fl ounces/934 ml) heavy cream

10 egg yolks from large eggs (see storing egg whites, below)

3/4 cup (6 ounces/170 grams) firmly packed light brown sugar

3/4 cup (5 1/4 ounces/149 grams) canned solid-pack pumpkin (not seasoned pumpkin pie filling)

1 teaspoon pure vanilla extract

3/4 teaspoon ground cinnamon

1/4 teaspoon ground nutmeg

1/4 teaspoon table salt

for the caramel topping:

2/3 cup (5 1/4 ounces/149 grams) granulated sugar

1. Position an oven rack on the middle rung. Heat the oven to 325 degrees (165°C). Place an 8-cup round or oval ceramic dish with 2 inch (5cm) sides or eight 3/4-cup ramekins in a large baking pan.

2. In a medium saucepan, heat the cream until very warm and steamy (there's no need to bring it to a boil). Alternatively, heat the cream in a 4-cup Pyrex measure in the microwave.

3. In a medium bowl, combine the egg yolks, brown sugar, pumpkin, vanilla, cinnamon, nutmeg, and salt. Whisk until well blended. Whisking constantly, slowly pour the hot cream into the yolk mixture. Use a spoon to skim off any bubbles and foam from the top of the cream mixture.

4. Pour the custard into the baking dish or ramekins. Carefully fill the baking pan with hot water to come halfway up the sides of the baking dish or ramekins. Bake until the custard wiggles like Jell-O when the pan is nudged, 40 to 50 minutes if using a large dish or 30 to 40 minutes if using ramekins. Transfer the baking pan to a rack, carefully lift out the baking dish or ramekins, and set on a rack to cool completely. Cover with plastic wrap and refrigerate until ready to serve.

5. Just before serving, sift the sugar evenly over the top of the chilled custard. If using a mini propane torch, position the flame about 2 inches (5cm) above the custard and sweep the flame evenly across the top until the sugar is caramelized and glossy. If using a broiler, heat it on high. Slide the baking dish under the broiler and rotate it until the sugar is caramelized and glossy. Serve immediately.

storing egg whites: The white from 1 large egg weighs about 1 ounce and measures about 2 tablespoons (1 fl ounce/29 ml). Egg whites keep in the fridge for up to 1 month, and they also freeze beautifully. I like to freeze my extra whites in an ice-cube tray – putting 1 white in each cube. This way, I can defrost the exact amount called for in a recipe. Before filling the tray, make sure that the small containers hold 2 tablespoons and that they are impeccably clean. Wiping the tray with some white vinegar and then rinsing with warm water will get rid of any hint of grease that might spoil the whites' whipping power. Fill the tray and freeze. When the whites are frozen solid, pop them out of the tray and into a heavy-duty freezer bag.

bursting with raspberries
bread pudding

MAKES ONE 8-INCH (20CM) SQUARE PUDDING, OR 8 SERVINGS

Originally a nursery pudding served to toddlers, or a plain dessert made with stale bread, custard bread pudding was revitalized by restaurant chefs about 20 years ago. It quickly became popular, especially when served with a rich butter sauce laced with whiskey. Drawing on the original, I favor a less firm, creamier custard version, and I like to add chopped bittersweet chocolate or fruit (blueberries or raspberries are favorites) in lieu of the more customary raisins. The Dodge clan serves the pudding a bit on the warm side (20 to 30 seconds in the microwave does the job nicely) doused with chocolate or blueberry sauce instead of the usual whiskey sauce.

do aheads

• The pudding can be prepared through step 3 and refrigerated for up to 1 day before proceeding with the recipe.

• The pudding can be prepared through step 5 and refrigerated for up to 2 days.

1 medium (about 12 ounces/340 grams) loaf day-old French or country-style bread (avoid sourdough)

4 whole large eggs plus 2 yolks from large eggs

1/2 cup (4 ounces/113 grams) firmly packed light brown sugar

1 teaspoon pure vanilla extract

1/2 teaspoon finely grated lemon zest

1/4 teaspoon table salt

3 cups (24 fl ounces/700 ml) half-and-half, or 1 1/2 cups (12 ounces/350 ml) each heavy cream and whole milk

1/2 pint (5 ounces/42 grams/about 1 cup) raspberries, blueberries, or blackberries, rinsed and well dried

go-withs: Bittersweet Chocolate Sauce (page 44) or Blueberry Sauce (page 45) for garnish (optional)

1. Trim away the tough ends and bottom crust from the bread. Cut into slices 3/4 inch (2cm) thick, and then into 3/4-inch (2cm) cubes (don't fuss too much with the size as they won't all be uniform). Measure 5 cups (10 ounces/284 grams) of the cubes.

2. Lightly grease the bottom and sides of an 8-cup baking dish (I often use an 8-inch/20cm square Pyrex) and add the bread cubes in an even layer.

3. In a medium bowl, combine the whole eggs, egg yolks, brown sugar, vanilla, lemon zest, and salt. Whisk until well blended. Pour in the half-and-half or cream and milk and whisk until combined. Pour the custard over the bread cubes. Cover with plastic wrap and let sit at room temperature, pressing down on the bread occasionally, until the bread is evenly soaked, 20 minutes to 1 hour.

4. Meanwhile, position the oven rack on the middle rung. Heat the oven to 350 degrees (180°C). Have ready a large baking pan with 3-inch (7.75cm) sides.

5. Scatter the berries evenly on top of the pudding and gently press on them so that they are submerged but still slightly visible. Set the baking dish in the baking pan. Carefully fill the baking pan with hot water to come halfway up the sides of the baking dish. Bake until a small paring knife inserted near the center of the pudding comes out almost clean, about 45 minutes. Transfer the baking pan to a rack, carefully lift out the baking dish and set on a rack to cool. Serve warm, or let cool completely, cover with plastic wrap, and refrigerate until ready to serve. Drizzle each serving with the chocolate or berry sauce, if desired.

all-star custards

MAKES 8 SERVINGS

a custard is different from a pot de crème or a crème brûlée. Think firmer texture and a less rich, slightly eggier taste. The flavors and sweetness are so gentle and soft that you'll be soothed and satisfied with every spoonful. When my daughter, Tierney, was very young, she was a very particular eater, and the vanilla version of this custard was one of her favorite foods. And, believe me, when Tierney liked something, I rejoiced.

I originally intended on giving you only Tierney's favorite custard (the traditional vanilla-flavored one), but more and more flavor variations occurred to me during testing. So I offer you my top four flavor options – vanilla, maple, lemon, and coconut. While the ingredients vary for each, the mixing and baking methods are the same. This keeps the recipe easy and undemanding – just the way I like it.

do aheads

• The unbaked custard can be prepared through step 3. Let cool completely and cover with plastic wrap. Refrigerate for up to 1 day before proceeding with the recipe. Please note that the chilled custard will take a few more minutes to bake.

• The baked custards can be prepared through step 4 and refrigerated for up to 2 days.

for the vanilla custard:

1 1/2 cups (12 fl ounces/350 ml) heavy cream

1 1/2 cups (12 fl ounces/350 ml) whole milk

4 large eggs

2/3 cup (5 1/4 ounces/149 grams) granulated sugar

1 teaspoon pure vanilla extract

1/4 teaspoon table salt

for the lemon custard:

1 1/2 cups (12 fl ounces/350 ml) heavy cream

1 1/2 cups (12 fl ounces/350 ml) whole milk

4 large eggs

2/3 cup (5 1/4 ounces/149 grams) granulated sugar

2 tablespoons lemon juice

1 teaspoon finely grated lemon zest

1/4 teaspoon table salt

for the maple custard:

2 1/4 cups (18 fl ounces/525 ml) heavy cream

4 large eggs

2/3 cup (5 fl ounces/146 ml) pure maple syrup

1/4 teaspoon table salt

for the coconut custard:

1 can (14 fl ounces/408 ml) unsweetened coconut milk

1 1/2 cups (12 fl ounces/350 ml) heavy cream

4 large eggs

2/3 cup (5 1/4 ounces/149 grams) granulated sugar

1/4 teaspoon table salt

go-withs: toasted coconut or chopped walnuts (see page 40), blueberries, or raspberries for garnish (optional)

1. Position the oven rack on the middle rung. Heat the oven to 325 degrees (165°C). Arrange eight 3/4-cup ramekins in a large baking pan with 3-inch (7.75cm) sides.

2. Select a medium saucepan. If making **vanilla** custard or **lemon** custard, pour the cream and milk into the pan. If making **maple** custard, pour the cream into the pan. If making the **coconut** custard, pour the coconut milk and cream into the pan. Heat until very warm and steamy (no need to bring to a boil). Alternatively, use a 4-cup Pyrex measure and the microwave to heat the liquid.

3. Select a medium bowl. If making **vanilla** custard, combine the eggs, sugar, vanilla, and salt in the bowl. If making **lemon** custard, combine the eggs, sugar, lemon juice, lemon zest, and salt in the bowl. If making **maple** custard, combine the eggs, maple syrup, and salt in the bowl. If making **coconut** custard, combine the eggs, sugar, and salt in the bowl. Whisk until well blended. Slowly pour in the hot liquid while whisking constantly. Using a spoon, skim off any bubbles and foam from the surface.

4. Pour the custard into the ramekins. (I like to pour the custard into a 4-cup Pyrex measure and pour it from there into the ramekins – the spout makes pouring easy.) Carefully fill the baking pan with hot water to come halfway up the sides of the ramekins. Bake until the custards wiggle like Jell-O when the ramekins are nudged, 25 to 35 minutes, depending on the thickness of the ramekin walls. Transfer the baking pan to a rack, carefully lift out the ramekins, and set on a rack to cool completely. Cover with plastic wrap and refrigerate until ready to serve.

ready-when-you-are
chocolate-raspberry soufflés

MAKES 8 SERVINGS

refrigerators and freezers are set at different temperatures, so results can vary from home to home when this recipe is baked for the same amount of time. The good news is that I've tested these soufflés – both from fridge and freezer – at different baking times and all results were yummy, albeit slightly different. A little underdone and the center is a bit runny; a little overdone and the center is more cakelike. Any way you bake these soufflés they're delicious, and they're the perfect dessert to load up in your freezer. But best of all, they're ready when you are.

do aheads

• The soufflés can be prepared through step 4 and refrigerated for up to 1 day or frozen for up to 2 weeks before baking. To refrigerate: slide the ramekins into the fridge, chill for about 30 minutes, and then cover the ramekins with plastic wrap and keep refrigerated for up to 1 day. To freeze: pop the ramekins into the freezer and chill for about 20 minutes, then wrap each ramekin in plastic wrap and freeze for up to 2 weeks.

granulated sugar for coating the
   ramekins
3 tablespoons dark rum, brandy,
   Grand Marnier, or water
1 1/2 teaspoons instant coffee
   granules (any type, even decaf,
   will do)
6 ounces (170 grams) bittersweet
   chocolate, finely chopped

6 tablespoons (3 ounces/85 grams)
   unsalted butter, cut into pieces
1/4 teaspoon table salt
3 large eggs, separated
3/4 cup (3 ounces/85 grams) confectioners' sugar

go-withs: 1 pint (10 ounces/284 grams/about 2 cups) raspberries, rinsed and well dried; Sweetened Whipped Cream (page 46) for garnish (optional)

1. Lightly grease eight 3/4-cup ramekins and dust them with granulated sugar, gently tapping out the excess sugar. Set the ramekins on a small cookie or baking sheet.

2. In a small bowl, stir together the liqueur or water and instant coffee. Set aside and stir occasionally until the coffee is dissolved.

3. Melt the chocolate and butter in a double boiler (see What Is It? on page 74) or in the microwave (see page 51). Remove from the heat and whisk until glossy and smooth. Stir in the coffee mixture and salt. Add the egg yolks one at a time, whisking well after each addition. Add about one-third of the confectioners' sugar and whisk until well blended and smooth. Set aside.

4. In a medium bowl, beat the egg whites with an electric mixer (stand mixer fitted with the whisk attachment or handheld mixer) on medium-high speed until they form soft peaks. Increase the speed to high and gradually sprinkle in the remaining confectioners' sugar. Continue beating until firm, glossy peaks form. Scoop about one-fourth of the beaten whites onto the chocolate mixture and whisk until blended. Add the remaining whites and fold in gently with a rubber spatula just until blended. Pour into the prepared ramekins, filling them half full. Scatter the raspberries evenly over the top and then pour in the remaining batter. The mixture will almost completely fill the ramekins. Refrigerate or freeze as directed in Do Aheads.

5. TO BAKE STRAIGHT FROM THE FRIDGE

Position an oven rack on the middle rung. Heat the oven to 400 degrees (200°C). Uncover the ramekins and place them on a cookie or baking sheet. Bake the soufflés until they are puffed and have risen about 1 inch (2.5cm) above the rim of the ramekins, about 15 minutes. The top will still be slightly sunken in the center. Don't worry – think of it as a well to fill with a dollop of whipped cream. Remove from the oven and serve immediately with the whipped cream, if desired.

5. TO BAKE STRAIGHT FROM THE FREEZER

Position an oven rack on the middle rung. Heat the oven to 400 degrees (200°C). Unwrap the ramekins and place them on a cookie sheet or baking sheet. Bake the soufflés until they are puffed and have risen about 1 inch (2.5cm) above the rim of the ramekins, about 18 minutes. The top will be slightly sunken in the center. Don't worry – think of it as a well to fill with a dollop of whipped cream. Remove from the oven and serve immediately. Top with a dollop of the whipped cream, if desired.

raspberry charlotte

MAKES 6 SERVINGS

C asual summer picnics or dinners call for undemanding desserts. Cool, light, and creamy, this raspberry charlotte fits the bill. It's based on an Italian *panna cotta* (cooked cream), chilled eggless custard thickened with unflavored gelatin. I've enhanced the presentation, turning it into a charlotte by adding ladyfingers. Simply line a bowl or mold with store-bought or homemade ladyfingers and fill it up with the creamy raspberry *panna cotta* made in the blender. Once the gelatin is set, turn the chilled charlotte upside down, cut into wedges, and serve.

do aheads

• The raspberry mixture can be prepared through step 3, covered, and refrigerated for up to 2 days before gently softening the mixture to the correct consistency and proceeding with the recipe.

• The charlotte can be prepared through step 6 and refrigerated for up to 3 days before serving.

2 cups (16 fl ounces/467 ml) whole milk

1 tablespoon unflavored powdered gelatin (measured from 2 packets), see What Is It? below

1 cup (8 fl ounces/233 grams) heavy cream

2/3 cup (5 1/4 ounces/149 grams) granulated sugar

1/2 pint (5 ounces/142 grams/about 1 cup) raspberries, rinsed and well dried

1 tablespoon lemon juice

1 teaspoon finely grated lemon zest (optional)

Pinch table salt

1 to 2 packages (3 ounces/85 grams each) plain ladyfingers (24 to 48 ladyfingers each 3 inches long)

or

24 Hazelnut Ladyfingers (page 271)

go-withs: Red Berry Sauce (page 43) for garnish (optional) or Sweetened Whipped Cream (page 46) and raspberries, for garnish (optional)

1. Pour 1/2 cup (4 fl ounces/117 ml) of the milk into a blender. Sprinkle the gelatin evenly over the milk and let stand until the gelatin is no longer dry looking and has softened, about 5 minutes.

2. In a small saucepan, combine the cream and the remaining 1 1/2 cups (12 fl ounces/350 ml) milk. Heat just until boiling. (This can also be done in a 4-cup Pyrex measure in the microwave.) Once boiling, carefully pour into the blender to cover the gelatin. Let stand for 1 minute. Cover the blender and blend until the gelatin is dissolved, about 3 minutes. Dip a spoon or spatula into the liquid. It should look clear and feel smooth to the touch.

3. Add the sugar, 3/4 cup (about 3 1/2 ounces/99 grams) of the raspberries, lemon juice, lemon zest (if using), and salt. Cover and blend until smooth, about 45 seconds. Pour into a medium bowl (or back into the 4-cup Pyrex measure) and refrigerate, stirring frequently, until the mixture is cooled and thickened, about 15 minutes. For faster chilling, set the bowl in an ice bath (see What Is It? page 000).

4. Meanwhile, lightly grease a 6-cup round bowl or charlotte mold (see equipment note, below). Arrange 2 pieces of plastic wrap in a cross shape and press into the bowl or mold, covering the inside of the bowl completely and allowing the ends to hang a few inches over the rim. Snugly arrange the ladyfingers, flat side up (trimming with a serrated knife when necessary), against the plastic wrap, lining the bowl completely. Set aside.

5. Once the raspberry mixture has thickened (it should be as thick as unbeaten egg whites), stir in the remaining raspberries. The berries should be suspended in the mixture and not sink to the bottom or float to the top. If the mixture is too thick to stir in the berries, heat gently in a double boiler (see What Is It? on page 74) until more liquidy and repeat the chilling process. If the raspberries sink, continue chilling and stirring the mixture until it reaches the proper consistency.

6. Pour the mixture into the ladyfinger-lined bowl. Cover the top of the bowl completely with the overhanging plastic wrap and refrigerate until firm, about 4 hours.

7. To serve, uncover the top and then trim off the tips of the ladyfingers so they are flush with the filling. Invert a flat serving plate over the bowl and, holding the bowl and plate, invert them together. Use the plastic wrap to help remove the bowl and then peel away the plastic wrap from the charlotte. Using a serrated knife, cut into wedges to serve. Garnish with berry sauce or whipped cream, if desired.

equipment note

A traditional charlotte mold is shaped like a bucket, with a flat-bottom and slightly sloping sides. Traditionally, the ladyfingers are trimmed into long triangles and arranged in the bottom of the mold, flat side up, to form a flower shape, and the remaining ladyfingers are trimmed to fit snugly along the sides.

what is it? (unflavored gelatin)

Most often found in powdered form, unflavored gelatin is a thickener that helps give body to mousses and puddings. It's a great invisible helper, as it imparts neither color nor flavor to the finished product. Gelatin first needs to be softened in a small amount of cold liquid. The granules will swell and expand. Once dissolved, combine it with more liquid to unleash its thickening powers. On the other hand, you must never allow it to come to a boil, as its holding power will be reduced.

glazed apricot-plum galette

MAKES ONE 10-INCH (25CM) GALETTE, OR 8 SERVINGS

if you're one of the many afflicted with "pie anxiety" and so shy away from pie making, help has arrived. A galette is as close as you can come to a beginner pie. No pie plate, no crimping, no double crusts. All the equipment you need is a half sheet pan, a rolling pin, and a few metal spatulas. Plus, shaping isn't an issue, because a galette's free-from shape makes it the friendliest of all pies. Once you see how easy the dough is to handle, you may be inspired to move on to traditional pies.

As for the fruit filling, you can use an equivalent amount of any stone fruit. Plums and apricots make a magnificent galette to both see and taste. It's more important, however, that the fruit be ripe. Press the "shoulders" (the area surrounding the stem of the fruit) gently with your finger. If the fruit is ripe, it will yield slightly under the pressure. And don't forget to smell the fruit. The aroma should be sweet and flowery. If it isn't, substitute an equal amount of a fruit (or fruits) you find that is ripe.

do aheads

• The galette dough can be prepared as directed in step 1, wrapped in plastic wrap, and refrigerated for up to 3 days or frozen for up to 3 months. Thaw in the refrigerator before proceeding with the recipe.

• The galette can be prepared through step 4, wrapped well in plastic, and frozen for up to 1 month before baking. Make sure to check your freezer and clear some space before embarking on the recipe. I find it easiest to freeze the galette before attempting to wrap it in plastic. Shape it on a plastic-lined dinner-sized plate. Slide the filled and shaped galette, plate and all, into the freezer uncovered and let it firm up, about 1 hour. Using 2 long metal spatulas (or your hands if it's frozen enough), carefully lift the galette (remember, it's not completely frozen) onto a large sheet of plastic wrap, then wrap in several layers of plastic and freeze. To bake a frozen galette: Position an oven rack on the middle rung and set a foil-lined half sheet pan on the rack. Heat the oven to 350 degrees. Unwrap the frozen galette (don't thaw it) and brush with the heavy cream or milk (step 5). Carefully slide the galette onto the heated sheet pan and bake until the crust is golden and the fruit is tender, about 1 1/2 hours. If the crust browns too quickly, cover it loosely with foil. Let cool slightly, then glaze as directed in step 6.

for the dough:

2 cups (9 ounces/255 grams) all-purpose flour

3 tablespoons granulated sugar

1 teaspoon finely grated lemon zest

1/4 teaspoon table salt

10 tablespoons (5 ounces/142 grams) very cold unsalted butter, cut into 1/2-inch pieces

1/4 cup (2 fl ounces/58 ml) plus 2 tablespoons very cold water

2 tablespoons lemon juice

for the filling:

1/2 cup (4 ounces/113 grams) firmly packed light brown sugar

3 tablespoons all-purpose flour

1 teaspoon finely grated lemon zest

Pinch of table salt

1 pound (454 grams) ripe apricots, pitted and cut into wedges 3/4 inch (2cm) thick

1 pound (454 grams) ripe plums, pitted and cut into wedges 3/4 inch (2cm) thick

2 teaspoons minced fresh ginger

2 teaspoons lemon juice

2 tablespoons heavy cream or milk

2 tablespoons apricot jelly or preserves

1 1/2 teaspoons orange juice

go-withs: vanilla ice cream or Sweetened Whipped Cream (page 46) for garnish (optional)

1. TO MAKE THE DOUGH

Put the flour, sugar, lemon zest, and salt in a food processor and pulse briefly to combine. Add the butter pieces and pulse just until coarse crumbs form. Add the water and lemon juice and pulse just until a rough, shaggy dough forms. Dump the dough onto the work surface and gently shape into a disk about 6 inches (15.25cm) in diameter. Wrap in plastic wrap and refrigerate until chilled, at least 1 hour.

2. Position an oven rack on the middle rung. Heat the oven to 400 degrees (200°C). Line a half sheet pan with parchment or foil.

3. Unwrap the dough, place it on a lightly floured work surface, and roll out into a large round about 15 inches (38cm) in diameter and between 1/8 and 1/4 inch (3 and 6.5mm) thick. Lift and rotate the dough a quarter turn several times as you roll to prevent sticking, and dust the surface and the rolling pin with flour as needed. Use a bench scraper or spatula to loosen the rolled dough as needed. Trim off the excess dough to make a 14-inch (35cm) round. Remember this is a rustic dessert, so a few ragged edges are fine. Carefully roll the dough round around the pin and transfer it to the prepared pan. The dough will hang over the edges of the pan for now. Cover loosely with plastic wrap and set aside. If your kitchen is warm, carefully transfer the pan to the refrigerator.

4. TO MAKE THE FILLING

In a large bowl, combine the brown sugar, flour, lemon zest, and salt. Whisk until no lumps remain. Add the apricot and plum slices, ginger, and lemon juice and toss until the fruits are evenly coated with the dry ingredients. Pile the fruits and any juices in the center of the dough, leaving a 3-inch (7.75cm) bordered uncovered. Fold the dough edge up and over the filling, pleating the dough as you go. Using your fingers, dab a little water under each pleat and gently press down on the pleats to seal.

5.

Brush the pleated dough with the cream or milk. Bake until the crust is browned and the fruit is tender, about 40 minutes. Transfer the half sheet pan to a rack and let cool slightly. Using 2 long metal spatulas, lift the galette onto a large, flat serving plate.

6. TO GLAZE THE GALETTE

In a small bowl, stir together the apricot preserves and orange juice. Drizzle the glaze over the fruit and spread with the back of the spoon. Serve warm or at room temperature with a scoop of vanilla ice cream or a dollop of whipped cream, if desired.

flaky cinnamon apple tart

MAKES ONE 8-BY-14-INCH (20-BY-35CM) TART, OR 6 SERVINGS

When I studied in Paris, one of my favorite pastimes was strolling by pastry shops and taking notes on the displays. As a student of pastry, I noted that the staple item in every window was a puff pastry tart topped with apples. Be it a round, square, or rectangle, I always admired how perfectly the slices were cut and arranged. I marveled at how long it must have taken to get the apples "just so," and pledged that I would never be that deliberate or fussy. Little did I realize that even in those days, I was already a Weekend Baker, prizing convenience as much as quality.

True to my word, my Americanized version of the French tart features a casual scattering of apples (and a hint of cinnamon). Store-bought puff pastry bakes up crisp and buttery and pairs well with sweet and tender apple slices.

do aheads

• The tart can be prepared through step 3, covered with plastic wrap, and refrigerated for up to 1 day ahead before proceeding with the recipe.

• I'm reluctant to advise cutting the apples too far in advance because they discolor easily. However, in a pinch, they can be sliced, tossed with a generous amount of lemon juice, and slipped into a zipper-top plastic bag. Take care to squeeze out as much air as possible from the bag before sealing it to keep the slices from browning. Refrigerate for up to 6 hours. Before scattering the slices on the pastry, dump the apple slices onto a couple of paper towels and blot away some of the excess lemon juice. (Any remaining lemon will perfume, but not overwhelm, the baked tart.) The slices will be a bit discolored but, once baked, they will look just fine.

1 sheet frozen puff pastry, 9 1/2
    inches square
1/4 cup (2 ounces/57 grams)
    granulated sugar
1/2 teaspoon ground cinnamon
3 apples (about 7 ounces/198
    grams each), peeled, cored, and
    sliced 1/8 to 1/4 inch (3 to
    6.25mm) thick (I like Golden
    Delicious, but any firm, medium-
    tart apple will do.)

2 tablespoons milk or heavy cream
2 tablespoons (1 ounce/28 grams)
    unsalted butter, cut into 1/2-inch
    (1.25cm) pieces

go-withs: vanilla ice cream, Sweetened Whipped Cream (page 46), or Caramel Sauce (page 44) for garnish (optional)

1. Remove 1 sheet of frozen puff pastry from the box, set it on a lightly floured surface, and cover it with plastic wrap. Do *not* unfold. Wrap the remaining sheet in plastic wrap and return to the freezer. Let the covered puff pastry sit on the countertop until thawed and just pliable, about 20 minutes.

2. Meanwhile, position the oven rack on the middle rung. Heat the oven to 375 degrees (190°C). Line a cookie sheet with parchment or a nonstick baking liner (I like the Silpat). In a small bowl or ramekin, combine the granulated sugar and cinnamon. Stir with a spoon until well blended. Set aside.

3. On a lightly floured work surface, carefully place the thawed pastry (do not unfold). Dust the top of the puff pastry with a little flour. Roll out the dough, lightly dusting with flour as needed to prevent the dough from sticking to the rolling pin and work surface, into an 8-by-14-inch (20-by-35cm) rectangle. Using a large knife, trim about 1/4 inch (6.25mm) from all the sides. Transfer the pastry to the lined cookie sheet.

4. Brush the top of the pastry evenly with some of the milk or cream (you won't use it all). Scatter the apple slices over the pastry, forming an even, yet casual layer and leaving a 1/2-inch (1.25cm) border uncovered. Sprinkle the cinnamon sugar over the entire tart, including the exposed border. Scatter the small butter pieces evenly over the apple layer.

5. Bake until the pastry border is golden brown and the apples are tender, about 35 minutes. Transfer the cookie sheet to a rack and let cool for about 15 minutes. Using a long metal spatula, slide the tart onto the rack to cool, or, if serving immediately, onto a large, flat serving plate or decorative cutting board. Serve warm or at room temperature. While the tart is delicious on its own, a scoop of vanilla ice cream, a dollop of whipped cream, or a drizzle of Caramel Sauce makes it a real standout.

got extra time?

For a French pastry shop–window look, arrange the apple slices in neat, precise, slightly overlapping rows.

You can glaze the baked tart for a shimmering presentation. In a small bowl or ramekin, stir together 2 tablespoons apricot preserves or apple jelly and 1 1/2 teaspoons water until well blended. Drizzle the glaze over the apples and spread with the back of the spoon, if desired.

double-ginger ricotta tart

every once in a while, I'm lucky enough to receive a shipment of crystallized ginger from Lou Palma, my cousin's husband. (Lou buys crystallized ginger of exceptional quality in the Chinatown section of Patterson, New Jersey.) His last delivery inspired this tart. The crust is made from crushed gingersnaps and is pressed easily into the tart pan. The ricotta–cream cheese filling is smooth and flecked with finely chopped crystallized ginger. The velvety texture of the filling balances well with the slightly peppery ginger flavor.

do aheads

• The crust can be prepared through step 4, wrapped in plastic wrap, and stored at room temperature for up to 3 days or frozen for up to 1 month before proceeding with the recipe.

• The tart can be prepared through step 6, covered with plastic wrap, and refrigerated for up to 2 days or frozen for up to 1 month. Thaw in the refrigerator overnight.

for the crust:

1 cup (5 ounces/142 grams) ginger-snap crumbs (from about 20 crisp gingersnaps)
1 tablespoon granulated sugar

3 tablespoons (1 1/2 ounces/43 grams) unsalted butter, melted

for the filling:

2 cups (17 1/2 ounces/496 grams) whole-milk ricotta cheee	2 tablespoons all-purpose flour
4 ounces (113 grams) cream cheese, at room temperature	1/4 teaspoon table salt
2/3 cup (5 1/4 ounces/149 grams) granulated sugar	3 egg yolks from large eggs
	2 1/2 tablespoons finely chopped crystallized ginger
	3/4 teaspoon pure vanilla extract

1. Position an oven rack on the middle rung. Heat the oven to 350 degrees (180°C). Have ready a 9 1/2-inch (24cm) tart pan with a removable bottom.

2. **TO MAKE THE CRUST**

In a medium bowl, combine the gingersnap crumbs and sugar. Stir until well blended. Drizzle the melted butter over the crumbs and mix with a fork until evenly moistened and well blended.

3. Dump the crumbs into the tart pan and cover with a large sheet of plastic wrap. Place your hands on the plastic wrap and spread the crumbs to coat the bottom of the pan evenly. (The plastic wrap will keep the crumbs from sticking to your hands.) Once the crumbs are in place, and with the plastic wrap still in place, use your fingers to pinch and press some of the crumbs around the inside edge of the pan to cover the sides evenly and completely. Redistribute the remaining crumbs evenly over the bottom of the pan and firmly press down to make a compact layer. I like to use a metal measuring cup with straight sides and a flat bottom for this task.

4. Bake the crust until it is slightly darker, about 10 minutes. Meanwhile, prepare the filling. If the crust is baked before the filling is ready, slide the tart pan onto a rack. Leave the oven set to 350 degrees (180°C).

5. TO MAKE THE FILLING

In a medium bowl, combine the ricotta and cream cheeses. Beat with an electric mixer (stand mixer fitted with the paddle attachment or handheld mixer) on medium speed until the cream cheese is incorporated and no lumps remain. Add the sugar, flour, and salt and beat until well blended. Add the egg yolks, crystallized ginger, and vanilla and beat just until incorporated.

6. Scrape the filling into the baked crust. Return the tart to the oven and bake until the filling just barely jiggles when the pan is nudged, about 30 minutes. Transfer the tart pan to a rack and let cool completely. Refrigerate until well chilled and firm, about 3 hours. To remove the tart from the pan, place the pan on a widemouthed can and allow the outside ring to fall away. If it's a bit stubborn, gently grip the ring with your fingers to coax its release. Once the ring is removed, move the tart to a flat surface. Slide a long, thin metal spatula between the pan bottom and the crust to separate the two. Using a spatula or two, transfer the tart to a flat serving plate. Serve chilled.

velvety pumpkin tart

MAKES ONE 9 1/2-INCH (24CM) TART, OR 8 SERVINGS

i've never eaten a tart this velvety. The not-so-secret ingredient is cream cheese, but don't think of this as a cheesecake in a tart shell. There's just enough cream cheese to bring out the silken texture without making the filling heavy. The cream cheese also adds a subtle tartness that balances beautifully with the pumpkin.

Claire Van de Berghe, my friend and trusted recipe tester, finds this is not only one of the easiest tarts to make but also one of the most beautiful. This recipe just may replace your traditional Thanksgiving pumpkin pie.

do aheads

• The crust can be prepared through step 4, covered with plastic wrap, and stored at room temperature for up to 3 days or frozen for up to 1 month before proceeding with the recipe.

• The filling can be prepared as directed in step 5, covered, and refrigerated for up to 2 days. Bring to room temperature before proceeding with the recipe.

for the crust:

1 cup (5 ounces/142 grams) ginger-snap crumbs (from about 20 crisp gingersnaps)
1 tablespoon granulated sugar

3 tablespoons (1 1/2 ounces/43 grams) unsalted butter, melted

for the filling:

1 package (8 ounces/227 grams) cream cheese, at room temperature

3/4 cup (6 ounces/170 grams) firmly packed light brown sugar

1/2 cup (3 1/2 ounces/99 grams) canned, solid-packed pumpkin (not seasoned pumpkin pie filling)

1 teaspoon ground cinnamon

1/4 teaspoon ground nutmeg

1/4 teaspoon table salt

Pinch of ground cloves

1 large egg

1 egg yolk from a large egg

1/2 teaspoon pure vanilla extract

1. Position an oven rack on the middle rung. Heat the oven to 350 degrees (180°C). Have ready a 9 1/2-inch (24cm) tart pan with a removable bottom.

2. TO MAKE THE CRUST
In a medium bowl, combine the gingersnap crumbs and sugar. Stir until well blended. Drizzle the melted butter over the crumbs and mix with a fork until evenly moistened and well blended.

3. Dump the crumbs into the tart pan and cover with large sheet of plastic wrap. Place your hands on the plastic wrap and spread the crumbs to coat the bottom of the pan evenly. (The plastic wrap will keep the crumbs from sticking to your hands.) Once the crumbs are in place, and with the plastic wrap still in place, use your fingers to pinch and press some of the crumbs around the inside edge of the pan to cover the sides evenly and completely. Redistribute the remaining crumbs evenly over the bottom of the pan and firmly press down to make a compact layer. I like to use a metal measuring cup with straight sides and a flat bottom for this task.

4. Bake the crust until it is slightly darker, almost 10 minutes. Meanwhile, prepare the filling. If the crust is baked before the filling is ready, slide the tart pan onto a rack. Reduce the oven temperature to 300 degrees (150°C).

5. TO MAKE THE FILLING

In a medium bowl, combine the cream cheese and brown sugar. Beat with an electric mixer (stand mixer fitted with the paddle attachment or hand-held mixer) on medium speed until the mixture is smooth with no lumps of cream cheese or sugar remaining. Add the pumpkin, cinnamon, nutmeg, salt, and cloves and beat until well blended. Add the egg, egg yolk, and vanilla and beat just until incorporated.

6.

Scrape the filling into the baked crust. Return the tart to the oven and bake until the filling just barely jiggles when the pan is nudged, 30 to 35 minutes. Transfer the tart pan to a rack and let cool completely. Refrigerate until well chilled and firm, about 3 hours. To remove the tart from the pan, place the pan on a widemouthed can and allow the outside ring to fall away. If it's a bit stubborn, gently grip the ring with your fingers to coax it to release. Once the ring is removed, move the tart to a flat surface. Slide a long, thin metal spatula between the pan bottom and the crust to separate the two. Using a spatula or two, transfer the tart to a flat serving plate. Serve chilled.

coconut-crusted pudding tart

MAKES ONE 9 1/2-INCH (24CM) TART, OR 8 SERVINGS

Creamy lemon pudding and a toasted-sweet coconut crust combine to make this tart the next best thing to escaping to the Caribbean in the middle of a New England winter. The tart itself evokes the warmth of summer. It also benefits from being topped with fresh fruit. In the winter, I like it with mango, kiwi, and orange.

do aheads

• The crust can be prepared through step 4, covered with plastic wrap, and stored at room temperature for up to 3 days or frozen for up to 1 month before proceeding with the recipe.

• The filling can be prepared as directed in step 5, covered, and refrigerated for up to 2 days before assembling the tart.

• The tart can be assembled, covered with plastic wrap, and refrigerated for up to 1 day before serving.

for the crust:

1 cup (5 ounces) vanilla wafer crumbs (I use about 27 Nilla Vanilla Wafers)

1/2 cup (2 1/2 ounces/71 grams) sweetened shredded dried coconut, finely chopped

3 tablespoons (1 1/2 ounces/43 grams) unsalted butter, melted

1/2 cup (4 ounces/113 grams) granulated sugar

3 tablespoons cornstarch

Pinch of table salt

2 large eggs

1 1/4 cups (10 fl ounces/292 ml) whole milk

1/3 cup (2 1/2 fl ounces/73 ml) lemon juice

1 teaspoon finely grated lemon zest

3 tablespoons (1 1/2 ounces/43 grams) unsalted butter, cut into 3 pieces

for the topping:

3 cups (15 ounces/425 grams) cut-up mixed fresh fruit

1. TO MAKE THE CRUST

Position an oven rack on the middle rung. Heat the oven to 350 degrees (180°C). Have ready a 9 1/2-inch (24cm) tart pan with a removable bottom.

2.

In a medium bowl, combine the cookie crumbs and coconut. Stir until well blended. Drizzle the melted butter over the crumbs and mix with a fork until evenly moistened and well blended.

3.

Dump the crumbs into the tart pan and cover with a large sheet of plastic wrap. Place your hands on the plastic wrap and spread the crumbs to coat the bottom of the pan evenly. (The plastic wrap will keep the crumbs from sticking to your hands.) Once the crumbs are in place, and with the plastic wrap still in place, use your fingers to pinch and press some of the crumbs around the inside edge of the pan to cover the sides evenly and completely. Redistribute the remaining crumbs evenly over the bottom of the pan and firmly press down to make a compact layer. I like to use a metal measuring cup with straight sides and a flat bottom for this task.

4.

Bake the crust until slightly darker, about 10 minutes. Transfer the tart pan to a rack and let cool completely.

5. TO MAKE THE FILLING

In a medium, heavy saucepan off the heat, combine the sugar, cornstarch, and salt. Whisk until well blended. Add the eggs and whisk until blended. Pour in the milk and lemon juice and whisk until the mixture is smooth. Set the pan over medium-high heat and cook, whisking constantly, until the mixture just begins to boil. Remove from the heat and add the butter pieces. Whisk until the butter is melted and the pudding is smooth. Pour the pudding into a medium bowl and press a piece of plastic wrap directly on the pudding surface to cover completely (this will keep a skin from forming). Refrigerate until well chilled.

6. Using an offset spatula, spread the chilled pudding evenly in the baked crust. Scatter the fruit over the pudding. To remove the tart from the pan, place the pan on a widemouthed can and allow the outside ring to fall away. If it's a bit stubborn, gently grip the ring with your fingers to coax its release. Once the ring is removed, move the tart to a flat surface. Slide a long, thin metal spatula between the pan bottom and the crust to separate the two. Using a spatula or two, transfer the tart to a flat serving plate. Serve chilled.

got extra time?

Just before serving, sprinkle the fruit topping with 1/3 cup (2 ounces/57 grams) sweetened shredded dried coconut, lightly toasted (see page 40).

never-fail pie dough

i f you're one of the millions who are reluctant to make and handle pie dough, this recipe, I promise, will make a pie baker out of you. It comes complete with directions for rolling, lining the pie plate, blind baking (pre-baking), a double crust, and an incredibly easy prefab lattice top. It's the only pie dough you'll ever need.

do aheads

• The dough disks can be well wrapped in plastic wrap and refrigerated for up to 2 days or frozen for up to 3 months. Thaw in the refrigerator.

• The pastry-lined plate can be well wrapped and frozen for up to 3 months before baking.

• The baked and cooled pie crust can be covered with plastic wrap and stored at room temperature for up to 1 day before proceeding with the recipe.

• The lattice top can be well wrapped and frozen on the cookie sheet for up to 3 months. Be sure to keep it level in the freezer. Remove it from the freezer about 15 minutes before topping the pie with it.

2 1/2 cups (11 1/4 ounces/319 grams) all-purpose flour

1 tablespoon granulated sugar

1/2 teaspoon table salt

8 tablespoons (4 ounces/113 grams) very cold unsalted butter, cut into 1/2-inch pieces

4 tablespoons (2 ounces/57 grams) very cold vegetable shortening, cut into 1/2-inch pieces

2 teaspoons lemon juice

6 tablespoons (3 fl ounces/87 ml) very cold water

Put the flour, sugar, and salt in a food processor and pulse briefly to combine. Add the butter and shortening pieces and pulse just until the mixture looks like coarse crumbs. Add the lemon juice and water and pulse just until a rough, shaggy dough forms. Dump the dough onto a work surface and gently shape into 2 equal disks each about 5 inches (13cm) in diameter. Wrap each in plastic and refrigerate until chilled, at least 1 hour.

for a single-crust pie:

Lightly dust the work surface and a rolling pin with flour. Unwrap 1 disk, place it on the floured surface, and roll out into a 14-inch (35cm) round. Lift and rotate the dough a quarter turn several times as you roll to prevent sticking, and dust the surface and the rolling pin with flour as needed. Use a bench scraper or spatula to loosen the rolled dough as needed. Carefully roll the dough around the pin and position the pin over a 9-inch (22.75cm) pie plate (I use Pyrex). Unroll the dough onto the pie plate and gently nudge it into the bottom and sides of the plate. Gently but firmly press the dough against the sides and bottom, being careful not to stretch or tear it. Trim the edges, leaving a 3/4-inch (2cm) overhang. Roll the overhang under itself to shape a high edge that rests on top of the plate rim. Position the thumb and forefinger of one hand on the outside edge of the plate rim and the forefinger of the other hand directly opposite on the inside. Then, pinch-crimp the edge, working your way completely around the rim.

for blind baking (prebaking):

Follow the directions for a single-crust pie. Freeze the crust until very firm, at least 30 minutes. Position an oven rack on the middle rung. Heat the oven to 400 degrees (200°C). Line the frozen crust with a large piece of foil and fill with pie weights or dried beans. Bake for 15 minutes. Remove the foil and weights and continue baking until the crust is golden brown, about 10 minutes longer. Transfer to a rack and let cool completely.

for a double-crust pie:

Roll out 1 dough disk and line a 9-inch (22.75cm) pie plate as directed for a single-crust pie, leaving the excess dough untrimmed and hanging over the sides. Cover loosely with plastic wrap while you roll out the other disk as directed for a single-crust pie. Load the filling into the pastry-lined pie plate and brush the edge of the bottom crust with water. Roll the remaining dough round around the pin and position over the filling. Gently unroll over the filling. Press the edges of the top and bottom crusts together and trim both crusts, leaving a 3/4-inch (2cm) overhang. Roll the overhang under itself to shape a high edge that rests on top of the plate rim. Position the thumb and forefinger of one hand on the outside edge of the plate rim and the forefinger of the other hand directly opposite on the inside. Then, pinch-crimp the edge, working your way completely around the rim. With a paring knife, slash 2 or 3 vents in the top crust, and bake according to the recipe directions.

for a prefab lattice crust:

Roll out 1 dough disk and line a 9-inch pie (22.75cm) plate as directed for a single-crust pie, leaving the excess dough untrimmed and hanging over the sides. Cover loosely with plastic wrap and set aside. Roll out the remaining disk into a rectangle slightly larger than 9 by 14 inches (22.75 by 35cm). Trim the dough to an exact 9-by-14-inch (22.75-by-35cm) rectangle. Cut the rectangle into 12 strips each 14 inches (35cm) long and 3/4 inch (2cm) wide. Line a cookie sheet with parchment. Arrange 6 strips horizontally on the cookie sheet, setting them 3/4 inch (2cm) apart. These are the "bottom" strips. Set aside the remaining 6 strips. They will be the "top" strips.

Position the cookie sheet so that the strips are horizontal to you. Starting with the bottom strip nearest you, and working from the right end, fold back every other strip. Slightly right of center, lay down 1 top strip vertically. Unfold the folded strips. Then, working from the left end of the strips, fold back the other 3 bottom strips. Lay a second top strip 3/4 inch (2cm) to the left of the first. Unfold the folded strips. Now fold back alternating strips on the right. Lay a third top strip 3/4 inch (2cm) to the right of the center strip; unfold the strips. Repeat the process on the left and right sides with the remaining top strips.

Dab a little water between the strips where they overlap, pressing gently to seal. Cover with plastic wrap and pop the lattice – cookie sheet and all – into the fridge for 15 minutes; be sure to keep it level.

Put the filling in the lined pie plate as directed in the recipe. Brush the edge of the bottom crust with water. Remove the lattice from the fridge and uncover. Slide your palm under the parchment and center it under the lattice. Lift the paper and invert the lattice onto the filling, using your palm as a guide to center the lattice on the filling. Press the edges together and trim both crusts, leaving a 3/4-inch (2cm) overhang. Roll the overhang under itself to shape a high edge that rests on top of the plate rim. Position the thumb and forefinger of one hand on the outside edge of the plate rim and the forefinger of the other hand directly opposite on the inside. Then, pinch-crimp the edge, working your way completely around the rim. Bake according to the recipe directions.

dark chocolate–pecan pie

MAKES ONE 9-INCH (22.75CM) PIE, OR 10 SERVINGS

i'm apt to put chocolate in just about anything, including this pecan pie.
Pecan pie doesn't really need improving on (this gives you permission to
leave out the chocolate, if you choose), but this variation is definitely
worth trying.

do aheads

• The pie crust can be prepared as directed in step 1, well wrapped, and
refrigerated up to 2 days or frozen for up to 1 month before baking.

• The pie crust can be prepared through step 2, covered with plastic wrap,
and stored at room temperature for up to 1 day before proceeding with the
recipe.

• The custard can be prepared through step 3, covered, and refrigerated for
up to 2 days before proceeding with the recipe. If using the custard straight
from the fridge, expect to add a few minutes to the baking time.

1/2 recipe (1 disk) Never-Fail Pie
  Dough, chilled (page 244)
1 1/4 cups (10 fl ounces/292 ml)
  light corn syrup
3/4 cup (6 ounces/170 grams)
  firmly packed light brown sugar
5 tablespoons (2 1/2 ounces/71
  grams) unsalted butter, melted
  and cooled slightly

1 tablespoon dark rum or 1 1/2 teaspoons pure vanilla extract
1/4 teaspoon table salt
5 large eggs
1 1/3 cups (5 1/2 ounces/156
  grams) chopped pecans, toasted
  (see page 40)
2 ounces (57 grams) bittersweet
  chocolate, finely chopped

1. Lightly dust the work surface and a rolling pin with flour. Unwrap the disk, place it on the floured surface, and roll out into a 14-inch (35cm) round. Lift and rotate the dough a quarter turn several times as you roll to prevent sticking, and dust the surface and the rolling pin with flour as needed. Use a bench scraper or a spatula to loosen the rolled dough as needed. Carefully roll the dough around the pin and position the pin over a 9-inch (22.75cm) pie plate (I use Pyrex). Unroll the dough onto the pie plate and gently nudge it into the bottom and sides of the plate. Gently but firmly press the dough against the sides and bottom, being careful not to stretch or tear it. Trim the edges, leaving a 3/4-inch (2cm) overhang. Roll the overhang under itself to shape a high edge that rests on top of the plate rim. Position the thumb and forefinger of one hand on the outside edge of the plate rim and the forefinger of the other hand directly opposite on the inside. Then, pinch-crimp the edge, working your way completely around the rim. Slide the lined pie plate into the freezer and chill until the dough is very firm, at least 30 minutes.

2. Position an oven rack on the middle rung. Heat the oven to 425 degrees (220°C). Line the frozen crust with foil and fill with pie weights (or dried beans). Bake for 15 minutes. Remove the foil and weights and continue to bake until the shell is pale golden brown, about 5 minutes. Transfer the pie plate to a rack. Reduce the oven temperature to 350 degrees (180°C).

3. In a medium bowl, combine the corn syrup, brown sugar, melted butter, rum or vanilla, and salt. Whisk until well blended and smooth. Add the eggs and whisk just until blended.

4. Scatter the nuts and the chocolate evenly in the baked pie shell. Carefully pour the custard into the shell to coat the nuts and chocolate, being careful not to dislodge them. Rearrange the nuts, if necessary. Bake until the filling is puffed and the center jiggles slightly when the pie plate is nudged, about 50 minutes. Transfer the pie plate to a rack and let cool completely. Serve at room temperature or chilled.

crumble-topped pear–rum raisin pie

MAKES ONE 9-INCH (22.75CM) PIE, OR 8 SERVINGS

the rum-drenched raisins enrich the flavor of this crumble-topped pear pie. I love to serve this pie at the first hint of a chill in the air. You can also substitute a solid top crust or a lattice top (see page 244).

do aheads

• The pie crust can be prepared as directed in step 1, well wrapped, and refrigerated for up to 2 days or frozen for up to 1 month before proceeding with the recipe.

• The topping can be prepared as directed in step 3, covered, and refrigerated for up to 2 days or frozen for up to 1 month before proceeding with the recipe. To use, soften slightly at room temperature so that it can be crumbled over the pie.

• The pie can be prepared through step 5, well wrapped in plastic, and frozen for up to 1 month before baking. To bake the frozen pie: Position an oven rack on the middle rung and set a foil-lined half sheet pan on the rack. Heat the oven to 375 degrees (190°C). Unwrap the frozen pie (don't thaw it), place it on the heated sheet pan, and bake until the crust is golden and the fruit is tender, about 1 hour and 20 minutes. If the crust browns too quickly, cover it loosely with foil.

1/2 recipe (1 disk) Never-Fail Pie Dough (page 244)

for the crumble topping:

3/4 cup (3 1/2 ounces/99 grams) all-purpose flour

1/3 cup (2 3/4 ounces/78 grams) firmly packed light brown sugar

3/4 teaspoon ground cinnamon

8 tablespoons (4 ounces/113 grams) unsalted butter, cut into 6 pieces

1/2 cup (2 ounces/57 grams) chopped walnuts, toasted (see page 40)

for the filling:

3/4 cup (4 ounces/113 grams) dark raisins

1/2 cup (4 fl ounces/117 ml) dark rum

3/4 cup (6 ounces/170 grams) firmly packed light brown sugar

3 tablespoons all-purpose flour

1/2 teaspoon ground cinnamon

1/4 teaspoon ground cloves

1/4 teaspoon table salt

3 pounds (1,361 grams) firm, ripe pears, peeled, cored, and sliced 3/4-inch thick

2 tablespoons lemon juice

1. Lightly dust the work surface and a rolling pin with flour. Unwrap the disk, place it on the floured surface, and roll out into a 14-inch (35cm) round. Lift and rotate the dough a quarter turn several times as you roll to prevent sticking, and dust the surface and the rolling pin with flour as needed. Use a bench scraper or a spatula to loosen the rolled dough as needed. Carefully roll the dough around the pin and position the pin over a 9-inch (22.75cm) pie plate (I use Pyrex). Unroll the dough onto the pie plate and gently nudge it into the bottom and sides of the plate. Gently but firmly press the dough against the sides and bottom, being careful not to stretch or tear it. Trim the edges, leaving a 3/4-inch (2cm) overhang. Roll the overhang under itself to shape a high edge that rests on top of the plate rim. Position the thumb and forefinger of one hand on the outside edge of the plate rim and the forefinger of the other hand directly opposite on the inside. Then, pinch-crimp the edge, working your way completely around the rim. Pop the pastry-lined plate into the fridge while you prepare the filling.

2. Position the oven racks in the lower and middle rungs. Slide a foil-lined cookie sheet on the lower rack to catch any juicy pear drippings. Heat the oven to 425 degrees (220°C).

3. TO MAKE THE TOPPING

In a medium bowl, combine the flour, brown sugar, and cinnamon. Stir until well blended. Add the butter pieces and, using a fork (or your fingers), mix while pressing on the ingredients until they're blended and crumbly. Stir in the walnuts. Cover and refrigerate until ready to use.

4. TO MAKE THE FILLING

In a small saucepan, combine the raisins and rum. Set over high heat and bring to a boil. Reduce the heat and simmer until the raisins are plump and the rum is reduced to about 3 tablespoons, about 5 minutes. Set aside.

5. In a large bowl, combine the brown sugar, flour, cinnamon, cloves, and salt. Stir until well blended. Add the pear slices, lemon juice, and raisins and remaining rum. Toss until the pears are evenly coated with the sugar mixture. Scrape into the prepared pie shell, mounding slightly higher in the center. Remove the topping from the fridge and, using your fingers or a fork, break it into large crumbs. Scatter the crumbs evenly over the top of the pie.

6. Set the pie on the middle rack, positioning it over the cookie sheet. Bake until the pears are tender when pierced with the tip of a knife, about 40 minutes. If the topping browns too quickly, loosely cover the pie with foil. Transfer the pie plate to a rack to cool. Serve warm or at room temperature.

productions

In my 25-plus years of baking professionally, I've developed some pretty astonishing and complicated desserts. Years of study, apprenticeship, practice, and an arsenal of specialized gadgets have enabled me to make these spectacular productions. Throughout my career as a recipe developer, teacher, and food writer, I've been on a mission to teach the nuts and bolts of baking and to write doable recipes for enthusiastic bakers at all levels of experience. I've always believed passionately that the keen sense of accomplishment I get from knowing how to make such stunning creations shouldn't be limited to people like me. You really don't need professional training or fancy tools to make impressive desserts. The recipes in this section aren't difficult; they just require a bit more time. You can do it, and I'm here to show you how.

Here, in Productions, I've demystified seemingly complex desserts by breaking the recipes into smaller, manageable parts that can be executed over the course of several days – a way of working that can fit into anyone's schedule. Layered Chocolate Mousse Cake (page 299) is a fancy-looking dessert, yet it consists of only two elements: an easy-to-make cake and a straightforward chocolate mousse. Making Vanilla Stand-Ups (page 277) is a wonderful project for the whole family. They are fun to bake, delicious to eat, and they make terrific table or mantle decorations. The recipes in this section are a bit longer and a little more involved than the ones in Baker's Express and Baking in Stages, but they aren't any harder. They are just a sum of simple parts that often can be made in advance, sometimes as long as a month.

Turn to this section when you want to make the extra effort – and when you have the time to do it. Making sure you have the time is crucial. Setting your sights higher than your schedule allows is a pitfall that's easy for any baker, either novice or experienced, to stumble into. For example, when I'm planning a holiday breakfast, I start making the Glazed Cinnamon Rolls (page 334) three days ahead. The recipe is broken down into three stages that can easily be completed over consecutive days. Or I bake up a coffee cake, like Nut-Crusted Chocolate-Banana Swirl Cake (page 288), up to one month before the holiday and store it in the freezer. If you find yourself housebound on a winter afternoon, turn to the Slow-Baked Brown Rice Pudding with a Sugary Nut Topping (page 343). It cooks in the oven for 1 1/2 hours of hands-free baking, and the results will soothe and warm your soul.

Why bother with a Production? Because it's fun. It's exhilarating to make a splash or add a good dose of zjoo-zjee (zjoo-zjee is my fashion-editor friend Harriet's favorite word for sex appeal) to your dinner party or holiday table. And it's a great feeling to take well-deserved bows in front of your awed guests and friends when you present a glitzy dessert. You don't have to tell them how effortless it was to put together. Keep that to yourself.

Productions are all about the plan. When faced with a crash schedule or a project that needs doing in a hurry, one of my brother Darv's favorite recommendations is "let's script it out." (The planning gene seems to run in the family.) Scripting it out is what makes baking a big creation enjoyable and, most important, possible to achieve. For instance, it is what makes home-made English Muffins (page 326) and Apple Cider Pie with Toasted-Walnut Lattice Crust (page 369) easy to prepare and fun to eat. The muffins can be assembled over two days and placed on the griddle any morning of the week. It just takes planning. Trust me on this. If you don't script it out, you'll disappoint your guests, lose your mind, throw this book across the room, and give up on baking.

Here are a few tips: Read the recipe with time in mind. Scan it to figure out how many components you'll need to make. Get a pen and paper. Working backward from when you're serving the dessert, plot a timeline. (And while you're at it, if you're the one hosting the party, include tasks like setting the table, cleaning the house, shopping, chilling the wine, and the like.) Fit the recipe components into your schedule. Take care to consider all the interruptions that will enter into your days, like conference calls, errands, pickups, and drop-offs. You'll be making a dessert within the context of your life. This makes the difference between a smash success and a big disappointment.

Productions is divided into three categories:

1.
storable do aheads

These recipes have simple, separate components that can handle long-term storage in the fridge, in the freezer, or at room temperature before final assembly and then can be stored even longer before serving. Old-Fashioned Ice Cream Sandwiches (page 317) can be made over the course of a month and then kept in the freezer for up to another four weeks. They're fun to serve and add a touch of whimsy to your menu, no matter what time of year you serve them. No-Bake Graham Cracker Mini-Houses (page 284) are an ideal holiday project to work on with your kids at home or at school as a class activity. Either way, the houses can be started up to two months in advance. The pitted cherries, galette dough, and topping for the Almond-Crunch Cherry Galette (page 362) can be done and put in the freezer up to a month in advance before thawing and proceeding with the recipe. If you're planning ahead, the assembled galette can then be frozen for up to one month before baking and serving.

2.
desserts made in stages

Desserts in this category have simple components that can be made in advance. Unlike the Storable Do Aheads, these desserts, once assembled, are best when served soon after completion. You can make elements of the Four-Layer Carrot Cake (page 305) or the Classic Fruit Tart (page 366) one to four weeks in advance, component by component, depending on when you have available time. That way, you'll get the greatest enjoyment out of what I think is the most fun part – putting all the different pieces together, and then serving your cake or tart to an eager audience.

glazed plum galette
page 228

four-layer carrot cake
page 305

chocolate-chip brownie double-deckers
page 263

no-bake graham cracker mini-house
page 284

glazed cinnamon rolls
page 334

chocolate-dipped macadamia brittle
page 274

lemon chiffon pie with pretzel crust
page 358

layered chocolate mousse cake
page 299

3.
hands-free baking

These recipes are more intensive simply because of the time commitment. The brown rice pudding (page 343) spends 1 1/2 hours in the oven. While that's 90 minutes, it's hands-free time, offering you a chance to weed the garden, clean out a closet, or prepare a report. Overnight Brioche Braid (page 339) is a yeasted dough and thus needs time to rise, but some of the rising can happen in the fridge while you sleep or go about your day, and the recipe can be spread out over three days.

special equipment and ingredients

Because the desserts in this section are a little more involved, they require a few pieces of equipment and some ingredients that haven't been necessary up to this point.

Stand Mixer

While I've listed this workhorse before (see page 29), you'll find it most helpful – though still not mandatory – when you set out to make a Production. For example, you can mix the dough for Overnight Brioche Braid (page 339) by hand, but the going is much easier with a stand mixer. The same is true for Mrs. Hall's Brandy Snaps (page 269). They can be mixed by hand – the way Mrs. Hall has always done them – but a stand mixer really comes to the rescue for this thick batter, saving time and energy.

Cake Flour

Lower in protein than all-purpose flour, cake flour (*not* self-rising) produces a more tender, finer crumb. It's not better than all-purpose flour, it simply results in a different style cake. I use cake flour for the Strawberries-and-Cream Layer Cake (page 309). The cake's texture is soft and refined. Unlike all-purpose flour, cake flour needs to be sifted before measuring. It's an extra step, but it's the only way to get an accurate measurement.

Half Sheet Pan

This pan, which measures 11 3/4 by 16 3/4 inches (29.75 by 42.5cm; measured on the bottom), will save you a lot of time and effort. It's the pan that you'll use to bake thin cake layers for Four-Layer Carrot Cake (page 305) and Spiced Ginger Roll (page 291), so you won't need to slice thicker layers into thinner ones, and it's also handy for baking a galette (pages 228 and 362). A half sheet pan is well worth having for weeknight savory cooking as well as for desserts. I use mine all the time for roasting vegetables.

Pastry Bag and Tips

Having at least one large – about 13 inches (33cm) long – and one small – about 8 inches (20cm) long – pastry bag will prove invaluable when piping Hazelnut Ladyfingers (page 271) or assembling and decorating Vanilla Stand-Ups (page 277) or No-Bake Graham Cracker Mini-Houses (page 284). For easy cleanup, I prefer the polyurethane or plastic disposable varieties. If you are an enthusiastic cookie decorator, you'll want to have a few bags on hand, so that you can have a number of colored icings at the ready. For accurate piping, the bags require metal or plastic tips. For beginners, a plain 1/2-inch (1.25cm) tip opening for the large bag and a plain 3/16-inch (8mm) tip opening for the small one will suffice. The tips are available in many sizes and shapes, making it possible to add to your collection as your interest dictates.

Quarter Sheet Pan

This pan, which measures 8 1/2 by 12 inches (21.5 by 30.5cm; measured on the bottom), makes easy work out of Individual Tiramisus (page 295). Plus,

I love these for carrying ingredients around the kitchen, for toasting nuts, and for making dinner on the nights when I'm working at home alone.

Sheet Cake Pan

A Pyrex baking dish will do, but a straight-sided 9-by-13-inch (22.75-by-33cm) metal pan has sharp corners, which gives sheet cakes a more finished appearance. Chocolate Cake for a Crowd (page 322) looks like it came straight from the bakery.

Cookies and Bars

• • •

pistachio tuiles

MAKES 2 DOZEN COOKIES

these curled, wafer-like cookies are often brought to the table at the end of a special dinner and served with chocolate truffles. Their name is the French word for "tiles," because they are shaped like the curved terra-cotta roof tiles so common in the South of France.

The tuiles are draped over a rolling pin when they're hot from the oven to create their curved form. It's not difficult if you work in small batches, baking just four or five at a time. To ensure the close-to-paper-thin quality, a tablespoon of batter needs to be spread in a thin, even layer. A small offset spatula is the traditional tool for this procedure, but to save time, I use plastic wrap and a lid 4 1/2 inches (11.5cm) wide from a plastic quart, pint, or half-pint container to press the batter into the perfect shape and thickness.

do aheads

• The batter can be prepared through step 2, covered, and stored at room temperature for up to 8 hours before baking.

• The tuiles can be prepared through step 4, cooled, and carefully packed in an airtight container. They'll keep well at room temperature for up to 5 days.

2 egg whites from large eggs (1/4 cup/2 fl ounces/58 ml)

1/2 cup (4 ounces/113 grams) granulated sugar

Pinch of table salt

6 tablespoons (3 ounces/85 grams) unsalted butter, melted and cooled slightly

1/2 teaspoon pure vanilla extract

2/3 cup (3 ounces/85 grams) all-purpose flour

1/2 cup (2 ounces/57 grams) finely chopped unsalted pistachios (no need to toast)

1. Position an oven rack on the middle rung. Heat the oven to 350 degrees (180°C). Line 2 cookie sheets (or four if you have them – otherwise, reuse the sheets once they've cooled off) with parchment or nonstick baking liners (I like the Silpat). Steady a rolling pin between 2 bottles or cans so that it's ready to shape the cookies.

2. In a medium bowl, combine the egg whites, sugar, and salt. Whisk until blended and a bit foamy. Add the melted butter and vanilla and whisk until blended. Pour in the flour and continue to whisk until smooth and blended.

3. Drop the batter by 1 tablespoonfuls onto the prepared cookie sheets, positioning them about 4 inches (10cm) apart (I can fit 5 to a cookie sheet). Spread each round of batter into a 4-inch (10cm) circle with a small offset spatula, or try my newest tuile trick: Give each tablespoon of batter a spray of nonstick cooking spray. Tear off a piece of plastic wrap, 5 inches (13cm) wide, and place it directly onto the surface of a mound of batter. Position the bottom of a flat plastic lid 4 1/2 inches (11.5cm) across from a quart, pint, or half-pint container on the plastic-covered mound. Using your fingers, press down onto the center of the lid. The batter will spread easily. Keep pressing on the lid – on different areas if the round is lopsided – until the batter is a 4-inch (10cm) round. Remove the lid and peel away the plastic. Reuse the plastic and repeat the flattening process with the remaining mounds. Sprinkle a scant 1 teaspoon of the pistachios over each cookie.

4. Bake 1 sheet at a time (make sure to use a cooled sheet for the next batches) until the cookies are golden brown around the edges, about 9 minutes. Working quickly, transfer the cookie sheet to a rack. Using a metal spatula, lift off the hot cookies, one by one, and immediately drape them over the rolling pin. Let cool until set, about 1 minute. Carefully remove the tuiles from the rolling pin and set them on a rack to cool completely.

chocolate-chip brownie double-deckers

MAKES 2 DOZEN 2-INCH (5CM) DOUBLE-DECKERS

One afternoon, I was testing both the brownie and chocolate chip cookie recipes for this book and my husband Chris was in the kitchen looking for a sample or two. Eyeing both batters, Chris asked what would happen if they were baked layered together. A great idea and, as it turned out, with a few tweaks to the chocolate chip recipe, I ended up with bar cookies that offer the best of both cookies.

do aheads

• The double-deckers can be prepared through step 7, cut, tightly wrapped, and frozen for up to 1 month. There's almost no thawing necessary, about 20 minutes, as these brownies are delicious even when partially frozen.

for the chocolate chip layer:

12 tablespoons (6 ounces/170 grams) unsalted butter

1 cup (8 ounces/227 grams) firmly packed light brown sugar

1 1/2 cups (6 3/4 ounces/191 grams) all-purpose flour

1/2 teaspoon baking soda

1/4 teaspoon table salt

1 large egg

1 teaspoon pure vanilla extract

1 cup (6 ounces/170 grams) semi-sweet chocolate chips

for the brownie layer:

12 tablespoons (6 ounces/170
   grams) unsalted butter, cut into 6
   equal pieces
3/4 cup (2 1/4 ounces/64 grams)
   unsweetened Dutch-process
   cocoa powder, sifted if lumpy
1 1/2 cups (12 ounces/340 grams)
   granulated sugar

1/4 teaspoon table salt
2 large eggs
1 1/2 teaspoons pure vanilla extract
3/4 cup (3 1/2 ounces/99 grams)
   all-purpose flour

1. Position an oven rack on the middle rung. Heat the oven to 325 degrees (165°C). Lightly grease the bottom and sides of a 9-by-13-inch (22.75-by-33cm) baking pan.

2. TO MAKE THE CHOCOLATE-CHIP LAYER
Put the butter in a medium saucepan and set over medium heat, stirring occasionally, until the butter is melted. Slide the pan from the heat and add the brown sugar. Whisk until no lumps remain. Set aside to cool while you make the brownie layer.

3. TO MAKE THE BROWNIE LAYER
Put the butter in a medium saucepan and set over medium heat, stirring occasionally, until the butter is melted. Slide the pan from the heat and add the cocoa powder. Whisk until the mixture is smooth. Add the sugar and salt and whisk until blended. Add the eggs one at a time, whisking after each addition just until blended. Whisk in the vanilla with the second egg. Sprinkle the flour over the chocolate mixture and stir with a rubber spatula just until blended.

4. Scrape the batter into the prepared baking dish and spread evenly with an offset or rubber spatula. Set aside while you finish the chocolate-chip layer.

5. TO FINISH THE CHOCOLATE CHIP LAYER

In a small bowl, combine the flour, baking soda, and salt. Whisk until well blended. Once the butter mixture has cooled, add the egg and vanilla to it and whisk until blended. Pour in the flour mixture and stir with a rubber spatula until blended. Stir in the chocolate chips.

6.

Drop the dough over the brownie batter in large scoopfuls and spread evenly with the offset or rubber spatula. Bake until a toothpick or cake tester inserted in the center comes out with small, gooey clumps of brownie sticking to it, about 40 minutes. Don't overbake or they won't be fudgy. Transfer the baking pan to a rack to cool completely.

7.

Using a bench scraper or a knife, cut into small squares measuring about 2 inches (5cm) each. The cooler the double-deckers are, the cleaner the cutting will be, but these fudgy treats will always leave some sticky crumbs on the knife.

black and whites

MAKES 16 FROSTED COOKIES

this big, saucer-shaped frosted cookie, a staple in New York bakeries and delis, is a childhood favorite that I still adore. Some folks call them half-moons or half-and-half cookies because one half is glazed with dark chocolate and the other with vanilla, but I grew up calling them black and whites.

Actually, they really aren't cookies at all, but free-form cupcake tops that bake on a cookie sheet. The top puffs up while the bottom stays flat, which makes a perfect canvas for the bittersweet chocolate glaze and its white counterpart. Yellow cake is traditional, but I prefer my chocolate version.

do aheads

• The cookies can be prepared through step 3, wrapped in plastic, and stored at room temperature for up to 2 days or frozen for up to 1 month.

• Both the chocolate and white icings can be prepared, covered, and stored at room temperature for up to 2 days. Reheat the chocolate icing until spreadable before frosting the cookies.

• The cookies can be prepared through step 6, covered with plastic, and stored at room temperature for up to 5 days.

2 cups (9 ounces/255 grams) all-purpose flour

2/3 cup (2 ounces/57 grams) unsweetened natural cocoa powder (not Dutch process), sifted if lumpy

1 teaspoon baking powder

1/2 teaspoon baking soda

1/2 teaspoon table salt

12 tablespoons (6 ounces/170 grams) unsalted butter, at room temperature

1 1/2 cups (12 ounces/340 grams) granulated sugar

2 large eggs

1 teaspoon pure vanilla extract

1/2 cup (4 1/2 ounces/128 grams) sour cream

2/3 cup (5 fl ounces/146 ml) hot water

for the chocolate icing:

8 ounces (227 grams) bittersweet chocolate, finely chopped

5 tablespoons heavy cream

1 tablespoon light corn syrup

for the white icing:

2 1/4 cups (9 ounces/255 grams) confectioners' sugar

6 tablespoons heavy cream

3 tablespoons light corn syrup

1. TO MAKE THE COOKIES

Position an oven rack on the middle rung. Heat the oven to 375 degrees (190°C). Line 3 large cookie sheets with parchment or nonstick baking liners (I like the Silpat).

2. In a medium bowl, combine the flour, cocoa powder, baking powder, baking soda, and salt. Whisk until well blended. In another bowl, beat the butter with an electric mixer (stand mixer fitted with the paddle attachment or handheld mixer) on medium-high speed until smooth. Gradually add the sugar and continue beating until fluffy. Add the eggs one at a time, beating just until blended after each addition. Beat in the vanilla with the second

egg. Sprinkle half of the flour mixture over the butter and mix on low speed just until the flour disappears. Add the sour cream and mix just until blended. Add the remaining flour and mix just until blended. Finally, pour in the hot water and mix just until blended.

3. Using a 1/4-cup measure or an ice-cream scoop about 2 1/3 inches (6cm) in diameter, drop the batter onto the prepared cookie sheets, spacing the mounds about 3 1/2 inches (9cm) apart (I can fit 5 or 6 to a cookie sheet). Spread each mound into a 3-inch (7.75cm) circle (I use a small offset spatula). Bake 1 sheet at a time (make sure to use a cooled sheet for the next batches) until the cookies are puffed and a toothpick or cake tester inserted in the center of 1 cookie comes out clean, about 10 minutes. Transfer the cookie sheet to a rack to cool for about 10 minutes. Using a spatula, lift the cookies from the sheet onto a rack and let cool completely.

4. **TO MAKE THE CHOCOLATE ICING**
Combine the bittersweet chocolate, cream, and corn syrup and melt in a double boiler (see What Is It? on page 74) or in the microwave (page 51). Stir until smooth.

5. **TO MAKE THE WHITE ICING**
In a small bowl, combine the confectioners' sugar, cream, and corn syrup. Stir until smooth and shiny.

6. Turn the cooled cookies flat side up. Using your hands, gently brush away any loose crumbs. Using a small spatula, spread about 1 tablespoon of the white icing over half of each cookie. Spread about 1 tablespoon of the chocolate icing over the other half. Set aside until the icing is set, about 1 hour, or place them into the fridge for about 15 minutes.

mrs. hall's brandy snaps

MAKES ABOUT 33 COOKIES

every Christmas of my childhood, our neighbor Susan Hall delivered a bucket of her extraordinary brandy snaps. "Has Mrs. Hall dropped off her cookies yet?" was December's daily question. One year, no cookies came. Mrs. Hall's bursitis was acting up and she couldn't stir the thick, heavy batter. The next year, around Thanksgiving, we began asking "So, how's Mrs. Hall's bursitis?" When you taste the deep, bittersweet flavor of these chewy cookies, you'll understand. Back then a stand mixer with the paddle attachment wasn't as common as it is today. This batter is a bear to stir by hand and a handheld mixer isn't up to the task, so bring out the stand mixer if you have one.

There isn't a drop of brandy in these cookies, but thanks to all the brown sugar and molasses, they sure taste as though there is. They keep for weeks and the flavors deepen and intensify as they sit. The dough puffs up during baking, but settles down as it cools to make a uniformly thin, round cookie. Mrs. Hall likes to refrigerate the dough until very cold and then shape it into balls (no flour needed) just before baking. I prefer to shape the soft dough and refrigerate. Both methods deliver the same excellent results.

do aheads

• The dough can be prepared through step 2, covered with plastic wrap, and refrigerated for up to 3 days or frozen for up to 1 month.

• The cookies can be prepared through step 3, wrapped in plastic wrap, and stored at room temperature for up to 1 week or frozen for up to 1 month.

16 tablespoons (8 ounces/227 grams) unsalted butter, at room temperature

1 cup (8 ounces/227 grams) firmly packed dark brown sugar

1/4 teaspoon table salt

1/2 cup (4 fl ounces/117 ml) light molasses

2 1/2 cups (11 1/4 ounces/319 grams) all-purpose flour

1. In the large bowl of a stand mixer, combine the butter, brown sugar, and salt. Fit the mixer with the paddle attachment and beat on medium speed until well blended. Add the molasses and beat until combined. Pour in the flour and beat on low speed until the dough begins to clump together and the flour is thoroughly incorporated, about 4 minutes.

2. Using a small ice-cream scoop about 1 2/3 inches (4.25cm) in diameter or 2 tablespoons, shape round mounds of about 1 heaping tablespoon (they will be about 1 1/3 inches (3.5cm) in diameter and weigh 1 ounce/28 grams). Using your palms, roll the dough into smooth balls (no flour needed). Arrange the dough balls close together on a plastic-lined plate or small cookie sheet. Cover with plastic wrap and refrigerate until very firm, about 6 hours.

3. Position an oven rack on the middle rung. Heat the oven to 325 degrees (165°C). Line 2 cookie sheets with parchment. (Do not use nonstick baking liners or the cookies will spread too much.) Arrange the dough balls on the lined cookie sheets about 2 inches (5cm) apart.

4. Bake 1 sheet at a time (make sure to use a cooled sheet for the second batch) until the tops are puffed and don't leave an indent when lightly touched, about 15 minutes. Transfer the cookie sheet to a rack to cool for about 15 minutes. During cooling, the cookies will shrink and flatten. Using a spatula, lift the cookies from the sheet onto a rack and let cool completely.

hazelnut ladyfingers

MAKES 3 DOZEN 3 1/2-INCH (9CM) LADYFINGERS

i remember ladyfingers as my mom's favorite cookie, especially with her afternoon tea. Light, spongy, not too sweet, and with a lovely nutty flavor and crunch, these are worlds away from the store-bought kind. They're delicious eaten on their own, as my mom used to do, or in the Raspberry Charlotte (page 225). Using a pastry bag to pipe the batter works best. In a pinch, though, you can fashion a pastry bag: use a large, heavy-duty zipper-top bag with a corner snipped off.

do aheads

• The "fingers" can be prepared through step 5, well wrapped, and stored at room temperature for up to 3 days or frozen for up to 1 month.

3/4 cup (3 1/4 ounces/92 grams) all-purpose flour

1/3 cup (1 ounce/28 grams) very finely chopped, toasted hazelnuts (see page 40)

1/4 teaspoon baking powder

4 large eggs, separated

1 teaspoon pure vanilla extract

1/2 cup (4 ounces/113 grams) granulated sugar

Pinch of table salt

2 tablespoons finely chopped, toasted hazelnuts, mixed with 1 tablespoon granulated sugar

1. Position 2 oven racks on the top and bottom third rungs of the oven. Heat the oven to 375 degrees (190°C). Fit a large pastry bag with a no. 7 plain tip (about 1/2 inch/1.25cm). Line 2 large cookie sheets with parchment or nonstick baking liners (I like the Silpat).

2. In a small bowl, combine the flour, hazelnuts, and baking powder. Whisk until well blended. In a large bowl, combine the egg yolks and vanilla. Beat with an electric mixer (stand mixer fitted with the whisk attachment or handheld mixer) on medium-high speed until foamy. Gradually add all but 2 tablespoons of the sugar while beating. Continue beating until the mixture is pale yellow and tripled in volume, almost 3 minutes. When the whisk or beaters are lifted, the mixture will fall back into the bowl and form a ribbon; it should linger a bit on the surface.

3. In a clean bowl, using a clean whisk attachment or beaters, beat the egg whites with the salt on medium speed until the whites are frothy and have doubled in volume. With the mixer on high speed, gradually add the remaining 2 tablespoons sugar and beat until the whites are glossy and form medium-firm peaks (the peaks will hold their shape but the tips will flop over). Using a rubber spatula, scoop about one-third of the whites into the yolk mixture. Gently stir just until combined. Add half of the remaining whites and fold in carefully. Sprinkle half of the flour mixture over the surface of the yolk-white mixture and fold in with a couple of gentle strokes. Gently fold in the remaining whites. Sprinkle the remaining flour mixture over the top and gently fold in just until well blended.

4. Using a large rubber spatula, carefully scoop some of the batter into the pastry bag, using deep, cutting strokes to keep the batter from deflating. Fill the pastry bag about two-thirds full. Twist the top of the bag closed. Hold the bag about 2 inches (5cm) above a prepared cookie sheet. Gently squeezing from the top of the bag, pipe the batter into short, narrow strips each about 3 inches (7.75cm) long and 3/4 inch (2cm) wide, spacing them about 2 inches (5cm) apart. For optimum lightness, let the batter fall gently from the bag, and finish each ladyfinger by releasing any pressure on the bag and lifting up the pastry tip. Remember to stop between ladyfingers and twist down the top of the bag to keep the batter flowing smoothly. Refill the bag as needed and continue piping the ladyfingers.

5. Sprinkle the hazelnut-sugar mixture over the tops of the batter strips. Place a cookie sheet on each rack and bake until puffed and the tops are golden brown, about 13 minutes. Swap the positions of the cookie sheets and rotate front to back halfway through baking. Remove from the oven, slide the parchment or baking liners with the strips intact onto racks, and let cool until barely warm, about 15 minutes. Carefully peel the strips from the parchment, place on racks, and let cool completely.

chocolate-dipped macadamia brittle

MAKES ABOUT 1 POUND OF BRITTLE, OR ABOUT 2 DOZEN

1- TO 2-INCH (2.5- TO 5CM) PIECES

i remember the first time my friend Ann Mileti made this brittle. It was more than a decade ago, but I recall it as if it were yesterday. One bite of this smooth, crisp caramel lulled me into reverent silence.

Over the years, Ann has given the recipe to many of her friends. But caramel can be finicky, and occasionally reports would filter back that a batch was grainy. I consulted Flo Braker (cookbook author, instructor), who confirmed that the key to caramel success is to dissolve the sugar completely *before* it comes to a boil. So, please be patient when making this brittle. Don't rush the caramel-making process in step 2, and smooth, creamy results will be your reward.

do aheads

• The brittle (without the glaze) can be prepared through step 4, layered between parchment or waxed paper in an airtight container or a heavy-duty zipper-top bag, and stored at room temperature for up to 2 weeks.

• The chocolate-covered brittle can be layered between parchment or waxed paper in an airtight container or a heavy-duty zipper-top bag and stored at room temperature for up to 2 weeks.

for the brittle:

1 teaspoon pure vanilla extract

1/4 teaspoon baking soda

2/3 cup (5 ounces/142 grams) granulated sugar

6 tablespoons (3 ounces/85 grams)
unsalted butter, cut into 6 pieces

2 tablespoons light corn syrup

2 tablespoons water

1/4 teaspoon table salt

1 1/4 cups (6 ounces/170 grams)
unsalted macadamia nuts,
toasted (see page 40), and very
roughly chopped

for the chocolate glaze:

6 ounces (170 grams) bittersweet
chocolate, finely chopped

4 tablespoons (2 ounces/57 grams)
unsalted butter, cut into 4 equal
pieces

1. TO MAKE THE BRITTLE

Measure the vanilla and baking soda into separate, small ramekins or metal
measuring cups. Generously oil a cookie sheet or line it with a nonstick baking liner (I like the Silpat).

2.
In a large, heavy saucepan, combine the sugar, butter, corn syrup,
water, and salt. Set the pan over low heat and cook, stirring frequently with
a heatproof spoon or spatula (I use a silicone spatula), until the butter is
melted and the sugar is dissolved, about 10 minutes. Be patient and don't
try to speed this process. If you're worried that the liquid is about to boil,
just slide the pan from the heat for a minute. If the mixture boils before the
sugar is dissolved, it will crystallize and make the brittle grainy, rather than
smooth and satiny. The easiest way to check if the sugar has fully dissolved
is to give the mixture a stir and then quickly and carefully (it's very hot)
run a finger over the spatula. If you feel any graininess, the sugar needs to
cook a bit longer.

3. Once the sugar is dissolved, increase the heat to medium and bring the mixture to a boil. Cook, without stirring, until the bubbles begin to slow down and the mixture begins to turn light golden brown, about 4 minutes. Swirl the pan (don't stir!) over the heat until the liquid is a uniform light golden brown. Slide the pan from the heat and immediately add the chopped nuts, vanilla, and baking soda. The sugar will bubble up and the steam will be very, very hot, so be careful. Using a heatproof silicone spatula, quickly stir until well blended.

4. Pour the brittle onto the prepared cookie sheet, scraping the inside of the pan. Using the silicone spatula, spread the brittle into an even, single layer of caramel-coated nuts. Set the cookie sheet on a rack and let cool completely. When the brittle is completely cool, cut it into random, jagged pieces measuring 1 to 2 inches (2.5 to 5cm).

5. TO MAKE THE CHOCOLATE GLAZE
Melt the chocolate and butter in a double boiler (see What Is It? on page 74) or in the microwave (see page 51). Stir until smooth.

6. Dip the cooled brittle pieces in the warm chocolate to cover about halfway. Set each chocolate-covered piece, flat side down, on a clean cookie sheet lined with parchment or a nonstick baking liner (I like the Silpat). Set aside until the chocolate is firm.

vanilla stand-ups

MAKES 15 STAND-UP COOKIES ABOUT 4 3/4 INCHES (12CM) TALL

When I worked as an editor at *Woman's Day* magazine in the 1980s, I got to know some talented food stylists, and Deborah Mintcheff was at the top of the list. All her creations were impressive, but her decorated Christmas cookies were exceptional. They were as gorgeous to look at as they were delicious to eat. One year she made cutout cookies for the magazine that stood up! These cookies are my tribute to her genius.

Along with baking large cookie cutouts, you'll bake cookie-dough support triangles (similar to the back of a picture frame) that, when "glued" together with royal icing, will allow the cookies to stand tall. Decorating them is fun and, depending on your time and level of interest, it can be as simple as a few colored sprinkles, or as elaborate as multicolored icings and a variety of candies. The cookies make unique decorations for your mantle, table, or counter. Claire, the *Weekend Baker* recipe tester, uses Vanilla Stand-Ups as dinner-party place cards. She writes each guest's name in royal icing on a cookie.

Unlike many cookie doughs, this one does not need to be chilled before rolling. It's soft, pliable, and easily rolled out on parchment paper. For the cookie shapes, select cutters about 4 3/4 inches (12cm) tall, with a wide, sturdy base to hold the support triangles. Fresh or powdered egg whites (see What Is It? on page 281) can be used for the icing. The recipe yields enough for you to have a field day piping and decorating. But if you're a minimalist, the cookies are striking on their own.

do aheads

• The cookie dough can be prepared as directed in step 2, wrapped in plastic wrap, and stored in the fridge for up to 2 days or frozen for up to 1 month (thaw the dough in the fridge overnight) before proceeding with the recipe.

• The baked and cooled cookies can be prepared through step 5, wrapped in plastic, and stored at room temperature for up to 3 days or frozen for up to 1 month before proceeding with the recipe.

• The icing can be prepared as directed in step 6, covered, and refrigerated for up to 4 days before proceeding with the recipe.

• The decorated cookies are best when wrapped individually in plastic and eaten within 3 days, but as decorations they will last for 6 weeks.

for the cookies:

2 cups (9 ounces/255 grams)
   all-purpose flour
1/4 teaspoon baking powder
1/4 teaspoon table salt
12 tablespoons (6 ounces/170
   grams) unsalted butter, at room

temperature
3/4 cup (6 ounces/170 grams)
   granulated sugar
2 yolks from large eggs
1 teaspoon pure vanilla extract

for the icing:

2 tablespoons powdered egg whites (see What Is It? page 281) and
   6 tablespoons warm water

or

3 whites from large eggs (1/3 cup/3 fl ounces/87 ml)

4 cups (16 ounces/454 grams) confectioners' sugar
Food coloring, colored sprinkles and/or other edible decorations for
   garnish

1. TO MAKE THE COOKIES

Line 2 cookie sheets with parchment or nonstick baking liners (I like the Silpat).

2. In a medium bowl, combine the flour, baking powder, and salt. Whisk until well blended. In a large bowl, combine the butter and sugar. Beat with an electric mixer (stand mixer fitted with the paddle attachment or hand-held mixer) on medium speed until well blended. Add the egg yolks and vanilla and beat until combined. Pour in the flour mixture and beat on low speed until the dough begins to clump together. Dump the dough onto a work surface and gently shape into a disk 7 inches (18cm) in diameter. If the dough is very soft, wrap it in plastic and refrigerate briefly. Otherwise, get ready to roll.

3. Position the disk on a large piece of lightly floured parchment and lightly flour the top of the disk. Roll out the dough 1/4 inch (6.25mm) thick, lightly flouring both sides as needed to prevent sticking. (This measurement is important. Too thin and the cookies will burn and be too fragile to stand up; too thick and they will taste doughy and be too heavy to stand up.) Using a round cookie cutter 4 to 5 inches (10 to 13cm) in diameter, cut out as many cookies as possible, cutting them close together. Pull away any dough scraps from the cutouts. Using a metal spatula, transfer the cutouts to the prepared cookie sheets, spacing them about 3/4 inch (2cm) apart. Gather up the dough scraps and gently shape into a flat disk. Repeat the rolling and cutting and transfer the cutouts to the cookie sheets. You should have 15 cutouts in all. Slide the cookie sheets into the fridge. (It's easy to balance the sheets on top of milk cartons.)

4. Gather up the remaining dough scraps and shape into a long rope about 3/4 inch (2cm) in diameter. Using the rolling pin, flatten the rope and roll it into a strip 11 inches (28cm) long and 1/4 inch (6.25mm) thick. Using a paring knife or a bench scraper, trim to create a strip 1 inch (2.5cm) wide. Cut the strip into small, straight-edged triangles with the longest side measuring 1 1/2 inches (4cm). Gather up the dough scraps and roll and cut out more triangles. These are the supports for your stand-ups. You'll need 2 triangles per cookie, or a total of 30. Arrange the support triangles on the cookie sheets in among the cookies, spacing them about 1/2 inch (1.25cm) apart. Return the sheets to the fridge to chill the dough until very firm, about 1 hour.

5. Position an oven rack on the middle rung. Heat the oven to 375 degrees (190°C). Bake 1 sheet at a time (make sure to use a cooled sheet for the second batch) until the tops look dry and the edges are golden brown, about 12 minutes. The support triangles will be a bit darker, but that's okay, as they're hidden behind the stand-ups. Transfer the cookie sheet to a rack to cool for about 10 minutes. Using a spatula, lift the cookies and supports from the sheet onto a rack and let cool completely.

6. TO MAKE THE ICING
In a large bowl, combine the powdered egg whites and warm water and let stand, whisking frequently, until the powder is dissolved, about 5 minutes. If using fresh whites, simply put them in the bowl. Beat with an electric mixer (stand mixer fitted with the whisk attachment or handheld mixer) on medium speed until frothy. Add the confectioners' sugar and continue beating until blended. Increase the speed to high and beat until the mixture is thick and shiny, about 5 minutes. Place a damp paper towel directly on the icing to keep a skin from forming. If not using within 2 hours, cover the bowl with plastic wrap and refrigerate.

7. TO ASSEMBLE THE STAND-UPS
Arrange the cookies and support triangles on the work surface. Have ready a small-tipped pastry brush (or a clean small paintbrush from the art store) or a small metal spatula (an offset with a tapered point is best) and a small pastry bag fitted with a small plain tip (or a heavy-duty zipper-top bag with a corner snipped off). If you like, divide the icing into 2 or more bowls (one for each color) and stir drops of food coloring into each bowl until the color is just right.

8. Spoon some of the icing into the pastry bag, and twist the top of the bag closed. Holding the bag close to the cookie, squeeze gently to outline the rim of the cookie with the icing. Dampen the brush in water or use the offset spatula and spread a small amount (about 2 teaspoons, depending on the size of your cookie) of additional icing on the cookie to form an even layer. (If the icing is too thick to spread evenly, stir in water, a drop or two at a time, until the icing can be spread to coat the cookie evenly. But don't thin the entire batch. You'll need the thick stuff to "glue" the supports onto the cookies.) Decorate the cookie, if desired, with sprinkles or other decorations. Set the cookie aside until the icing is set. Repeat with the remaining cookies.

9. When the icing is set, use a pastry bag to squeeze about 1/2 teaspoon icing on 2 spots on the back of each cookie, positioning the spots near the bottom edge of the cookie so that it will eventually stand up without wobbling. Press a short side of a triangle into each spot of icing, then pipe additional icing around the triangles where they meet the cookie. Set aside, front side down (triangle supports up in the air), until the icing is set. Then stand them up!

what is it? (powdered egg whites)

Powdered egg whites are pure dried and pasteurized egg whites. I use the brand Just Whites by Deb-El. They are fat free, cholesterol free, bacteria free, and have an extremely long shelf life (at least six months). The powder stands in beautifully for fresh egg whites in royal icing, making it safe to lick the bowl. The powder tends to be sticky, so use the dip-and-sweep method for the most accurate measurement. Also, for the best result, be sure to reconstitute the powder in the warm water as directed.

annie's mocha-cinnamon chocolate chip cookies

MAKES 4 DOZEN COOKIES

annie Giammattei, an art director at *Fine Cooking* magazine, started making these cookies ten years ago, and her friends and family still can't get enough of them. I'm grateful that she has allowed me to include her recipe. Cinnamon and coffee flavor sets these apart from classic chocolate chip cookies, and, like lace cookies, they are buttery and deliciously crisp.

do aheads

• The cookies can be prepared through step 4, covered, and stored at room temperature for up to 4 days or frozen for up to 1 month.

2 cups (9 ounces/255 grams) all-purpose flour

1/2 teaspoon baking powder

3/4 teaspoon ground cinnamon

1/4 teaspoon table salt

20 tablespoons (10 ounces/284 grams) unsalted butter, soft enough so that it barely holds its shape when poked with a finger

3 tablespoons instant espresso powder, or 4 tablespoons instant coffee granules, crushed (any kind, even decaf, will do)

1 cup (4 ounces/113 grams) confectioners' sugar

1/2 cup (4 ounces/113 grams) firmly packed light brown sugar

1 1/2 cups (9 ounces/255 grams) semisweet chocolate chips

About 1/4 cup (2 ounces/57 grams) granulated sugar for dipping

1. Position an oven rack on the middle rung. Heat the oven to 350 degrees (180°C). Have ready 3 cookie sheets. Line a cooling rack with paper towels.

2. In a medium bowl, combine the flour, baking powder, cinnamon, and salt. Whisk until well blended. In a large bowl, combine the butter and espresso powder or crushed coffee granules. Beat with an electric mixer (stand mixer fitted with the paddle attachment or handheld mixer) on medium speed until well combined. Add the confectioners' sugar and brown sugar and beat until combined. Add the flour mixture about 1/2 cup (2 ounces/57 grams) at a time, mixing on low speed until well blended. Stir in the chocolate chips with a rubber spatula.

3. Put the granulated sugar in a small, shallow bowl. Scoop out about 1 tablespoon dough and flatten it slightly into a disk. Dip one side into the granulated sugar and then set the disk, sugar side up, on an ungreased cookie sheet. Repeat with the remaining dough, spacing the disks about 2 inches (5cm) apart.

4. Bake 1 sheet at a time (make sure to use a cooled sheet for the next batches) until the edges start to darken, 12 to 14 minutes. (Begin checking after 12 minutes, but don't be tempted to remove them too soon.) Transfer the cookie sheet to a rack to cool for 1 to 2 minutes. Using a metal spatula, lift the cookies from the sheet onto the paper towel–lined rack and let cool completely.

no-bake graham cracker mini-houses

MAKES 6 HOUSES

When my children Alex and Tierney were in elementary school, I taught cooking lessons to their classes through a program called Cooking in the Classroom. I covered subjects like how cakes rise, the difference between baking powder and baking soda, and how ice cream is made. Around the holidays, I would set aside time for a group project, an easy variation on the classic gingerbread house. The kids loved building their own little houses and really got creative with the decorations.

This recipe makes six houses, but it can easily be tripled or quadrupled. It makes a great at-home project for a parent and child to work on together, and I've also included instructions on setting up the project for a class.

Setting Up for a Classroom

Delegate various steps to different parents. Volunteers are always plentiful, just ask. Have the kids gather the empty milk or orange juice cartons (the tall 1/2-pint size). You'll need one for every child, but I always have a few extras on hand in case of an accident. The kids can collect them from the cafeteria after lunch and rinse them out.

You'll need to make the royal icing ahead, gather assorted candy decorations (see the ingredients list below), and buy a large piece of foam board from an art-supply store. Ask the teacher to set aside about an hour, and have the kids bring plastic grocery bags for carrying the decorated houses home. If possible, set the houses aside to dry (overnight is best) before wrapping them in the plastic grocery bags for transport.

Divide the kids into groups of 4 or 5. Scoop the royal icing into paper cups (this can be done in advance, if you prefer) and give one to each child along with a wooden Popsicle stick to serve as an applicator. Jumble the assorted candies onto paper plates (about 2 plates per group).

You'll need to explain to the kids how to glue the decorations to the house and board using the icing as "glue." Emphasize creativity, remind them to decorate the whole house and yard (not just the roof), and set down some rules about eating as they go.

do aheads

• The icing can be prepared as directed in step 2, covered with a damp paper towel and plastic wrap, and stored in the fridge for up to 2 weeks.

• The graham cracker side and roof panels can be prepared through step 3, wrapped, and stored at room temperature for up to 2 months.

• The houses can be prepared through step 4, covered, and stored at room temperature for up to 1 month.

• The decorated houses can be prepared through step 5 and displayed at room temperature for up to 2 months.

for the houses:

1 or 2 boxes (14.4 ounces/408 grams each) graham crackers (you'll use 4 crackers per house, unless there's breakage)

6 small (1/2 pint each and about 4 1/3 inches/11cm high) milk or orange juice cartons, emptied, rinsed, dried, and stapled closed

for decorating:

Assorted candies, cereals, crackers, and cookies; the most popular items are gumdrops, Necco wafers (for roofs), mini marshmallows, frosted mini wheat cereal (for roofs or paths), Hershey's chocolate bars (great for doors, paths, shutters), hard peppermint candies, whole almonds, Good & Plenty, pretzel sticks, M&M's, red or black licorice sticks, Life Savers

6 paper cups
6 wooden Popsicle sticks
12 paper plates
6 foam board rectangles, about 5 by 8 inches (13 by 20cm)

for the icing:

2 tablespoons powdered egg whites (see What Is It? on page 281) and 6 tablespoons warm water

or

3 whites from large eggs (1/3 cup/3 fl ounces/87 ml)

4 cups (16 ounces/454 grams) confectioners' sugar

1.
Assemble all the items you need for the houses and for decorating.

2. TO MAKE THE ICING

In a large bowl, combine the egg white powder and warm water and let stand, whisking frequently, until the powder is dissolved, about 5 minutes. If using fresh egg whites, simply put them in the bowl. Beat with an electric mixer (stand mixer fitted with the whisk attachment or handheld mixer) on medium speed until frothy. Add the confectioners' sugar and continue beating until blended. Increase the speed to high and beat until the mixture is thick and shiny, about 5 minutes. Place a damp paper towel directly on the icing to keep a skin from forming. If not using within 2 hours, cover the bowl with plastic and refrigerate.

3. TO ASSEMBLE THE HOUSES

Position a graham cracker on a cutting board and set a milk carton on top, with the triangular top face down. Using a serrated knife and the carton as your guide, trim away the top corner triangles of the graham cracker. The cracker will form a point at the top. Next, cut the short sides (usually the label side) and roof panels. Using the serrated knife and a ruler as your guide, carefully saw away two-thirds of the cracker, leaving you with one rectangle 3 inches (7.75cm) long (the side piece) and one rectangle 1 3/4 inches (4.5cm) long (the roof piece). You'll need 2 of each of these sections for each house. Repeat with another 11 crackers. Pile the scraps and any broken crackers into a large plastic bag and save for graham cracker crusts. Carefully set the pieces aside.

4.

Using a small metal spatula (an offset one is good), spread about 2 teaspoons of the icing on one side of a carton. Gently press the corresponding cracker piece onto the carton. Repeat with the other 3 sides. Stand the carton up, and dab about 2 teaspoons icing on each side of the stapled top. Gently press the roof pieces onto the icing. Repeat with the remaining houses. Set the houses aside to dry completely, about 12 hours.

5. TO DECORATE THE HOUSES

Dab a bit of icing onto the foam board rectangle and position a house on top. Working on one section at a time, spread with icing and arrange decorations as you like. I recommend saving the roof and the yard decorations for last.

nut-crusted chocolate-banana swirl cake

MAKES ONE 10-INCH (25CM) BUNDT CAKE, OR 10 TO 12 SERVINGS

this cake is yet another good use for overripe bananas. Like the Supermoist Banana-Nut Muffins variation for muffin tops with chocolate chips (page 83) and the Banana Layer Cake with Fudgy Frosting (page 171), this is a riff on a Dodge family favorite: chocolate and bananas. Here the banana-chocolate combination reaches a more sophisticated level. Baked in a Bundt or other fluted tube pan (see equipment note on page 166), the cake makes an elegant brunch coffee cake or a not-too-sweet dinner party dessert. Bittersweet chocolate is stirred into half of the buttermilk-banana batter, and the two batters are gently swirled together in the pan. Though the coarse but especially moist crumb of the baked cake is not as sweet and tender as the crumb of a layer cake, it is more delicate than a muffin top. And the nut crust makes a handsome presentation, while adding a crunchy texture and nutty taste.

do aheads

• The cake pan can be prepared as directed in step 1, covered, and stored at room temperature for up to 2 days.

• The cake can be prepared through step 4, covered, and stored at room temperature for up to 5 days.

Softened unsalted butter

2 tablespoons granulated sugar

1/3 cup (1 1/4 ounces/35 grams) medium-fine chopped walnuts (no need to toast)

for the cake:

2 cups (9 ounces/255 grams) all-purpose flour

2 teaspoons baking powder

1/4 teaspoon baking soda

1/4 teaspoon table salt

3/4 cup (6 ounces/170 grams) unsalted butter, completely softened at room temperature

1 1/4 cups (10 ounces/284 grams) granulated sugar

3 medium very, very ripe bananas (about 14 ounces/397 grams total, including peels), peeled

2 teaspoons pure vanilla extract

3 large eggs

6 tablespoons buttermilk

4 ounces (113 grams) bittersweet chocolate, melted and cooled slightly

1. TO PREPARE THE PAN

Position an oven rack on the middle rung. Heat the oven to 350 degrees (180°C). In a small bowl, mix the sugar with the chopped walnuts. Generously butter the bottom and sides of a 12-cup Bundt or other fluted tube pan. Coat with the nuts and sugar, pressing the nuts with your fingers to help them stick. The pan sides will be coated and some of the nuts will fall to the bottom – that's fine.

2. TO MAKE THE CAKE

In a medium bowl, combine the flour, baking powder, baking soda, and salt. Whisk until well blended. In a large bowl, combine the butter, sugar, bananas, and vanilla. Beat with an electric mixer (stand mixer fitted with the paddle attachment or handheld mixer) on medium-high speed until well blended and the bananas are almost smooth, stopping to scrape down the sides of the bowl as needed. Add the eggs one at a time, beating after each addition just until blended. Add half of the flour mixture and stir gently with a rubber spatula just until blended. Add the buttermilk and stir just until blended, and then add the rest of the flour mixture and stir just until blended. Spoon half the batter into a medium bowl and gently stir in the melted chocolate just until combined.

3. Using a large spoon, alternately add a scoopful of each batter to the prepared pan, working around the pan until all the batter is used. Gently run a knife or the tip of a rubber spatula through the batter, once clockwise and once counterclockwise, to swirl the batters slightly. Gently tap the pan on the counter to settle the contents.

4. Bake until a toothpick or cake tester inserted in the center comes out with just a few crumbs sticking to it, about 40 minutes. Transfer the pan to a rack to cool for 15 minutes. If you wait too long, the cake will stick to the pan, and if you unmold it too early, it can break into chunks. Run a thin knife around the pan sides, being careful not to dislodge the nuts, to loosen the cake. Invert the cake onto the rack, lift off the pan, and let cool completely.

spiced ginger roll

MAKES 1 ROLLED CAKE, OR 12 SERVINGS

Spiraled with cream filling, a rolled cake makes a striking presentation, one that looks impossible to achieve at home. I remember my first attempt. Following the recipe directions, I pulled the thin sheet cake from the oven, immediately inverted it onto a sugar-coated towel, and rolled it up in the towel. I was sure my roll cake would be a disaster, but, instead, the results were perfect. It looked exactly like the picture, and it wasn't nearly as difficult to prepare as I had imagined. The key to success is, simply, following the recipe directions to a tee.

Over the years, I've jazzed up the traditional vanilla rolled cake and developed a spice version with a mascarpone filling studded with crystallized ginger. When it's first baked and filled, the cake is a delicate, airy contrast to the rich filling. But when chilled in the fridge for a day or three, the cake takes on a new personality. While the cake and filling flavors stay balanced, they each become more pronounced, and the texture changes to a moister, denser cake that melds with the gingery mascarpone filling.

do aheads

• The filling can be prepared as directed in step 6, covered, and refrigerated for up to 1 day before proceeding with the recipe.

• The cake can be prepared through step 7, covered, and refrigerated for up to 3 days before serving.

for the cake:

1 cup (4 1/2 ounces/128 grams) all-
   purpose flour
3/4 teaspoon baking powder
1/4 teaspoon baking soda
2 teaspoons ground ginger
1 teaspoon ground cinnamon
1/4 teaspoon table salt

4 large eggs
1/2 cup (4 ounces/113 grams) firmly
   packed light brown sugar
1 teaspoon pure vanilla extract
About 3/4 cup (3 ounces/85 grams)
   confectioners' sugar for dusting

for the filling:

1 cup (8 fl ounces/233 ml) heavy
   cream
1 container (8 ounces/227 grams)
   mascarpone cheese
1/2 cup (2 ounces/57 grams) confectioners' sugar

Pinch of table salt
1/3 cup (1 ounce/28 grams) finely
   chopped crystallized ginger
2 teaspoons finely grated fresh ginger (I use a Microplane grater)

go-with: finely chopped crystallized ginger for garnish (optional)

1. TO MAKE THE CAKE

Position an oven rack on the middle rung. Heat the oven to 350 degrees (180°C). Lightly grease the bottom and sides of a half sheet pan and line the bottom with parchment. Lightly grease and flour the parchment and flour the sides of the pan, tapping out the excess flour.

2. In a medium bowl, combine the flour, baking powder, baking soda, ginger, cinnamon, and salt. Whisk until well blended. In a large bowl, beat the eggs with an electric mixer (stand mixer fitted with the whisk attachment or handheld mixer) on medium-high speed until pale yellow and tripled in volume, about 3 minutes. Add the brown sugar and vanilla and continue beating until thick enough to form a ribbon. To test, lift the whisk or beaters, the mixture should fall back into the bowl in the form of a rib-

bon that lingers a bit on the surface. Sift the flour mixture over the egg mixture and, using a rubber spatula, fold just until blended. Scrape the batter into the prepared pan and spread it evenly.

3. Bake until the top springs back when lightly touched (the cake is too thin to use the cake tester or toothpick test), about 13 minutes.

4. While the cake is baking, lay a clean kitchen towel on a counter and generously dust it with about 3/4 cup sifted confectioners' sugar (I use a sifter to get an even coating). The sugar should cover an area the same size as the cake pan.

5. When the cake is done, transfer the pan to a rack. Immediately run a thin knife around the pan sides to loosen the cake. Invert the cake onto the prepared towel, lift the pan, and carefully peel away the parchment. Beginning on a short side, roll up the cake and towel together. Do this immediately – while the cake is hot – or it will crack. Set the towel-wrapped cake on a rack and let cool completely.

6. TO MAKE THE FILLING

In a large bowl, combine the cream, mascarpone, confectioners' sugar, and salt. Beat with the electric mixer (stand mixer fitted with the whisk attachment or handheld mixer) on medium-low speed until well blended. Increase the speed to medium-high and continue beating until the mixture is thick enough to hold medium-firm peaks. Add the crystallized ginger and the fresh ginger. Beat just until blended. Scoop out about 3/4 cup, cover, and refrigerate until serving to use as a garnish.

7. TO ASSEMBLE

Unroll the cake. Spread the filling evenly over the cake, leaving a 1/2-inch (1.25cm) border uncovered on the long sides. Gently reroll the cake – this time without the towel – and set the roll, seam side down, on a cutting board. Using a serrated knife, trim each end on a sharp angle. Save the ends for a baker's treat. Transfer the cake to a flat, rectangular serving plate, and cover with plastic wrap. Refrigerate until ready to serve.

8. Just before serving, drop small dollops of the reserved cream filling down the center of the top of the cake and sprinkle with the crystallized ginger, if using.

individual tiramisus

While officially Italian, tiramisu has been adopted by Americans as one of their favorite after-dinner desserts. The combination of coffee-infused cake layered with sweetened mascarpone cheese and topped with bittersweet chocolate shavings tempts almost everyone.

When I'm hosting a dinner party, especially a buffet, I like to present tiramisu in individual glasses or dishes. Assembling the dessert in advance allows me time to fuss a bit over the presentation (something I never have time for during a party), and the individual glasses make serving easier and neater. As an added bonus, this tiramisu contains no egg yolks, which means you don't have to cook it and you can lick the bowl.

do aheads

• The cake can be prepared through step 3, wrapped with plastic, and stored at room temperature for up to 2 days or frozen for up to 1 month before proceeding with the recipe.

• The syrup can be prepared as directed in step 4, covered, and refrigerated for up to 4 days before using.

• The tiramisus can be prepared through step 8, covered with plastic wrap, and stored in the fridge for up to 2 days.

for the cake:

3/4 cup (3 1/4 ounces/92 grams)
   all-purpose flour
1/2 teaspoon baking powder
1/4 teaspoon table salt

3 large eggs
1/3 cup (2 1/2 ounces/71 grams)
   granulated sugar
3/4 teaspoon pure vanilla extract

for the syrup:

1 cup (8 fl ounces/233 ml) water

2/3 cup (5 ounces/142 grams) granulated sugar

3 tablespoons coffee-flavored
liqueur

4 teaspoons instant coffee granules
or instant espresso powder (any
kind, even decaf, will do)

for the filling:

2 containers (8 ounces each/227
grams) mascarpone cheese

1/2 cup (4 ounces/113 grams) firmly
packed light brown sugar

1 teaspoon instant coffee granules
or instant espresso powder (any
kind, even decaf, will do)

1 cup (8 fl ounces/233 ml) whole
milk

1/4 cup (2 fl ounces/58 ml)
coffee-flavored liqueur

2 whites from large eggs (1/4 cup/
2 fl ounces, 58 ml)

1 tablespoon granulated sugar

1 cup (4 1/2 ounces/128 grams)
bittersweet or semisweet
chocolate shavings
(see page 42) for garnish

1. TO MAKE THE CAKE

Position an oven rack on the middle rung. Heat the oven to 350 degrees
(180°C). Lightly grease the bottom and sides of an 8 1/2-by-12-inch (21.5-
by-30.5cm) jelly-roll pan with 1-inch sides (this is a quarter sheet pan) and
line the bottom with parchment. Lightly grease and flour the parchment and
flour the sides of the pan, tapping out the excess flour.

2. In a small bowl, combine the flour, baking powder, and salt. Whisk until
well blended. In a medium bowl, beat the eggs with an electric mixer (stand
mixer fitted with the whisk attachment or handheld mixer) on medium-high
speed until pale yellow and tripled in volume, about 3 minutes. Add the sugar
and vanilla and continue beating until thick enough to form a ribbon. When
the whisk or beaters are lifted, the mixture will fall back into the bowl and
form a ribbon; it should linger a bit on the surface. Sift the flour mixture over

the egg mixture and, using a rubber spatula, gently fold just until blended. Scrape the batter into the prepared pan and spread it evenly.

3. Bake until the top springs back when lightly touched (the cake is too thin to use the cake tester or toothpick test), about 15 minutes. Transfer the pan to a rack to cool for 15 minutes. Run a thin knife around the pan sides to loosen the cake. Lightly grease (or coat with nonstick cooking spray) another rack and invert the cake onto it. Lift off the sheet pan and carefully peel away the parchment. Let cool completely.

4. TO MAKE THE SYRUP
In a small saucepan, combine the water and sugar and cook over medium heat, stirring frequently, until the sugar is dissolved. Bring to a boil and remove from the heat. Add the coffee liqueur and the instant coffee and stir until dissolved. Set aside to cool to room temperature.

5. TO MAKE THE FILLING AND ASSEMBLE THE TIRAMISUS
It's important to have the cake and syrup ready before preparing the filling. In a large bowl, combine the mascarpone, brown sugar, and instant coffee. Beat with the electric mixer (stand mixer fitted with the whisk attachment or handheld mixer) on medium speed until blended. At this point, don't worry if the coffee hasn't fully dissolved. It will have done so by the time you're finished making the filling. Add 1/2 cup (4 fl ounces/116 ml) of the milk and beat on low speed just until incorporated. Add the remaining milk and the coffee liqueur and mix until blended and smooth.

6. In a small bowl, using clean beaters, beat the egg whites with the electric mixer on medium-high speed until soft peaks form. Add the granulated sugar and continue beating until firm, glossy peaks form. Scrape the beaten whites into the mascarpone mixture and, using a rubber spatula, gently fold just until blended. Cover the bowl with plastic wrap and leave at room temperature while assembling the desserts.

7. Have ready eight 10-ounce stemmed glasses. Cut the cake into 8 equal rectangles, then cut each rectangle into small pieces no bigger than 3/4 inch (2cm). Put about one-third of each stack of small cake pieces into the bottom of each glass. Drizzle the cake in each glass liberally with some of the coffee syrup and spoon about 3 tablespoons (or a scant 1/4 cup) of the filling over the cake. Sprinkle with about 2 teaspoons of the shaved chocolate. Repeat the layers twice, ending with chocolate. There should be 3 layers each of cake, cream, and chocolate shavings. (You'll use about 2/3 cup filling and 2 tablespoons chocolate per glass.)

8. Cover each glass with plastic wrap and refrigerate for at least 2 hours. For the best taste, serve the tiramisus at room temperature, not straight from the fridge.

layered chocolate mousse cake

MAKES ONE 9-INCH (22.75CM) CAKE, OR 12 TO 16 SERVINGS

this exciting cake is surprisingly uncomplicated to put together. The easy-to-make components lend themselves to working ahead, even up to a month in advance. But don't let ease and convenience fool you. This dessert gets raves. While the cake can be served unadorned, I've included three different garnishing suggestions from simple to elaborate. Pressing chopped walnuts against the frosted sides is the easiest way to dress up the cake and add crunch. Melting some of the remaining mousse for a shiny glaze is also easy and produces a dramatic appearance. Making chocolate (white or dark) shavings takes a bit more time, but is still easy. Pressed against the sides, the shavings add a touch of sophistication to the cake's appearance. And when you have time for a real project, you can both glaze the top of the cake and cover the sides with the walnuts or the chocolate shavings.

This cake is ideal for a dinner party, or for when you need to make a birthday cake that's a little bit fancy. I've also made it for Christmas, New Year, and Fourth of July parties, and it has traveled many places in the back of my car – it's that reliable.

Transporting the Cake

If you do choose to bring the cake to a summer party that's more than a 15-minute drive away, make sure to use a cooler to transport it. If the party is a fancy occasion, I'll assemble the cake on a serving plate. If the setting is more casual, I use my Tupperware cake carrier. I set a large cooler (one that's roomy enough to hold the cake) on its side in the back of my car, so that the cooler lid can be flipped up. This way the cake slides easily in and out of the cooler. Load the cake into the cooler just before leaving. If your destination does not have a refrigerator, you'll need to keep the cake chilled in the cooler. Two or three freezer packs will do the job. When I use my Tupperware cake carrier, I slide the packs in on either side of the container, which protects the cake from being damaged. If I'm using a serving plate, I position one or two freezer packs (depending on the cooler space available) flat on their sides next to, but not leaning against, the plate. Once I reach my destination, I park the car in a shaded location and carefully position another pack or two in the cooler.

do aheads

• The cake can be made through step 3, wrapped, and frozen for up to 1 month. Thaw in the refrigerator overnight before proceeding with the recipe.

• The cake can be prepared through step 8, covered with plastic wrap, and refrigerated for up to 48 hours. The assembled cake can also be frozen – in the springform – for up to 2 weeks. Thaw in the refrigerator overnight before proceeding with the recipe.

• The cake can be prepared through step 9, including the garnish, covered loosely with plastic so as not to mar the icing, and refrigerated for up to 2 days before serving.

for the cake:

1 1/2 cups (6 ounces/170 grams) cake flour

1/3 cup (1 ounce/28 grams) unsweetened natural cocoa powder (not Dutch process)

2 teaspoons baking powder

1/4 teaspoon baking soda

1/4 teaspoon table salt

1 cup (8 ounces/227 grams) granulated sugar

1 cup (8 fl ounces/233 ml) water

1 large egg

1/4 cup (2 fl ounces/58 ml) canola or corn oil

2 teaspoons pure vanilla extract

2 1/4 cups (18 fl ounces/525 ml)
   heavy cream
1/3 cup (1 ounce/28 grams)
   unsweetened Dutch-process
   cocoa powder, sifted if lumpy
14 ounces (397 grams) bittersweet
   chocolate, chopped
10 tablespoons (5 ounces/142 grams)
   unsalted butter, cut into 8 pieces

2 teaspoons pure vanilla extract, or
   1 to 2 tablespoons brandy,
   Cointreau, or bourbon
1/4 teaspoon table salt
8 whites from large eggs (1 cup, 8 fl
   ounces/233 ml)
2/3 cup (5 ounces/142 grams) granulated sugar

go-withs: 2 cups (9 ounces/255 grams) medium-fine chopped walnuts, toasted (see page 40), for garnish (optional); 10- to 12-ounce (284- to 340-gram) thick block bittersweet, semisweet, milk, or white chocolate for garnish (optional)

1. TO MAKE THE CAKE

Position an oven rack on the middle rung. Heat the oven to 325 degrees (165°C). Lightly grease the bottom and sides of a 9-by-2-inch (22.75-by-5cm) round cake pan. Line the bottom with parchment and flour the sides, tapping out the excess flour.

2.
Sift together the cake flour, cocoa, baking powder, baking soda, and salt into a large bowl. Add the sugar and whisk until well blended. Measure the water in a 2-cup Pyrex measure. Add the egg, oil, and vanilla. Using a fork, mix until blended. Scrape the wet ingredients into the dry ingredients. Whisk until the dry ingredients are just moist. Resist the urge to overbeat, or the baked cake will be dense and form a dome while baking. Pour the batter into the prepared pan.

3.
Bake until a toothpick or cake tester inserted in the center comes out clean, about 33 minutes. Transfer the pan to a rack and let cool for 20 min-

utes. Lightly grease a wire rack and invert the cake onto it. Lift off the pan and peel off the parchment. Let cool completely.

4. TO MAKE THE MOUSSE

Pour the cream into a large saucepan and set over medium heat. Add the cocoa powder. Bring the cream to a full boil, whisking occasionally to blend in the cocoa. Slide the pan from the heat and immediately add the chocolate and butter. Whisk slowly until melted and smooth. Scrape the mixture into a large mixing bowl and set over another large mixing bowl filled with ice and some water. Add the vanilla or liquor and salt. Stir frequently with a rubber spatula until the mixture has cooled to room temperature.

5.

While the chocolate mixture is chilling, gather together the supplies for assembling the cake. You'll need a large, flat serving plate, toothpicks (for cake slicing; optional), a long serrated knife, a rubber spatula, a long, metal spatula (offset is fine), and a 2-cup measure (I use the kind for dry-weight measuring).

6.

In a large bowl, beat the egg whites with an electric mixer (stand mixer fitted with the whisk attachment or handheld mixer) on medium-low speed until they are frothy. Increase the speed to medium-high and beat until the whites form soft peaks. Continue beating while gradually sprinkling in the sugar. When all the sugar has been added, increase the speed to high and whip until firm, glossy peaks form.

7.

Scoop about one-third of the whites into the cooled chocolate mixture and whisk gently until blended. Scrape the remaining whites into the chocolate and fold together gently but thoroughly with a rubber spatula. Scoop out about 2 1/2 cups of the mousse, cover, and refrigerate for the final touchups and glaze, if using. (Otherwise, it's a treat for the chef). Cover and set aside the remaining mousse at room temperature.

8. TO ASSEMBLE THE CAKE

Remove the bottom of a 9-inch (22.75cm) springform pan and set the ring on a large, flat serving plate. If using toothpicks to help slice the cake, stand a ruler against the side of the cake and evenly insert 2 picks vertically along the outside edge, dividing the cake into 3 equal horizontal layers. Repeat around cake. (Think of the cake as a clock, and stick the picks in at 12, 3, 6, and 9 o'clock.) Set your hand atop the cake, position a long serrated knife just barely above the top toothpick, and, using a sawing motion with long, gentle strokes, slice off the top layer of the cake. Flip the top layer upside down and place it in the bottom of the springform ring. Using the toothpicks as a guide, repeat to cut the remaining cake into 2 layers. Set aside. Scoop about 2 cups of the mousse onto the first cake layer in the ring and gently spread to cover. Place the next (middle) cake layer onto the mousse and press gently to level. This will push the mousse to the edge of the pan. Spread about 2 more cups of the mousse over the second layer. Turn the remaining (bottom) cake layer upside down and place it on top of the mousse. Press gently on the layer to level. Spread the remaining mousse on the final cake layer and smooth the top. The cake should fill the springform ring. Cover the assembled cake with plastic wrap and refrigerate until well chilled and the mousse is firm, about 6 hours.

9. TO GARNISH THE CAKE

Remove the chilled cake from the fridge and uncover. Warm a long, thin knife or metal spatula and slide it between the cake and the ring to loosen the cake. Carefully unlock the springform clasp and slowly release it until it is open all the way. Lift the ring away from the cake. Clean the plate edge, if necessary, and slide thin strips of parchment or foil slightly under the cake if you'd like to keep the plate clean while you garnish the cake. Check the sides of the cake. If they aren't completely covered with mousse, use a small metal spatula and about 1 cup of the reserved mousse to cover any bare patches and smooth the sides.

To garnish with chocolate glaze:

Melt about 1 cup of the remaining reserved mousse in a double boiler (see What Is It? on page 74) or in a 2-cup Pyrex measure in the microwave. Pour the glaze onto the top center of the chilled cake until a large pool forms and begins to spread to the edges. The top should be completely covered and the glaze should drip down the sides of the cake in a few spots and form small pools on the plate. If there are any bald spots around the edges, drizzle a little glaze on them to cover. This will also coax the glaze over the edge. Serve immediately, or cover and refrigerate until serving.

To garnish with walnuts:

Scoop up some of the walnuts with one hand and gently press them against the side of the cake. Rotate the cake plate slightly and repeat. Continue turning the plate and pressing the nuts onto the cake until the sides are completely covered. Brush any extra walnuts off the plate before removing the parchment or foil strips and save for another recipe. Serve immediately, or cover and refrigerate until serving.

To garnish with chocolate shavings and curls:

Place 2 sheets of parchment or waxed paper, each 11 by 17 inches (28 by 43cm), on a work surface, then make the chocolate shavings and curls as directed on page 42, letting the shavings fall onto one sheet of paper and the curls onto the other. You'll need 1 1/2 to 2 cups shavings; make enough curls to cover the sheet in an even, single layer. Use a tablespoon to scoop up some of the shavings. Starting at the bottom of the cake and using light pressure, gently drag the spoon up the side so the shavings stick; continue until the sides of the cake are completely covered. Arrange the curls on the top. Brush any extra shavings off the plate before removing the parchment or foil strips and save for another recipe. Serve immediately, or cover and refrigerate until serving.

four-layer carrot cake

this spectacular and professional-looking rectangular cake is made without worry or time commitment. I bake the batter in a half sheet pan. The single layer bakes in 15 minutes (about one-third the time of traditional layers) and is effortlessly cut into four strips that handle easily as they are stacked and frosted. The cake is moist yet delicate and the spicy, sweet flavors are well balanced. I use small currants instead of larger raisins, so they are more evenly distributed throughout the cake, and shredded coconut adds texture as well as a touch of additional sweetness.

While developing this recipe, I learned that there's much debate regarding which is the better frosting for a carrot cake: vanilla or lemon? After much testing and tasting (with special thanks to the Dianon Systems crew, my brother Tim's coworkers), I decided on the lemon, but, if you're a believer that the only icing for carrot cake is vanilla, leave out the lemon juice and zest and mix in the vanilla extract.

do aheads

• The cake can be prepared through step 3, covered with plastic wrap, and stored at room temperature for 1 day or frozen for up to 1 month before proceeding with the recipe.

• The frosting can be prepared as directed in step 4, covered, and stored at room temperature for up to 1 day or refrigerated for up to 3 days. Bring to room temperature before proceeding with the recipe.

• The cake can be prepared through step 7, covered, and stored in the refrigerator for up to 3 days before serving.

for the cake:

1 1/3 cups (6 ounces/170 grams) all-purpose flour

1 1/2 teaspoons baking powder

3/4 teaspoon baking soda

1 teaspoon ground cinnamon

1/2 teaspoon ground nutmeg

1/2 teaspoon table salt

1/4 teaspoon ground cloves

3/4 cup (6 ounces/170 grams) firmly packed light brown sugar

1/2 cup (4 fl ounces/117 ml) canola or corn oil

2 large eggs

1 teaspoon pure vanilla extract

1 cup finely grated carrots (from 2 medium/6 ounces/170 grams)

1/2 cup (1 ounce/28 grams) sweetened shredded dried coconut

1/2 cup (2 ounces/57 grams) currants

for the frosting:

12 ounces (340 grams) cream cheese, at room temperature

1 cup (8 ounces/227 grams) unsalted butter, at room temperature

2 1/2 cups (10 ounces/284 grams) confectioners' sugar

1/2 teaspoon table salt

3 tablespoons lemon juice and 2 teaspoons finely grated lemon zest

or

2 teaspoons pure vanilla extract

2 cups (9 ounces/255 grams) medium-fine chopped walnut or pecans, toasted (see page 40), for garnish

1. TO MAKE THE CAKE

Position an oven rack on the middle rung. Heat the oven to 350 degrees (180°C). Lightly grease the bottom and sides of a half sheet pan and line the bottom with parchment. Lightly grease and flour the parchment and flour the sides of the pan, tapping out the excess flour.

2. In a large bowl, combine the flour, baking powder, baking soda, cinnamon, nutmeg, salt, and cloves. Whisk until well blended. In a medium bowl, combine the brown sugar, oil, eggs, and vanilla. Whisk until well blended, and then add the carrots, coconut, and currants and whisk until blended. Pour the wet ingredients over the dry ingredients and, using a rubber spatula, mix just until blended. Scrape the batter into the prepared pan and spread it evenly. It will be a thin layer.

3. Bake until the top springs back when lightly pressed (the cake is too thin to use the cake tester or toothpick test), about 15 minutes. Transfer the pan to a rack. Immediately run a thin knife around the pan sides to loosen the cake. Invert the cake onto a rack, lift off the pan, and carefully peel away the parchment. Let cool completely.

4. TO MAKE THE FROSTING
In a large bowl, combine the cream cheese and butter. Beat with the electric mixer (stand mixer fitted with the paddle attachment or handheld mixer) on medium-high speed until very smooth and creamy. Add the confectioners' sugar, salt, and the lemon juice and zest or the vanilla. Beat on medium speed until blended and fluffy. Cover the bowl with plastic wrap and set aside at room temperature until the cake is completely cool and ready to be frosted.

5. TO ASSEMBLE THE CAKE
Using a long serrated knife, cut the cooled cake crosswise into four strips each 4 inches (10cm) wide. Set 1 layer on a flat, rectangular serving plate. To protect the plate from smears during frosting, slide small strips of parchment or foil slightly under the cake to cover the plate. Using a metal spatula or the blunt edge of a table knife, spread about 3/4 cup of the frosting evenly over the layer. Place the second layer on top of the frosted layer. Be sure the sides are lined up and then press gently on the layer. Spread

another 3/4 cup of the frosting evenly over the layer. Repeat with the third layer and the same amount of frosting. Position the remaining layer, top side down. Apply a very thin layer of frosting over the entire cake to seal in any crumbs. Set aside for 5 minutes (chill in the fridge, if possible). Spread the remaining frosting over the top and sides of the cake. Using your hand, press the nuts against the long sides of the cake, and then pull away the protective strips. Cover and refrigerate the cake until ready to serve.

strawberries-and-cream layer cake

my friend Pam, whose birthday is August 18, a day after mine, and I have established what's become a longstanding tradition of birthday-partying together. One year, another friend, Colleen Everett, gave us summer birthday girls a celebration lunch, beginning with massages and ending with this cake. The combination of vanilla-scented white cake layered with sweetened whipped cream (with a touch of gelatin for stability) and fresh strawberries is irresistible. If you can't find ripe strawberries, substitute raspberries or blueberries, or a mixture of the two.

do aheads

• The cake layers can be prepared through step 4, wrapped in plastic wrap, and stowed at room temperature for up to 2 days or frozen for up to 1 month.

• The cake can be prepared through step 7, covered, and refrigerated for up to 3 days.

for the cake:

3 cups (12 ounces/340 grams) cake flour

1 tablespoon baking powder

1/2 teaspoon table salt

12 tablespoons (6 ounces/170 grams) unsalted butter, at room temperature

1 1/2 cups (12 ounces/340 grams) granulated sugar

1 1/2 teaspoons pure vanilla extract

4 whites from large eggs (1/2 cup/ 4 1/4 fl ounces/124 ml)

1 cup (8 fl ounces/233 ml) butter-milk

for the frosting:

3 tablespoons water

2 1/4 teaspoons (1 packet) unflavored powdered gelatin (see What
Is It? on page 227)

2 cups (16 fl ounces/467 ml) heavy
cream

1 cup (4 ounces/113 grams) confectioners' sugar

1 teaspoon pure vanilla extract

Pinch of table salt

2 pints (20 ounces/567
grams/about 4 cups) strawberries
(raspberries or blueberries are
fine as well), rinsed and well
dried

go-with: 1 cup (2 ounces/57 grams) sweetened shredded dried coconut,
toasted (see page 40), for garnish (optional)

1. TO MAKE THE CAKE

Position an oven rack on the middle rung. Heat the oven to 350 degrees
(180°C). Grease the bottom and sides of two 9-by-2-inch (22.75-by-5cm)
round cake pans and line the bottoms with parchment. Lightly grease and flour
the parchment and flour the sides of the pans, tapping out the excess flour.

2. Sift together the flour, baking powder, and salt onto a paper plate or
into a medium bowl. In a large bowl, beat the butter with an electric mixer
(stand mixer fitted with the paddle attachment or handheld mixer) on
medium speed until smooth. Add 1 1/4 cups (10 ounces/284 grams) of the
sugar and the vanilla and beat until well combined. Pour in about 1/3 cup
(2 1/2 fl ounces/73 ml) of the buttermilk and mix on low just until
blended. Add half of the flour mixture and mix just until blended. Add the
remaining buttermilk and mix just until blended. Add the remaining flour
mixture and mix just until blended.

3. In a medium bowl, beat the egg whites with the electric mixer (stand
mixer fitted with the whisk attachment or handheld mixer) on medium-high
speed until they form soft peaks. Increase the speed to high and gradually

add the remaining 1/4 cup (2 ounces/57 grams) sugar. Beat until medium-firm peaks form. Using a rubber spatula, scoop up about one-fourth of the whites and stir gently into the cake batter. Add the remaining whites and fold gently just until blended. Scrape the batter into the prepared pans, dividing it evenly.

4. Bake until the tops are light brown and a toothpick or cake tester inserted in the center of each layer comes out clean, about 30 minutes. Transfer the pans to racks and let cool for about 15 minutes. Run a thin knife around the pan sides to loosen each cake. Invert the layers onto racks, lift off the pans, and peel away the parchment. Let cool completely.

5. **TO MAKE THE FROSTING**
Put the water in a small saucepan. Sprinkle the gelatin evenly over it and let stand until the gelatin is no longer dry looking and has softened, about 5 minutes. Set the saucepan over low heat and stir constantly until the gelatin is dissolved, about 3 minutes. Do not allow to boil.

6. In a large bowl, combine the cream, confectioners' sugar, vanilla, and salt. Beat with the electric mixer (stand mixer fitted with the whisk attachment or handheld mixer) on medium-high speed until the cream just begins to thicken enough to see trace marks from the beater. Increase the speed to high and gradually add the hot dissolved gelatin. Beat until the cream forms firm peaks.

7. **TO ASSEMBLE THE CAKE**
Hull the strawberries. Cut half of the strawberries in half lengthwise and the remainder into quarters. If you are using raspberries or blueberries, leave them whole. Using your hands, gently brush away any excess crumbs from the layers. Set 1 cake layer, top side down, on a flat serving plate. To protect the plate from smears during frosting, slide small strips of parchment or foil under the cake to cover the plate. Using a metal spatula or the blunt

edge of a table knife, spread about 1 cup of the frosting evenly over the layer. Scatter the quartered strawberries evenly over the cream and press them into the cream. Spread about 3/4 cup of the frosting over the strawberries. Place the second layer, top side down, on top of the cream and strawberries. Be sure the sides are lined up and then press gently on the layer. Apply a very thin layer of frosting over the entire cake to seal in any crumbs. Set aside for 5 minutes (chill in the fridge, if possible). Spread the remaining frosting over the top and sides of the cake. Garnish the top with the halved strawberries. I like to arrange them piggyback style in a circle around the edge. Serve the cake slightly chilled.

chocolate-glazed ricotta cake

MAKES ONE 9-INCH (22.75CM) CAKE, OR 10 TO 12 SERVINGS

y version of cassata, the luscious Sicilian layer cake, is inspired by a recipe from the great cooking teacher Michael Field. The dessert partners a moist yellow cake with a lightly sweetened, orange-scented ricotta filling and a chocolate glaze. During the assembly stage, the cake is sliced into three layers (it's easy because the cake is sturdy) and filled with the ricotta mixture. The filling is a bit thin to begin with, but as it chills in the fridge, the cake absorbs some of its moisture and flavor. The end result is a dessert with almost-puddinglike cake layers separated by distinctive, orange-scented ricotta filling.

do aheads

• The cake can be prepared through step 3, covered in plastic wrap, and stored at room temperature for up to 1 day or frozen for up to 1 month.

• The filling can be prepared as directed in step 4, covered, and refrigerated for up to 1 day. Bring to room temperature before proceeding with the recipe.

• The cake can be prepared through step 5, covered with plastic wrap, and refrigerated for up to 2 days before proceeding with the recipe.

• The glaze can be prepared as directed in step 6, covered, and refrigerated for up to 3 days. Gently melt it before proceeding with the recipe.

• The cake can be prepared through step 7, covered, and refrigerated for up to 3 days.

for the cake:

1 3/4 cups (7 3/4 ounces/220 grams) all-purpose flour

1 3/4 teaspoons baking powder

1/2 cup (4 ounces/113 grams) unsalted butter, at room temperature

1 cup (8 ounces/227 grams) granulated sugar

2 large eggs

1 teaspoon pure vanilla extract

2/3 cup (5 fl ounces/146 ml) whole milk

for the filling:

2 cups (17 1/2 ounces/496 grams) whole-milk ricotta cheese

1/3 cup (2 1/2 ounces/71 grams) firmly packed light brown sugar

3 tablespoons Grand Marnier or other orange-flavored liqueur

1 tablespoon finely grated orange zest

for the glaze:

6 ounces (170 grams) bittersweet chocolate, finely chopped

6 tablespoons (3 ounces/85 grams) unsalted butter

2 tablespoons light corn syrup

1. TO MAKE THE CAKE

Position an oven rack on the middle rung. Heat the oven to 350 degrees (180°C). Grease the bottom and sides of one 9-by-2-inch (22.75-by-5cm) round cake pan. Line the bottom with parchment and flour the sides, tapping out the excess flour.

2.
Sift together the flour, baking powder, and salt onto a paper plate or into a medium bowl. In a large bowl, beat the butter with an electric mixer (stand mixer fitted with the paddle attachment or handheld mixer) on medium speed until smooth. Add the sugar and beat until well blended. Add the eggs one at a time, beating well after each addition. Add the vanilla with the second egg. The mixture will look curdled and a bit lumpy. Don't worry, as it will all come together after you add the flour and milk. Add half

of the flour mixture and mix on low speed just until blended. Add the milk and mix just until blended. Add the remaining flour mixture and mix just until blended. Scrape the batter evenly into the prepared pan.

3. Bake until the top is light brown and a toothpick or cake tester inserted in the center comes out clean, about 30 minutes. Transfer the pan to a rack to cool for about 15 minutes. Run a thin knife around the pan sides to loosen the cake. Invert the cake onto a rack, lift off the pan, and peel away the parchment. Let cool completely.

4. TO MAKE THE FILLING
In a blender, combine the ricotta, brown sugar, and liqueur. Pop on the lid and blend until smooth, stopping frequently to stir the mixture so it blends evenly. Add the orange zest and blend just until combined.

5. TO ASSEMBLE THE CAKE
Using a long serrated knife, slice the cake horizontally into 3 layers (see the Technique Tip on page 316). Set the bottom layer on a flat plate or cutting board. Using a metal spatula or the blunt edge of a table knife, spread about one-third of the filling evenly over the layer to within 1/2 inch (1.25cm) of the edge. Place the second layer on top of the filling. Be sure the sides are lined up and then press gently on the layer. Spread another one-third of the filling evenly over the layer to within 1/2 inch (1.25cm) of the edge. Position the remaining layer, top side up. Apply the remaining filling over the entire cake; it will be a very thin layer. The layers will slide around a bit and some of the filling will ooze out on the sides. When necessary, use a spatula to realign the layers and spread any leaking filling evenly over the sides. Adjust the layers to line them up and refrigerate the cake until the filling begins to firm up, about 1 hour. Realign the layers, if necessary, and cover the cake's surface with plastic. Refrigerate until the cake has absorbed some of the filling and the layers no longer slide around, about 12 hours or for up to 2 days.

6. TO MAKE THE GLAZE

When the cake is chilled and firm, prepare the glaze. Melt the chocolate along with the butter and corn syrup in a double boiler (see What Is It? on page 74) or in the microwave (see page 51). Stir until smooth. Don't allow it to cool.

7.

Uncover the cake and, using a long metal spatula, transfer it to a rack set over a plate to catch any dripping glaze. Pour the entire batch of glaze onto the center of the top of the cake. It will spread to cover the top and slide down the sides. If necessary, use the spatula to nudge the glaze over the top so that it slides down the sides to cover them completely. Do not coax it so much that you lose the thick top covering, however. Use the spatula to spread the glaze evenly over the sides. It won't take much encouragement. Transfer the cake, rack and plate or board included, to the fridge and let the glaze set, about 30 minutes. Once the glaze is firm, use the spatula to transfer the cake to a flat serving plate.

technique tip for cutting a single cake into layers

To cut a single cake into layers, set a ruler against the side of the cake and evenly insert toothpicks vertically along the outside edge, dividing the cake into equal horizontal layers. Do the same in three other equally spaced locations on the cake's side (it's easiest to think of 12, 3, 6, and 9 o'clock). Set your hand atop the cake, position a long serrated knife just barely above the top toothpick, and, using a sawing motion with long, gentle strokes – taking care to keep the knife parallel to your work surface – slice off the top layer of the cake. Set aside. Using the toothpicks as a guide, repeat to cut the remaining cake into layers.

old-fashioned ice cream sandwiches

MAKES 1 DOZEN SANDWICHES, EACH 2 3/4 INCHES (7CM) SQUARE

a few summers ago, my friend Ann and I gave a casual dinner party on Long Island Sound. Deciding on the main course was easy (Ann's husband, Ed, is a master griller), but we wanted something fun and different for dessert. We chose ice cream sandwiches. As kids, ice cream sandwiches were a much-anticipated beach-time treat, so why not make a grown-up homemade version?

The success of this recipe hinges on the chocolate cookie layers. They need to be sturdy and easy to handle, yet soft enough to bite into without the ice cream squishing out the back. I like to pair the cookie layers with different ice cream flavors and then coat the ice cream edges with nuts or crushed candies. That way, everyone gets the flavor of choice and it makes serving fun. I've included a few flavor variations for the cookie layer and assorted garnishes, but feel free to improvise with your personal favorites.

To transport these meltable treats, Ann and I slipped the sandwiches into individual plastic bags and tucked them into a small cooler with a block of dry ice. Worked like a charm.

do aheads

• The cookie layer can be prepared through step 3, wrapped in plastic wrap, and stored at room temperature for up to 2 days or frozen for up to 1 month before proceeding with the recipe.

• The ice cream sandwiches can be prepared through step 6 or through step 9, wrapped in plastic wrap, and frozen for up to 1 month.

for the cookie:

1 1/4 cups (5 1/2 ounces/156 grams) all-purpose flour

1/2 cup (1 1/2 ounces/43 grams) unsweetened natural cocoa powder (not Dutch process), sifted if lumpy

1/2 teaspoon baking soda

1/4 teaspoon table salt

6 tablespoons (3 ounces/85 grams) unsalted butter, at room temperature

3/4 cup (6 ounces/170 grams) granulated sugar

1 1/2 teaspoons pure vanilla extract

2/3 cup (5 fl ounces/146 ml) cold milk

Flavor options (pages 320–21)

1 quart ice cream of 1 flavor, or 2 pints of 2 different flavors

1 1/2 cups garnish (page 321), optional

1. TO MAKE THE SOFT COOKIE

Position an oven rack on the center rung. Heat the oven to 350 degrees (180°C). Lightly grease the bottom of a half sheet pan. Line the pan with parchment to cover the bottom and the longer sides.

2.
Select a flavor option, if desired. In a medium bowl, combine the flour, cocoa powder, baking soda, and salt. Whisk until well blended. In a large bowl, combine the butter and sugar. Beat with a handheld electric mixer on medium-high speed until well blended and lightened in color, about 3 minutes. Beat in the vanilla. Add about one-third of the flour mixture and beat on medium-low speed just until blended. Add half of the milk and mix just until blended. Add another one-third of the flour and mix just until blended. Add the remaining milk and mix just until blended, and then the remaining flour and mix just until blended.

3.
For the best results, it's important to spread the dough in an even layer. Distribute the dough evenly over the prepared pan in small dollops. Using one hand to anchor the parchment, drag a rectangular offset spatula

or a bench scraper over the dough to smooth it into an even layer, rotating the pan as you work. To make the layer as smooth and even as possible, brush or spray a sheet of parchment or plastic wrap the same size as the pan with nonstick cooking spray and lay it, sprayed side down, on top of the dough. Roll a straight rolling pin or a straight-sided wine bottle (a good size to get into the corners of the pan) over the paper to level the batter. Carefully peel away the parchment or plastic wrap. Bake until a toothpick or cake tester inserted in the center comes out clean, 10 to 12 minutes. Transfer the pan to a wire rack and let cool completely.

4. TO FILL THE SANDWICHES

Lay 2 long pieces of plastic wrap in a cross shape on a small baking sheet. Run a thin knife around the pan sides to loosen the cookie. Invert the cookie onto a large cutting board, lift off the pan, and peel off the parchment. Using a ruler as a guide, cut the cookie crosswise into 2 equal pieces. Place 1 piece, top side down, in the middle of the plastic-wrap cross (a wide, sturdy metal spatula will help the transfer) to create the bottom layer.

5.

Remove the ice cream from the freezer and take off the lid. It's important to work quickly from this point on. (If the ice cream becomes too soft, place it on a plate and back into the freezer to harden up.) Using scissors or a sharp knife, cut the container lengthwise in 2 places and tear away the container. Set the ice cream on its side. Cut the ice cream crosswise into even slices, 1/2 to 3/4 inch (1.25cm to 2cm) thick, and arrange the slices on top of the cookie layer in the pan, pairing the narrowest piece (from the bottom of the container) next to the largest (from the top of the container). If you have chosen 2 flavors, cover half of the cookie with 1 flavor and the other half with the other. Using a rubber spatula, gently yet firmly smear the ice cream to spread it evenly. (It helps to put a piece of plastic wrap on the ice cream and smear with your hands; remove the plastic before proceeding.)

6. Position the remaining cookie layer, top side up, over the ice cream. Press gently to spread the ice cream to the edges. Put a clean sheet of plastic on top and wrap the long ends of the bottom sheets up and over the filled layers. Put the baking sheet in the freezer and chill until the sandwich is hard, about 4 hours.

7. TO CUT AND GARNISH THE SANDWICHES

Take the baking sheet out of the freezer. Lift the package from the pan, transfer it to a cutting board, and line the pan with a fresh piece of plastic wrap. Peel the top layer of plastic off the sandwich (you can leave on the bottom layer).

8. Working quickly so the ice cream doesn't melt, use a ruler and a long, sharp chef's knife to score the cookie, dividing it into 1 dozen 2 3/4-inch (7cm) squares. Mark 3 equal strips on the short side and 4 equal strips on the long sides. Then, using the marks as a guide, cut the sandwiches, wiping the blade clean as needed. (If your kitchen is very warm, put the strips back into the freezer to firm, or work with 1 strip at a time, keeping the rest in the freezer.)

9. Garnish the sandwiches, if desired: Fill a small, shallow bowl with your chosen garnish and set it next to your work surface. Press some of the garnish onto some or all of the sides of the ice cream. Set the sandwiches back on the baking sheet and return them to the freezer immediately. (If your kitchen is warm, keep the sandwiches in the freezer and garnish one at a time.) Once the sandwiches are hard, wrap them individually in plastic and store in the freezer until serving.

Cookie Flavor Variations (optional)

Chocolate-Mint: Add 1/2 teaspoon peppermint extract when you add the vanilla.

Chocolate-Orange: Add 1/2 teaspoon natural orange flavor or orange extract when you add the vanilla.

Chocolate-Espresso: Add 1 tablespoon instant coffee granules (any kind, even decaf, will do) when you add the vanilla.

Chocolate-Ginger: Add 1/2 teaspoon ground ginger to the dry ingredients.

Garnishes (optional)

Hard peppermint candies, finely crushed
Bittersweet or semisweet chocolate, finely chopped or grated
Crystallized ginger, minced
Pecans, finely chopped and toasted (see page 40)
Sweetened dried coconut flakes, toasted (see page 40)
Amaretti cookies (see What Is It? on page 111), crushed
Toffee chips, crushed

chocolate cake for a crowd

MAKES ONE 2-LAYER SHEET CAKE, OR 16 TO 24 SERVINGS

Feeding a crowd is always a challenge, especially when you're talking dessert. When faced with a kid's birthday party or a neighborhood picnic, I know it's tempting to just call up the local bakery, but this cake is your answer. It is a classic two-layer sheet cake and will feed 16 to 24. The layers are moist, chocolaty, and delicious. The not-too-sweet vanilla frosting is amazingly spreadable and has a satiny finish. Depending on the occasion, you can top the frosted cake with fruit or decorate with some colored sprinkles, then stick in the birthday candles.

do aheads

• The cake layers can be prepared through step 3, wrapped in plastic wrap, and stored at room temperature for up to 2 days or frozen for up to 1 month before proceeding with the recipe.

• The frosting can be prepared as directed in step 4, covered, and stored at room temperature for up to 1 day or refrigerated for up to 3 days (bring to room temperature before using) before proceeding with the recipe.

• The cake can be prepared through step 5, covered loosely with plastic wrap so as not to mar the frosting, and stored in the refrigerator for up to 3 days before proceeding with the recipe.

• The cake can be garnished as directed in step 6, covered loosely with plastic wrap so as not to mar the garnish, and refrigerated for up to 6 hours. Bring to room temperature before serving.

3 cups (12 ounces/340 grams) cake flour

1 cup (3 ounces/85 grams) unsweetened natural cocoa powder (not Dutch process), sift if lumpy

2 1/4 teaspoons baking soda

3/4 teaspoon table salt

12 tablespoons (6 ounces/170 grams) unsalted butter, at room temperature

2 2/3 cups (21 1/4 ounces/602 grams) granulated sugar

3 large eggs

2 teaspoons pure vanilla extract

1 1/4 cups (11 1/4 ounces/319 grams) sour cream

1 cup (8 fl ounces/233 ml) boiling water

for the frosting:

15 ounces (425 grams) cream cheese, at room temperature

20 tablespoons (10 ounces/284 grams) unsalted butter, at room temperature

3 1/4 cups (13 ounces/369 grams) confectioners' sugar

2 1/2 teaspoons pure vanilla extract

3/4 teaspoon table salt

for the garnish (optional):

1 pint (10 ounces/284 grams/about 2 cups) blueberries, rinsed and well dried

1 pint (10 ounces/284 grams/about 2 cups) raspberries, rinsed and well dried

2 nectarines, pitted and thinly sliced

8 to 10 small strawberries, rinsed, well dried, hulled, and cut in half lengthwise

3 or 4 fresh mint sprigs

1. TO MAKE THE CAKE

Position an oven rack on the middle rung. (For smaller ovens, adjust 2 racks in the center third of the oven and switch the pans halfway through baking.) Heat the oven to 350 degrees (180°C). Lightly grease the bottom and sides of two 9-by-13-inch (22.75-by-33cm) baking pans (I prefer straight-sided metal baking pans, rather than glass baking dishes, to give a cleaner look to the finished cake) and line the bottom of each with parchment. Lightly dust the pan sides with flour, tapping out the excess flour.

2. Sift together the flour, cocoa powder, baking soda, and salt onto a paper plate or medium bowl. In a large bowl, beat the butter with an electric mixer (stand mixer fitted with the paddle attachment or handheld mixer) on medium speed until smooth. Add the sugar and beat until well blended. Add the eggs one at a time, beating well after each addition. Add the vanilla with the third egg. Add one-third of the flour mixture and mix on low speed just until blended. Stir in half of the sour cream. Add another one-third of the flour mixture and mix just until blended. Stir in the remaining sour cream. Add the remaining flour and mix just until blended. Pour in the boiling water and mix until blended and smooth. Immediately scrape the batter into the prepared pans, dividing and spreading it evenly. Tap the pans gently on the counter to settle the contents.

3. Bake until a toothpick or cake tester inserted in the center of each layer comes out with only a few moist crumbs attached, about 25 minutes. Transfer the cake pans to racks to cool for 15 minutes. Run a thin knife around the sides of the pans to loosen the cakes. Invert each cake onto a large rectangular rack, lift off the pans, and peel away the parchment. Let cool completely.

4. TO MAKE THE FROSTING
In a large bowl, combine the cream cheese and butter. Beat with the electric mixer (stand mixer fitted with the paddle attachment or handheld mixer) on medium-high speed until very smooth and creamy. Add the confectioners' sugar, vanilla, and salt and beat on medium speed until blended and fluffy. Cover the frosting and set aside at room temperature until the cake is completely cool and ready to be frosted.

5. TO ASSEMBLE THE CAKE

Using your hands, gently brush away any excess crumbs from the layers. Carefully place 1 layer, top side down, on a large, flat rectangular serving plate or cutting board. To protect the plate or board from smears during frosting, slide small strips of parchment or foil under the cake to cover the plate or board. Using a metal spatula or the blunt edge of a knife, spread about 2 cups of the frosting evenly over the layer. Place the second layer, top side up, on top of the frosting. Be sure the sides are lined up and then press gently on he layer. Apply a very thin layer of frosting over the entire cake to seal in any crumbs. Set aside for about 5 minutes (chill in the fridge, if possible). Spread the remaining frosting over the top and sides of the cake.

6. If you are using the garnish, decoratively arrange the fruits on top of the cake. Garnish with the mint sprigs. Serve immediately.

english muffins
MAKES 9 SQUARE MUFFINS

On a recent visit to Paris, my friend and colleague Amy Albert discovered a vendor who sells fresh English muffins at the Sunday outdoor market on the rue Raspail. The Frenchman, who calls himself Michael Muffin, pulls up in a truck, the back of which is actually a traveling bakery, complete with hearth oven, workbench, and a proofing box. While hungry Parisians queue up for freshly baked English muffins, Michael's Labrador sits patiently in the front of the truck throughout the day. The story inspired me to come up with my own English muffin recipe. After all, it's not just the English who love them.

My muffins are square, not round like the classic. Unlike round muffins, where the scraps from the first cutting are gathered up, rolled out a second time, and cut again, squares require only one rolling. (When the dough has to be rerolled, the texture becomes dense and heavy.)

You'll love how these homemade muffins look remarkably like store-bought muffins – nicely browned – and taste so much better! They are tender and moist and, for a low-fat bread, surprisingly rich.

do aheads

• Prepare the dough through step 6, spray the surface with a coating of nonstick spray, and cover the dough loosely but completely. Refrigerate the muffins for up to 10 hours before proceeding with the recipe. Remove from the fridge and set on the counter while heating the griddle.

• Prepare the muffins through step 8 and let cool completely. Store at room temperature for up to 2 days or freeze in a heavy-duty freezer bag for up to 1 month.

3 cups (13 1/2 ounces/383 grams) all-purpose flour

2 1/4 teaspoons (1 packet) instant yeast (see page 20)

1 tablespoon granulated sugar

1 1/4 teaspoons table salt

1 teaspoon baking powder

1 egg white from large egg

1/2 cup (4 fl ounces/117 ml) water, warmed to between 115 and 125 degrees (46 and 52°C)

1/2 cup (4 fl ounces/117 ml) whole milk, warmed to between 115 and 125 degrees (46 and 52°C)

Cornmeal for dusting

2 tablespoons (1 ounce/28 grams) unsalted butter, at room temperature

1. TO MIX BY HAND

In a large bowl, combine the flour, yeast, sugar, salt, and baking powder. Stir with a wooden spoon until blended. In a small mixing bowl, beat the egg white with a whisk or a handheld electric mixer on medium-high speed until soft peaks form.

2.

Check the temperatures of the water and milk; they should register about 120 degrees (49°C) on an instant-read thermometer. In order for the yeast to grow, the liquid needs to be between 115 and 125 degrees (46 and 52°C). Drizzle the warm liquids over the flour mixture and add the beaten egg white. Stir with the wooden spoon until a soft, sticky dough forms. Dump the dough onto a work surface (no need to flour the surface).

3.

Knead the dough with your hands. It will be sticky at first, but resist the urge to add more flour. First, gather the dough together. Next, using the heel of one hand, push the top part of the dough away from you. Fold that piece over the part of the dough nearest you. Give the dough a quarter turn clockwise and repeat. Keep kneading until the dough is smooth and no longer sticky, about 10 minutes. Shape the dough into a ball. Proceed as directed in step 4.

1. TO MIX IN A STAND MIXER

In the large bowl of a stand mixer, combine the flour, yeast, sugar, salt, and baking powder. Whisk until well blended. In a small bowl, beat the egg white with a whisk or a handheld electric mixer on medium-high speed until soft peaks form.

2. Check the temperatures of the water and milk; they should register about 120 degrees (49°C) on an instant-read thermometer. In order for the yeast to grow, the liquid needs to be between 115 and 125 degrees (46 and 52°C).

3. Fit the mixer with the dough hook. With the mixer on medium-low speed, slowly pour the warm liquids into the flour mixture and add the beaten egg white. Mix until the flour is completely incorporated. Increase the speed to medium and beat until the dough is smooth and pulls away from the bottom and sides of the bowl, about 10 minutes. If the dough begins to climb the hook, stop the mixer and scrape the dough back into the bowl. Don't venture too far away while the dough is mixing, as the mixer might dance around on the counter because of the large amount of dough. Proceed as directed in step 4.

4. LET THE DOUGH RISE

Scoop up the dough and shape it into a ball. Lightly grease the bowl and place the dough back into it. Cover the top securely with plastic wrap. (I like to use a large rubber band to hold the plastic in place.) Let the covered dough rise in a warm spot until doubled in size, about 45 minutes.

5. Sprinkle an even layer of cornmeal onto a large cookie sheet. Turn the dough out onto a clean work surface (there's no need to flour; the dough is soft but not sticky) and press down gently to deflate it. Shape the dough into a 7 3/4-inch (19.75cm) square about 1/2 inch (1.25cm) thick. Using a bench scraper or a chef's knife, trim off just a bit of the edges to make a neat 7 1/2-inch (19cm) square. Cut the dough into 2 1/2-inch (6.5cm) squares, and arrange them about 2 inches (5cm) apart on the cornmeal-dusted cookie sheet. Spray the tops of the squares with nonstick cooking spray and cover loosely but completely with plastic.

6. Let the dough rise in a warm spot until doubled in size, about 25 minutes.

7. When ready to cook, position a griddle on the stovetop (I use a double-sized griddle set over 2 burners) and heat over medium-low heat. Brush about 1 tablespoon of the butter evenly over the griddle. Carefully lift the muffins one at a time and place them gently (so as not to deflate the dough), cornmeal side down, on the hot griddle, spacing them about 2 inches (5cm) apart. I can fit 6 muffins on my griddle at once. Cook until the bottoms are well browned and the tops look dry around the edges, about 5 minutes. Using a spatula, carefully turn the muffins over and continue to cook until the bottoms are browned and the muffins sound hollow when tapped, another 5 to 7 minutes longer. Transfer the muffins to a rack and cook the remaining muffins in the same way. Using a serrated knife, split the muffins in half horizontally. Serve warm or toasted.

honey oatmeal bread

MAKES 1 LOAF

Oat and honey give this bread a lovely soft, moist texture and tender crumb, plus the honey adds a subtle sweetness. It's terrific freshly baked, but what I love best about this bread is that it keeps for days. It makes the most delicious toast topped with butter, jam, peanut butter, or an extra drizzle of honey.

do aheads

• Prepare the bread dough through step 5 and refrigerate for up to 24 hours before proceeding with the recipe. It will rise slowly in the fridge.

• Prepare the dough through step 6 and cover the loaf loosely but completely with plastic wrap. Refrigerate the loaf for up to 8 hours before proceeding with the recipe. Remove from the fridge and leave on the counter while the oven heats.

1 1/4 cups (10 fl ounces/292 ml) whole milk

3/4 cup (2 ounces/57 grams) old-fashioned rolled oats (not instant)

3 tablespoons (1 1/2 ounces/43 grams) unsalted butter, plus 1 tablespoon (1/2 ounce/14 grams), melted, for glazing (optional)

1 1/2 teaspoons table salt

1/3 cup (2 1/2 fl ounces/73 ml) honey

2 3/4 cups (12 1/4 ounces/347 grams) all-purpose flour

2 1/4 teaspoons (1 packet) instant yeast (see page 20)

1. Pour the milk into a small saucepan and set over medium-high heat. Bring to a boil and remove from the heat. Stir in the oats, the 3 table-

spoons butter, and the salt. Cover and set aside, stirring frequently, until the oatmeal is soft, about 20 minutes. Stir in the honey.

2. TO MIX BY HAND

In a large bowl, combine the flour and yeast. Stir with a wooden spoon until well blended.

3. Check the temperature of the oatmeal; it should register about 120 degrees (49°C) on an instant-read thermometer. In order for the yeast to grow, the liquid needs to be between 115 and 125 degrees (46 and 52°C). Add the warm oatmeal to the flour mixture and stir with a wooden spoon until a rough, shaggy dough forms. Lightly dust a work surface with a little flour. Dump the dough onto the surface.

4. Knead the dough with your hands. It will be sticky at first, but resist the urge to add more flour. First, gather the dough together. Next, using the heel of one hand, push the top part of the dough away from you. Fold that piece over the dough nearest you. Give the dough a quarter turn clockwise and repeat. Keep on kneading until the dough is smooth and no longer sticky, about 10 minutes. Shape the dough into a ball. Proceed as directed in step 5.

2. TO MIX IN A STAND MIXER

In the large bowl of a stand mixer, combine the flour and yeast. Whisk until well blended.

3. Check the temperature of the oatmeal; it should register about 120 degrees (49°C) on an instant-read thermometer. In order for the yeast to grow, the liquid needs to be between 115 and 125 degrees (46 and 52°C).

4. Fit the mixer with the dough hook. With the mixer on medium-low speed, add the warm oatmeal to the flour mixture and beat until the flour is

completely incorporated. Increase the speed to medium-high and beat until the dough is smooth and no longer sticky, about 10 minutes. If the dough begins to climb the hook, stop the mixer and scrape the dough back into the bowl. Don't venture too far away while the dough is mixing, as the mixer might dance around on the counter because of the large amount of dough. Proceed as directed in step 5.

5. LET THE DOUGH RISE

Scoop up the dough and shape it into a ball. Lightly grease the bowl and pop the dough back into it. Cover the top securely with plastic wrap. (I like to use a large rubber band to hold the plastic in place.) Let the covered dough rise in a warm spot until doubled in size, about 45 minutes.

6. Lightly grease an 8 1/2-by-4 1/2-inch (21.5-by-11.5cm) loaf pan (I use Pyrex). Turn the dough out onto a clean work surface (there's no need to flour; the dough is soft but not sticky) and press down gently to deflate it. Press the dough into a 7-by-10-inch (17.75-by-25cm) rectangle. Starting at a short side, roll up like a jelly roll. Pinch the bottom and side seams closed. Place the dough on the counter, seam side down and perpendicular to you. Using the outside edge of your slightly curved palms, press gently but firmly on the bottom seam until the dough forms a smooth rectangle 8 inches (20cm) long, with a rounded, taut-skinned top. Place the dough, seam side down, into the prepared pan. Press on the dough to flatten and fill the pan in an even layer.

7. Cover the pan loosely (to allow for rising) with plastic wrap and let the dough rise in a warm spot until almost doubled in size, about 45 minutes. The center of the dough will rise about 1 1/2 inches (4cm) above the rim of pan.

8. When ready to bake, position an oven rack on the middle rung. Heat the oven to 375 degrees (190°C). Remove the plastic and, using the tip of a very sharp knife or razor blade, cut a slit about 1/2 inch (1.25cm) deep down the center of the loaf, traveling its length. Bake until the loaf is puffed and browned, about 40 minutes. Transfer the pan to a rack and brush the top with the melted butter, if using. (This will keep the top soft and especially buttery.) Tip the baked loaf onto a rack and remove the pan. Set the loaf on its side and let cool completely.

glazed cinnamon rolls

MAKES 12 CINNAMON ROLLS

here at the Dodge lodge, we've been making these cinnamon rolls for years. In fact, they are a family holiday staple, and Thanksgiving or Christmas morning would not be complete without them. My son, Alex, is the family's official Baker of the Cinnamon Roll, a title he carries with pride and a level of responsibility and enthusiasm. The tender rolls are moist and buttery, and they make a perfect vehicle for the swirled cinnamon-sugar filling.

When I'm baking for the holidays, I double this dough recipe, shape half of it into dinner rolls (Buttery Pull-Aparts, page 208), and make the other half into these cinnamon-laden breakfast treats. Come holiday time, both are welcome indulgences.

do aheads

• Prepare the dough through step 5, but let rise until only about 1 1/2 times its original size, about 30 minutes. Refrigerate the dough for up to 24 hours before proceeding with the recipe. It will continue to rise slowly in the fridge.

• Prepare the dough through step 7, but let the rolls rise until only about 1 1/2 times their original size, about 30 minutes. Refrigerate the rolls for up to 12 hours before proceeding with the recipe. Remove from the fridge and set on the counter while heating the oven.

• Prepare the rolls through step 9 and let cool completely. Freeze the rolls in a heavy-duty freezer bag for up to 2 months.

for the dough:

1 cup (8 fl ounces/233 ml) whole milk

8 tablespoons (4 ounces/113 grams) unsalted butter, cut into 6 pieces

3 1/2 cups (15 3/4 ounces/447 grams) all-purpose flour

2 1/4 teaspoons (1 packet) instant yeast (see page 20)

1/3 cup (2 1/2 ounces/71 grams) granulated sugar

1 teaspoon table salt

1 large egg

for the cinnamon filling:

1/2 cup (4 ounces/113 grams) firmly packed light or dark brown sugar

1/2 cup (4 ounces/113 grams) granulated sugar

1/3 cup (1 1/2 ounces/43 grams) all-purpose flour

2 1/2 teaspoons ground cinnamon

6 tablespoons (3 ounces/85 grams) unsalted butter, melted

for the glaze:

2 1/4 cups (9 ounces/255 grams) confectioners' sugar

6 tablespoons heavy cream

1/4 teaspoon pure vanilla extract

1. In a small saucepan, combine the milk and the 8 tablespoons butter. Set over medium heat and heat, stirring constantly, until the butter melts and the liquid registers about 125 degrees (52°C) on an instant-read thermometer. Remove from the heat.

2. TO MIX BY HAND

In a large bowl, combine the flour, yeast, sugar, and salt. Stir with a wooden spoon until well blended.

3. Check the temperature of the milk mixture; it should now register about 120 degrees (49°C) on an instant-read thermometer. In order for the yeast to grow, the liquid needs to be between 115 and 125 degrees (46 and

52°C). Add the warm liquid and the egg to the flour and stir with the wooden spoon until a rough, shaggy dough forms. Lightly dust a work surface with a little flour. Dump the dough onto the surface.

4. Knead the dough with your hands. It will be sticky at first, but resist the urge to add more flour. First, gather the dough together. Next, using the heel of one hand, push the top part of the dough away from you. Fold that piece over the part of the dough nearest you. Give the dough a quarter turn clockwise and repeat. Keep kneading until the dough is smooth and no longer sticky, about 10 minutes. Shape the dough into a ball. Proceed as directed in step 5.

2. TO MIX IN A STAND MIXER

In a large bowl of a stand mixer, combine the flour, yeast, sugar, and salt. Whisk until well blended.

3. Check the temperature of the milk mixture; it should now register about 120 degrees (49°C) on an instant-read thermometer. In order for the yeast to grow, the liquid needs to be between 115 and 125 degrees (46 and 52°C).

4. Fit the mixer with the dough hook. With the mixer on medium-low speed, slowly pour the warm milk mixture into the flour mixture and add the egg. Mix until the flour is completely incorporated. Increase the speed to medium-high and beat until the dough is smooth and elastic and pulls away from the bottom of the bowl (a little will stick to the sides), about 5 minutes. If the dough begins to climb the hook, stop the mixer and scrape the dough back into the bowl. Repeat as needed. Don't venture too far away while the dough is mixing, as the mixer might dance around on the counter because of the large amount of dough. Proceed as directed in step 5.

5. LET THE DOUGH RISE

Scoop up the dough and shape it into a ball. Lightly grease the bowl and pop the dough back into it. Cover the top securely with plastic wrap. (I like to use a large rubber band to hold the plastic in place.) Let the covered dough rise in a warm spot until nearly doubled in size, 45 to 55 minutes.

6. In a small bowl, combine the brown sugar, granulated sugar, flour, and cinnamon. Whisk until well blended. Set aside. Lightly grease a 9-by-13-inch (22.75-by-33cm) baking dish (I use Pyrex). Turn the dough out onto a clean surface (there's no need to flour; the dough is soft but not sticky) and press down gently to deflate it. Roll out the dough into a 12-by-17-inch (30.5-by-43cm) rectangle. Use your hand to stretch the dough gently when necessary. Pour the melted butter into the center of the rectangle and spread evenly over the dough with a spatula (a rubber one is fine, but I use a small offset spatula). Don't worry if a little spills over the edge. Sprinkle the sugar mixture evenly over the butter, spreading with your hand, if necessary.

7. Starting on a short side, roll up like a jelly roll. Pinch the long seam of the dough to the roll to seal. Position the roll, seam side down, on the work surface and cut into slices 1 inch (2.5cm) wide. Arrange the slices, cut side up, in the prepared pan, forming 4 rows of 3 slices each. Using a bench scraper, scoop up any escaped filling and sprinkle it over the rolls. Spray the tops lightly with nonstick cooking spray. Cover the baking dish with plastic wrap and let the rolls rise in a warm spot until they're about 1 1/2 times their original size and have risen about two-thirds of the way up the sides of the baking dish (they won't yet fill the dish), about 40 minutes.

8. While the rolls are rising, prepare the glaze. In a small bowl, combine the confectioners' sugar, cream, and vanilla. Stir until well blended, smooth, and thick. Cover with plastic wrap and stow at room temperature until ready to serve. Position an oven rack on the middle rung. Heat the oven to 350 degrees (180°C).

9. Remove the plastic wrap and bake the rolls until they are puffed and well browned, 35 to 40 minutes. Transfer the baking dish to a rack and let cool slightly. Check the consistency of the glaze; it should form a thick ribbon when it is dropped from a spoon. If it's too thick, add a drop or two more cream. Serve the rolls warm with a thick ribbon of glaze over each roll.

overnight brioche braid

MAKES 1 LOAF

brioche is one of the softest and richest breads in the yeast category – it almost melts in your mouth. The secret? It's loaded with eggs and butter, making the dough silky smooth and the baked interior a gorgeous shade of yellow. Traditionally, brioche is baked in a high-sided, fluted, and flared mold with a small round of dough centered on the top. Once risen and baked, it resembles a crown. Although this presentation is classic, I prefer to braid the dough. It's just as handsome, and easier to slice.

As with my other yeast bread recipes, I've included a hand-mixing method. It's important to note that this dough is very sticky and requires a different hand-kneading technique, along with some perseverance and faith. I learned this hand method when I was studying at La Varenne Cooking School in Paris. Not only is it fun, but it has also come in handy on many occasions, especially during my time as head baker at Hay Day Country Market in Greenwich, Connecticut. One busy Friday, the power went out, with gallons and gallons of brioche dough awaiting its butter addition, a crucial step. Without an electric mixer at the ready, everyone thought the entire batch was lost. The bakery crew looked on with amazement as I worked the dough by hand (in smaller batches) from a messy, supersticky dough to the satiny, supple dough that yields a great brioche. I was a magician that day, but there's nothing supernatural about it – just good technique and some old-fashioned elbow grease. When you have the time, I encourage you to mix this dough by hand. It's very rewarding.

do aheads

• Prepare the dough through step 4, but let rise until only about 1 1/2 times its original size, about 30 minutes. Refrigerate the dough for up to 12 hours before proceeding with the recipe. It will continue to rise slowly in the fridge.

• Prepare the dough through step 6, but let the braid rise until only about 1 1/2 times its original size, about 20 minutes. Refrigerate the braid for up to 12 hours before proceeding with the recipe. Remove from the fridge and set it on the counter while heating the oven.

• Prepare the brioche through step 7 and let cool completely. Freeze in a heavy-duty freezer bag for up to 2 months.

3 1/2 cups (15 3/4 ounces/447 grams) all-purpose flour

1/4 cup (2 ounces/57 grams) granulated sugar

2 1/4 teaspoons (1 packet) instant yeast (see page 20)

1 1/4 teaspoons table salt

3/4 cup (6 fl ounces/175 ml) whole milk, warmed (between 115 and 125 degrees)

3 large eggs

8 tablespoons (4 ounces/113 grams) unsalted butter, at room temperature, cut into 8 pieces

for the egg glaze:

1 large egg

1 tablespoon water

1. TO MIX BY HAND

In a large bowl, combine the flour, sugar, yeast, and salt. Stir with a wooden spoon until well blended.

2.
Check the temperature of the milk; it should register about 120 degrees (49°C) on an instant-read thermometer. In order for the yeast to grow, the liquid needs to be between 115 and 125 degrees (46 and 52°C). Drizzle the milk over the flour and add the eggs. Stir with the wooden spoon until a soft dough forms.

3.
Keep the dough in the bowl or scrape it onto an unfloured work surface (my preference) and knead it with one hand, using a slapping motion. It will be sticky at first, but resist the urge to add more flour. First, gather the dough in one hand. Next, lift the dough up (it will continue to stick to

the bowl) and slap it back down onto itself. With your clean hand, give the bowl a quarter turn and repeat. (If kneading on a work surface, use a bench scraper in your clean hand to help pick up and turn the dough.) Keep slap-kneading until the dough is smooth and begins to release from the bowl or the counter and is no longer sticky, about 10 minutes. Spread out the dough and smear the softened butter over the top. Fold the dough up and over itself to cover the butter. Continue kneading as before (it will get sticky and messy again) until the dough is smooth and satiny and doesn't stick to the bowl or counter. Proceed as directed in step 4.

1. TO MIX IN A STAND MIXER

In the large bowl of a stand mixer, combine the flour, sugar, yeast, and salt. Whisk until well blended.

2.

Check the milk temperature; it should register about 120 degrees (49°C) on an instant-read thermometer. In order for the yeast to grow, the liquid needs to be between 115 and 125 degrees (46 and 52°C).

3.

Fit the mixer with the dough hook. With the mixer on medium-low speed, slowly pour the milk into the flour mixture and add the eggs. Beat until the flour is completely incorporated. Increase the speed to medium and beat until the dough begins to pull away from the bottom and sides of the bowl, about 6 minutes. If the dough climbs up the hook, stop the mixer and scrape the dough back into the bowl. Don't venture too far away while the dough is mixing, as the mixer might dance around on the counter because of the large amount of dough. With the mixer running, gradually drop the butter pieces into the bowl. Continue mixing until the butter is incorporated and the dough is smooth and satiny. Proceed as directed in step 4.

4. LET THE DOUGH RISE

Scoop up the dough and shape it into a ball. Lightly grease the bowl and pop the dough back into it. Cover the top securely with plastic wrap. (I use a large rubber band to hold the plastic in place.) Let the covered dough rise in a warm spot until doubled in size, about 45 minutes.

5. Line a large cookie sheet with parchment or a nonstick baking liner. (I like the Silpat.) Turn the dough out onto a clean work surface (there's no need to flour; the dough is soft but not sticky) and press down gently to deflate it. Using a bench scraper or a chef's knife, divide the dough into 3 equal pieces. Roll each piece into a rope 20 inches (51cm) long. Position the 3 ropes side by side on the prepared cookie sheet. Pinch the ropes together at one end and braid the ropes together loosely by alternating lifting the far right rope over the middle rope and the far left rope over the middle rope. Repeat the process until you reach the end. Pinch the bottom ends together and tuck both ends under the braid. Lightly grease the braid and cover loosely but completely with plastic wrap.

6. Let the braid rise in a warm spot until doubled in size, about 30 minutes.

7. When ready to bake, position an oven rack on the middle rung. Heat the oven to 400 degrees (200°C). In a small bowl, make the glaze. Stir the egg and water with a fork until blended. Using a pastry brush, evenly coat the top and sides of the braid. Bake until the braid is well browned and has a hollow sound when tapped, about 30 minutes. Transfer the cookie sheet to a rack and slide the braid onto the rack. Let cool completely.

slow-baked brown rice pudding with a sugary nut topping

MAKES 6 SERVINGS

Okay, I'll say it up front: This pudding takes about 1 1/2 hours to bake. But, and it's a *big* but, this is totally hands-free baking. No stirring, no rolling. Use this down time to your advantage – weed the garden, clean out that front-hall closet, vacuum the basement.

Even with the long baking time, I have managed to add some time-savers. Precooking the rice shaves off half the baking time. So, too, does replacing some of the heavy cream with evaporated milk (it's already concentrated). The slow cooking reduces and thickens the heavy cream and evaporated milk to a rich, caramelized sauce, while the brown rice gives the pudding its deep, nutty flavor. The pudding is a creamy mixture of softened rice and raisins laced with cinnamon and nutmeg. It's delicious served unadorned, but the sugary toasted walnut topping adds a crisp textural contrast.

do aheads

• The rice can be prepared through step 1, covered, and refrigerated for up to 2 days before proceeding with the recipe.

• The pudding can be prepared through step 2, covered, and refrigerated for up to 2 days before serving.

• The topping can be prepared as directed in step 3, covered, and stored at room temperature for up to 1 day before proceeding with the recipe.

for the pudding:

1/2 cup (3 1/2 ounces/92 grams)
    raw long-grain brown rice

1/3 cup (2 1/2 ounces/71 grams)
    firmly packed dark brown sugar

1/4 cup (1 1/4 ounces/35 grams)
    dark raisins

1 teaspoon pure vanilla extract

1/4 teaspoon ground cinnamon

Pinch of ground nutmeg

Pinch of table salt

1 can (12 fl ounces/350 grams)
    evaporated milk (not sweetened
    condensed)

1 1/2 cups (12 fl ounces/350 ml)
    heavy cream

for the topping:

1 tablespoon unsalted butter

1 cup (4 ounces/113 grams)
    medium-coarse chopped walnuts
    (no need to toast)

2 tablespoons granulated sugar

1. TO MAKE THE PUDDING

Put the rice in a medium saucepan and pour in water to cover the rice by 2 inches (5cm). Bring to a boil over high heat, reduce the heat to low, and simmer, uncovered, until the rice is tender, about 30 minutes. It should still have a little bite to it. When the rice is cooked, drain it well in a fine-mesh strainer.

2.

Position an oven rack on the middle rung. Heat the oven to 300 degrees (150°C). Have ready a shallow, 2-quart baking dish. Combine the precooked rice, brown sugar, raisins, vanilla, cinnamon, nutmeg, and salt in the baking dish. In a medium saucepan (you can reuse the one you cooked the rice in, if you like), combine the evaporated milk and cream. Set over medium-high heat and bring barely to a boil. Remove from the heat, pour into the baking dish, and stir the mixture a few times until the ingredients are well dispersed and the sugar has dissolved. Bake until the top is browned, the liquid is reduced and thick, and the rice is tender, 1 1/2 to 2 hours.

3. TO MAKE THE TOPPING

While the pudding bakes, make the topping. In a small skillet, melt the butter over medium heat. Add the nuts and sprinkle on the sugar. Cook, stirring often to ensure even browning, until the nuts are toasted and the sugar is caramelized, about 10 minutes. Remove from the heat, immediately transfer to a bowl, and let cool completely.

4. Remove the pudding from the oven and set on a rack. To serve warm, let the pudding cool for about 15 minutes. The pudding can also be served at room temperature. Just before serving, break the cooled nut topping apart and scatter it over the entire pudding.

21st-century brandy alexander mousse cake

MAKES ONE 9-INCH (22.75CM) CAKE, OR 12 SERVINGS

While the cocktail might be yesterday's news, its namesake dessert is as popular as ever. My updated version of the brandy Alexander cocktail, made with white crème de cacao and brandy, is baked in a springform pan, so it looks more like a cake than a pie. The chocolate cookie crumb crust is easy to press into the pan and provides a strong flavor and texture contrast for the velvety filling. Smooth, mellow white chocolate takes the place of the harsher crème de cacao and the brandy is, well, the star.

do aheads

• The crust can be prepared through step 4, covered with plastic wrap, and stored at room temperature up to 2 days before proceeding with the recipe.

• The cake can be prepared through step 9, covered, and refrigerated for up to 3 days before serving.

for the crust:

1 1/2 cups (7 1/2 ounces/213 grams) chocolate cookie crumbs (from about 30 chocolate wafers – I use Famous Chocolate Wafers by Nabisco)

3 tablespoons granulated sugar

4 tablespoons (2 ounces/57 grams) unsalted butter, melted

1 cup (8 fl ounces/233 ml) whole milk

1 packet (2 1/4 teaspoons) unfla-vored powdered gelatin (see What Is It? on page 227)

6 ounces (170 grams) white choco-late, finely chopped

1/4 cup (2 fl ounces/58 ml) brandy

2 tablespoons granulated sugar

Pinch of ground nutmeg

1 cup (8 fl ounces/233 ml) heavy cream

1 container (8 ounces/227 grams) mascarpone cheese

1/2 teaspoon pure vanilla extract

Pinch of table salt

go-with: chocolate shavings or curls (see page 42) for garnish (optional)

1. TO MAKE THE CRUST

Position an oven rack on the middle rung. Heat the oven to 400 degrees (200°C). Have ready a 9-inch (22.75cm) springform pan.

2.
In a medium bowl, combine the cookie crumbs and sugar. Stir until well blended. Drizzle the melted butter over the crumbs and mix with a fork until evenly moistened and well blended.

3.
Dump the crumbs into the springform pan and cover with a large sheet of plastic wrap. Place your hands on the plastic wrap and spread the crumbs to coat the bottom of the pan evenly. (The plastic wrap will keep the crumbs from sticking to your hands.) Once the crumbs are in place, and with the plastic wrap still in place, pinch and press some of the crumbs around the inside edge of the pan to cover 2 inches (5cm) up the sides evenly and com-pletely. Redistribute the remaining crumbs evenly over the bottom of the pan and firmly press down to make a compact layer. I like to use a metal measuring cup with straight sides and a flat bottom for this task.

4.
Bake the crust for 10 minutes. Transfer the pan to a rack and let cool completely.

5. TO MAKE THE FILLING

Put the milk in a small saucepan. Sprinkle the gelatin evenly over it and let stand until the gelatin is no longer dry looking and has softened, about 5 minutes. Set the saucepan over medium heat, and stir constantly, until the milk is very hot, but not boiling, and the gelatin is dissolved, about 3 minutes. Dip a spoon or spatula into the liquid. It should look clear and feel smooth to the touch.

6.

Add the chocolate and whisk until melted and smooth. Slide the pan from the heat and whisk in the brandy, sugar, and nutmeg. Pour into a medium bowl and refrigerate, stirring frequently with a rubber spatula, until the mixture is cooled and thickened, about 15 minutes.

7.

While the mixture is chilling, combine the cream, mascarpone, vanilla, and salt in a large bowl. Beat with an electric mixer (stand mixer fitted with the whisk attachment or hand-held mixer) on medium-high speed until the cream just begins to thicken enough to see trace marks from the beater. Increase the speed to high and beat until firm peaks form.

8.

When the gelatin mixture is thickened (it should be as thick and gelatinous as unbeaten egg whites), scrape the whipped cream into the bowl and, using a rubber spatula, fold the two together until well blended. Pour into the cooled crust. Cover with plastic and refrigerate until firm, about 6 hours.

9.

To serve, release the springform clasp and lift off the ring. Run a long, thin metal spatula under the bottom crust and carefully slide the cake onto a flat serving plate. Garnish the top with chocolate shavings or curls, if desired. Cut into slices with a thin knife run under hot water and wiped dry, repeating the process for each slice.

orange soufflé

ost folks think of soufflés as elegant dinner-party fare. This soufflé often shows up at the end of our relaxed Sunday-night family dinners. No matter if the occasion is fancy or casual, I like to bake it in a shallow, oval baking dish. The top puffs to an impressive height and the interior is light and custardy throughout. For a casual dessert, I bring the baked soufflé directly from the oven onto the center of our round kitchen table. With bowls in front of them and spoons at the ready, no one stands on ceremony and everyone digs in. For a more formal dinner, the soufflé is still presented at the table, but I do the serving.

The base of my soufflé is orange juice infused with zest and a touch of orange liqueur. By avoiding the use of milk or cream in the base, the baked soufflé is exceptionally light and delicate and, as an added bonus, it keeps the fat content down.

do aheads

• The orange cream can be prepared through step 2, covered, and refrigerated for up to 3 days before proceeding with the recipe. The soufflé will need to bake an additional 5 to 10 minutes.

• The soufflé can be prepared through step 3, covered, and frozen for up to 1 month. Remove from the freezer and leave the dish on the counter while the oven heats. The soufflé will bake in about 40 minutes. It won't puff up as much, but it will still be light, refreshing, and delicate.

Granulated sugar for dusting baking dish

1 cup (8 fl ounces/233 ml) orange juice

3 tablespoons Grand Marnier or other orange-flavored liqueur

2 tablespoons finely grated orange zest

6 large eggs, separated

2/3 cup (5 1/4 ounces/149 grams) granulated sugar

1/4 cup (1 ounce/28 grams) all-purpose flour

Pinch of table salt

1. Position an oven rack on the middle rung. Heat the oven to 375 degrees (190°C). Lightly grease the bottom and sides of a 2-quart baking dish with 2-inch (5cm) sides. Dust with granulated sugar, tapping out the excess sugar.

2. In a medium saucepan, combine the orange juice, liqueur, and orange zest and bring to a simmer. Meanwhile, in a small bowl, combine the egg yolks, half of the sugar, the flour, and the salt. Whisk until well blended and pale in color. Slowly add the hot juice, whisking constantly. Pour the mixture back into the saucepan. Cook over medium-low heat, while whisking constantly, until the mixture is thick and comes to a boil, then cook, whisking constantly, for 1 minute. Scrape the thickened cream into a medium bowl. Gently press a piece of plastic wrap directly on the surface to prevent a skin from forming. Set aside.

3. In a large bowl, beat the egg whites with an electric mixer (stand mixer fitted with whisk attachment or handheld mixer) on medium-high speed until they hold soft peaks. Continue beating while gradually sprinkling in the remaining sugar. When all the sugar has been added, increase the speed to high and beat until firm, glossy peaks form. Spoon about one-fourth of the beaten whites into the orange mixture and whisk until blended. Add the remaining whites and fold in gently with a rubber spatula just until blended. Pour into the prepared baking dish and spread evenly. It will almost fill the dish.

4. Bake until well puffed and the top is deep gold brown, about 25 minutes. Serve immediately.

strawberry mousse

MAKES 6 CUPS, OR 8 SERVINGS

m y brother Steve is a fabulous cook and, like most good cooks, he began young. In high school, he worked in a local restaurant that served classic French cuisine. Occasionally, he'd bring home leftovers for my mom and me. The coq au vin was divine, but it was the strawberry mousse that won my heart. It was soft, airy, and had a deep strawberry flavor. Maybe it was just my formative years, but this dessert made a lasting impression. When I began developing my own recipes, strawberry mousse was one of the first.

Ripe, sweet strawberries are essential for this mousse. Without their fully developed flavor, the mousse will be bland. I find the choicest strawberries at my local farmers' market, and the growers always oblige me with a sample or two before I purchase them. In this recipe, I use ricotta cheese. It adds a creamy texture to the mousse and keeps the consistency light and airy.

do aheads

• The mousse can be prepared through step 2, covered, and refrigerated for up to 3 days before proceeding with the recipe. Reheat the mixture until it is the correct consistency as described in step 4.

• The mousse can be prepared through step 6, covered, and refrigerated for up to 4 days before serving.

2 pints (20 ounces/567
    grams/about 4 cups) ripe
    strawberries, rinsed, well dried,
    and hulled
3/4 cup (6 1/2 ounces/177 grams)
    ricotta cheese (part-skim or
    whole is fine)
3/4 cup (6 ounces/170 grams)
    granulated sugar

1 tablespoon lemon juice
1/4 teaspoon table salt
1 packet (2 1/4 teaspoons)
    unflavored powdered gelatin
    (see What Is It? on page 227)
4 whites from large eggs (1/2 cup/
    4 fl ounces/116 ml)

1. Combine the strawberries, ricotta, 1/2 cup (4 ounces) of the sugar, lemon juice, and salt in a food processor. Process until smooth, about 1 to 2 minutes.

2. Pour the strawberry mixture into a large bowl. Scoop out about 1 cup of the mixture into a small saucepan. Set the large bowl aside. Sprinkle the gelatin evenly over the liquid in the saucepan and let stand until the gelatin is no longer dry looking and has softened, about 5 minutes. Set the saucepan over medium heat and stir constantly until the liquid is very hot, but not boiling, and the gelatin is dissolved, about 3 minutes. Dip a spoon or spatula into the liquid. It should look clear and feel smooth to the touch.

3. Pour the hot liquid into the strawberry mixture in the large bowl and whisk to blend. Refrigerate, stirring frequently with a rubber spatula, until the mixture has cooled and thickened, about 20 minutes.

4. Once the strawberry mixture is thickened (it should be as thick as unbeaten egg whites), remove it from the fridge. The mixture should mound slightly. If it's too thick, heat it gently in a double boiler (see What Is It? on page 74) until it's more liquid and repeat the chilling process.

5. In a large bowl, beat the egg whites with an electric mixer (stand mixer fitted with the whisk attachment or handheld mixer) on medium-high speed until they hold soft peaks. Continue beating while gradually sprinkling in the remaining 1/4 cup (2 ounces/57 grams) sugar. When all the sugar has been added, increase the speed to high and beat until firm, glossy peaks form. Scrape the whites into the chilled strawberry mixture and, using a rubber spatula, fold together gently but thoroughly until blended.

6. Spoon the mousse into serving dishes and allow it to mound in the center. Cover and refrigerate until well chilled and set, at least 4 hours.

blueberry cornmeal cobbler

MAKES 8 SERVINGS

the blueberry juices that bubble and thicken as this cobbler bakes release an almost intoxicating aroma. The filling is spiced with cinnamon and lemon zest, which intensify the blueberry flavor without overwhelming it. The cobbler topping also has a hint of cinnamon and mixes up like biscuit dough. The cornmeal adds crunch, making it the ideal texture to soak up all the blueberry sauce.

Blueberry pie was a much-loved summer dessert in my house growing up. So, this recipe is dedicated to my brother Tim, who loves blueberries.

do aheads

• The topping can be prepared as directed in step 4, covered, and refrigerated for up to 8 hours before proceeding with the recipe.

for the filling:

3/4 cup (6 ounces/170 grams) firmly packed light brown sugar

1/4 cup (1 ounce/28 grams) all-purpose flour

1 teaspoon ground cinnamon

1 teaspoon finely grated lemon zest

1/4 teaspoon table salt

3 pints (24 ounces/680 grams/ about 6 cups) blueberries, rinsed and well dried

1 tablespoon lemon juice

for the topping:

1 cup (4 1/2 ounces/128 grams) all-
 purpose flour

1/3 cup (1 1/2 ounces/43 grams)
 finely ground yellow cornmeal

1/3 cup (2 1/2 ounces/71 grams)
 firmly packed light brown sugar

1 1/2 teaspoons baking powder

1/4 teaspoon ground cinnamon

1/4 teaspoon table salt

4 tablespoons (2 ounces/57 grams)
 very cold unsalted butter, cut into
 6 pieces

6 tablespoons heavy cream

go-withs: Sweetened Whipped Cream (see page 46) or vanilla ice cream for garnish (optional)

1. Position an oven rack on the middle rung. Heat the oven to 375 degrees (190°C). Lightly grease the bottom and sides of a 9-inch (22.75cm) square or 9-by-13-inch (22.75-by-33cm/10- to 12-cup) baking dish.

2. TO MAKE THE FILLING
In a large bowl, combine the brown sugar, flour, cinnamon, lemon zest, and salt. Stir with a fork until no lumps remain. Add the blueberries and lemon juice and toss until the berries are evenly coated with the dry ingredients. Pile the fruit into the prepared baking dish, scraping in any remaining juices or sugar from the bowl, and spread evenly.

3. Pop the baking dish into the oven. Don't worry if the oven isn't up to temperature just yet. This initial blast of heat will give the berries a head start and help the cobbler topping to cook more evenly. While the blueberries begin to bake, make the topping.

4. TO MAKE THE TOPPING
Combine the flour, cornmeal, brown sugar, baking powder, cinnamon, and salt in a food processor. Pulse briefly to blend the ingredients. Add the butter and pulse until the butter pieces are no larger than small peas. Pour the

cream over the dough and pulse just until the dough comes together in moist clumps. Dump the shaggy dough onto a work surface. Gather it up and press to form a square 1 inch (2.5cm) thick. Lightly flour the work surface and the dough. Roll out the dough, lightly flouring as needed, into a 5-by-9-inch (13-by-22.75cm) rectangle. Cut the rectangle in half lengthwise. Cut each strip crosswise into 4 equal pieces.

5. Slide the oven rack out slightly and place the dough pieces randomly on top of the filling, leaving spaces between them. The dough won't cover the filling completely. Bake until the filling is bubbling and the topping is browned around the edges, about 30 minutes. Transfer the baking dish to a rack. This cobbler tastes best served warm on the same day it's prepared. Oh, and a little whipped cream or ice cream served on the side isn't a bad idea either.

lemon chiffon pie with pretzel crust

MAKES ONE 9-INCH (22.75CM) PIE, OR 8 SERVINGS

i learned my first stripes as a food editor on the staff of *Woman's Day* magazine. The brilliant, gracious Elizabeth Alston was one of my most influential mentors. She headed up a staff full of talented people from whom I learned much – including how important it is to listen to readers. The inspiration for this pretzel crust comes from a *Woman's Day* recipe. It's been 20 years, but I still remember how the salty, buttery crust played against the citrus filling. The textural combination of the soft, billowy lemon chiffon and the crunchy, salty crust is addictive. You'll notice that I don't use egg yolks, just the whites, and that I call for ricotta in the filling instead of heavy cream. So, except for the butter in the crust, this dessert is almost lo-cal. Well, at the least, it's less rich than classic versions. I like to garnish each serving with a mini-pretzel or two. It gives guests a hint of what to expect.

do aheads

• The crust can be prepared through step 2, covered with plastic wrap, and stored in the refrigerator for up to 1 day or frozen for up to 1 month before proceeding with the recipe.

• The lemon mixture can be prepared through step 5, covered, and refrigerated for up to 2 days before gently softening the mixture to the correct consistency and proceeding with the recipe.

• The pie can be prepared through step 8 and stored in the fridge for up to 3 days before serving.

3 1/2 cups (4 1/2 ounces/128
  grams) salted mini-pretzels
1/4 cup (2 ounces/57 grams) granulated sugar

12 tablespoons (6 ounces/170
  grams) unsalted butter, melted
  and cooled slightly

for the filling:

1 packet (2 1/4 teaspoons) unflavored powdered gelatin (see What
  Is It? on page 227)
3/4 cup (6 fl ounces/175 ml) lemon
  juice
1 1/4 cups (10 ounces/284 grams)
  ricotta cheese (part-skim or
  whole is fine)

1 cup (8 ounces/227 grams) granulated sugar
Pinch of table salt
1 tablespoon finely grated lemon
  zest
4 whites from large eggs (1/2 cup/4
  fl ounces/116 ml)

go-withs: lemon slices, mini-pretzels, mint sprigs; Red Berry Sauce (page 43); or Sweetened Whipped Cream (page 46) for garnish (optional)

1. TO MAKE THE CRUST

Have ready a 9-inch (22.75cm) pie plate (I use Pyrex). Combine the pretzels and sugar in a food processor and process until the pretzels are medium-fine crumbs (some small chunks are okay, as they add crunch). Add the melted butter and process briefly until the crumbs are evenly moist.

2. Dump the crumbs into the pie plate and cover with a large sheet of plastic wrap. Place your hands on the plastic wrap and spread the crumbs to coat the bottom evenly. (The plastic wrap will keep the crumbs from sticking to your hands.) Once the crumbs are in place, and with the plastic wrap in place, use your fingers to pinch and press some of the crumbs around the inside edge and on the rim of the plate to cover evenly and completely.

Redistribute the remaining crumbs evenly over the bottom of the pie plate, and press down firmly to make a compact layer. I like to use a metal measuring cup with straight sides and a flat bottom for this task. Set aside.

3. TO MAKE THE FILLING

Sprinkle the gelatin in the bottom of a blender, making sure that it's all off the blades. Pour about 1/3 cup of the lemon juice over the gelatin and let stand until the gelatin is no longer dry looking and has softened, about 5 minutes.

4.
In a small saucepan, bring the remaining lemon juice just to a boil. (This can also be done in the microwave.) Carefully pour it into the blender to cover the gelatin. Let stand for 2 minutes. Cover the blender and blend until the gelatin is dissolved, about 1 minute. Dip a spoon or spatula into the liquid. It should look clear and feel smooth to the touch.

5.
Add the ricotta, 3/4 cup (6 ounces/170 grams) sugar, and the salt. Cover and blend until the mixture is smooth, about 45 seconds. Pour into a medium bowl and stir in the lemon zest. Refrigerate, stirring frequently, until the mixture is cooled and beginning to thicken, about 15 minutes.

6.
Once the lemon mixture is thickened (it should be as thick as unbeaten egg whites), remove it from the fridge. The mixture should mound slightly. If it's too thick, heat it gently in a double boiler (see What Is It? on page 74) until it's more liquid and repeat the chilling process.

7.
In a large bowl, beat the egg whites with an electric mixer (stand mixer fitted with the whisk attachment or handheld mixer) on medium-high speed until they hold soft peaks. Continue beating while gradually sprinkling the remaining 1/4 cup (2 ounces/57 grams) sugar. When all the sugar has been added, increase the speed to high and beat until firm, glossy peaks form. Using a rubber spatula, stir about one-fourth of the whites into

the chilled lemon mixture. Add the remaining whites and fold together gently but thoroughly until blended.

8. Pour the filling into the crust and allow it to mound in the center. Cover and refrigerate until well chilled and set, at least 4 hours. To serve, use a sharp, pointed knife to cut the pie into 8 wedges.

almond-crunch cherry galette

MAKES ONE 10-INCH (25CM) GALETTE, OR 8 SERVINGS

Cherries have such a small seasonal window that I like to seize the moment and enjoy them while I can. This prediliction has, on occasion, led me to purchase too many bags of cherries at one time. Realizing that I can't eat them all out of hand, I pit some and freeze them for later use.

Thanks to a supple dough, this galette, like the one on page 228, is easy to assemble, and the crumbly topping is a crunchy accent to the lightly sweetened filling.

do aheads

• The cherries can be pitted and frozen for up to 3 months.

• The topping can be prepared as directed in step 1, covered, and refrigerated for up to 2 days or frozen for up to 1 month before proceeding with the recipe. To use, soften slightly at room temperature so that it can be crumbled over the galette.

• The galette dough can be prepared as directed in step 1 on page 230, wrapped in plastic wrap, and refrigerated for up to 3 days or frozen for up to 1 month. Thaw in the refrigerator before proceeding with the recipe.

• The galette can be prepared through step 5, wrapped well in plastic, and frozen for up to 1 month before baking. Make sure to check your freezer and clear some space before embarking on the recipe. I find it easiest to freeze the galette before attempting to wrap it in plastic. Shape it on a plastic-lined dinner-sized plate. Slide the filled and shaped galette, plate and all, into the freezer uncovered and let it firm up, about 1 hour. Using 2 long metal spatulas (or your hands if it's frozen enough), carefully lift the galette (remember, it's not completely frozen) onto a large sheet of plastic wrap, then wrap in several layers of plastic and freeze.

To bake the frozen galette: Positon an oven rack on the middle rung and set a foil-lined half sheet pan on the rack. Heat the oven to 350 degrees (180°C). Unwrap the frozen galette (don't thaw it). Carefully slide the galette onto the heated sheet pan and bake until the crust is golden and the fruit is tender, about 1 hour and 10 minutes. If the crust browns too quickly, cover it loosely with foil.

for the topping:

1/3 cup (1 1/2 ounces/43 grams) all-purpose flour

3 tablespoons granulated sugar

Pinch of baking powder

Pinch of table salt

2 tablespoons (1 ounce/28 grams) unsalted butter, at room temperature, cut into 3 pieces

1/8 teaspoon pure almond extract

1/4 cup (1 ounce/28 grams) sliced or slivered almonds (no need to toast)

Galette dough (page 229)

for the filling:

1/2 cup (4 ounces/113 grams) granulated sugar

3 tablespoons cornstarch

1/2 teaspoon finely grated lemon zest

Pinch of table salt

1 3/4 pounds (794 grams) Bing cherries, pitted

1 teaspoon pure vanilla extract

2 tablespoons heavy cream or milk

go-withs: vanilla ice cream or Sweetened Whipped Cream (see page 46) for garnish (optional)

1. TO MAKE THE TOPPING

In a small bowl, combine the flour, sugar, baking powder, and salt. Whisk until well blended. Add the butter pieces and almond extract and, using a fork, mix while pressing on the ingredients until they're blended and crumbly. (Truth be told, I usually just use my fingers and squeeze the ingredients together.) Add the almonds and toss together. Cover and refrigerate until ready to use.

2. Position an oven rack on the middle rung. Heat the oven to 400 degrees (200°C). Line a half sheet pan with parchment or a nonstick baking liner (I like the Silpat).

3. Unwrap the galette dough, place it on a lightly floured work surface, and roll out into a large round about 15 inches (38cm) in diameter and between 1/8 and 1/4 inch (3 and 6.25mm) thick. Lift and rotate the dough a quarter turn several times as you roll to prevent sticking, and dust the surface and rolling pin with flour as needed. Use a bench scraper or spatula to loosen the rolled dough as needed. Trim off the excess dough to make a 14-inch (35cm) round. Remember, this is a rustic dessert, so a few ragged edges are fine. Carefully roll the dough around the pin and transfer it to the prepared pan. The dough will hang over the edges of the pan for now. Cover loosely with plastic wrap and set aside. If your kitchen is warm, carefully transfer the pan to the refrigerator.

4. TO MAKE THE FILLING

In a large bowl, combine the sugar, cornstarch, lemon zest, and salt. Whisk until no lumps remain. Add the cherries and vanilla and toss until the cherries are evenly coated with the dry ingredients. Pile the cherries and any juices in the center of the dough, leaving a 3-inch (7.75cm) border uncovered. Fold the dough edge up and over the filling, pleating the dough as you go. Using your fingers, dab a little water under each pleat and gently press down on the pleats to seal.

5. Brush the pleated dough with the cream or milk and crumble the topping over the fruit and dough. If too much of the topping rolls off the dough, pick it up off the pan and gently press it onto the dough.

6. Bake until the crust is browned and the cherries are tender, 45 to 50 minutes. Transfer the half sheet pan to a rack and let cool slightly. Using 2 long metal spatulas, lift the galette onto a rack to cool or, if serving immediately, onto a large, flat serving plate.

classic fruit tart

MAKES ONE 9-1/2 INCH (24CM) TART, OR 8 SERVINGS

françois Payard, owner of Payard Bistro in Manhattan, makes such gorgeous fruit tarts that he has inspired me to create my own. This dessert is one of the most beautiful-to-look-at recipes in my repertoire. I've made it countless times, varying the fruit topping as the market and season allow. Simple sweet strawberries are delicious and classic, but feel free to mix different fruits together and tuck in a few thinly sliced apples, just as Payard does.

The sweet tart crust is my version of the French *pâte sucrée*, but don't be intimidated. It's a snap to mix up and any rips or tears are easily pinched and pressed together.

do aheads

• The dough can be prepared as directed in step 1, wrapped in plastic wrap, and refrigerated for up to 2 days or frozen for up to 1 month.

• The baked crust can be prepared through step 3, covered, and stored at room temperature for up to 1 day before proceeding with the recipe.

• The pastry cream can be prepared as directed in step 4, covered, and refrigerated for up to 2 days before proceeding with the recipe.

• The tart can be prepared through step 6, covered loosely, and refrigerated for up to 6 hours. Bring to room temperature before serving.

for the crust:

1 cup (4 1/2 ounces/128 grams) all-
   purpose flour
1/4 cup (1 ounce/28 grams) confectioners' sugar
Pinch of table salt

6 tablespoons (3 ounces/85 grams)
   very cold unsalted butter, cut into
   6 pieces
1 yolk from large egg

for the pastry cream:

1 cup (8 fl ounces/233 ml) whole
   milk
3 yolks from large eggs
3 tablespoons granulated sugar

4 teaspoons all-purpose flour
1 teaspoon pure vanilla extract
1/4 cup (2 fl ounces/58 ml) heavy
   cream

for the fruit:

1 1/2 pints (15 ounces/425 grams/about 3 cups) mixed berries, rinsed
   and well dried

1. TO MAKE THE CRUST

Put the flour, confectioners' sugar, and salt in a food processor. Pulse briefly
to combine. Add the butter pieces and pulse just until coarse crumbs form.
Add the egg yolk and pulse just until the dough forms moist clumps. Dump
the dough onto an unfloured work surface and gently shape into a disk
about 5 inches (13cm) in diameter. Wrap the disk in plastic and refrigerate
until chilled, at least 30 minutes.

2. Lightly dust the work surface and a rolling pin with flour. Unwrap the
disk, place it on the floured surface, and roll out into a 14-inch (35cm)
round. Lift and rotate the dough a quarter turn several times as you roll to
prevent sticking, and dust the surface and the rolling pin with flour as
needed. Use a bench scraper or spatula to loosen the rolled dough as
needed. Carefully roll the dough around the pin and position the pin over a
9 1/2-inch (24cm) tart pan with a removable bottom. Unroll the dough onto
the tart pan and gently nudge it into the bottom and side of the pan. Gently

but firmly press the dough against the sides and bottom. This dough is a bit more fragile than regular pie dough. If it tears or cracks, just pinch the dough back together. Trim the edges with a paring knife or scissors, leaving a 1/2-inch (1.25cm) overhang. Fold the overhang over itself and press it against the inside of the pan, creating a double thickness around the edge to reinforce the sides of the tart shell. Slide the lined tart pan into the freezer and chill until the dough is very firm, at least 30 minutes.

3. Position an oven rack on the middle rung. Heat the oven to 400 degrees (200°C). Line the frozen crust with a large piece of foil and fill with pie weights or dried beans. Bake for 15 minutes. Remove the foil and weights and continue to bake until the crust is pale golden brown, about 5 minutes. Transfer the tart pan to a rack and let cool.

4. TO MAKE THE PASTRY CREAM
In a small saucepan, bring the milk to a simmer. Meanwhile, in a small bowl, combine the egg yolks, sugar, flour, and salt. Whisk until well blended and pale in color. Slowly add the hot milk, whisking constantly. Pour the mixture back into the saucepan. Cook over medium-low heat, whisking constantly, until the mixture is thick and comes to a boil, then cook, whisking constantly, for 1 minute. Scrape the pastry cream into a medium bowl. Gently press a piece of plastic wrap directly on the surface to prevent a skin from forming. Refrigerate until cold.

5. TO ASSEMBLE THE TART
Add the vanilla to the chilled pastry cream and whisk until well blended. In a small bowl, beat the heavy cream with a handheld electric mixer on medium-high speed or a whisk until it forms firm peaks. Scrape the whipped cream into the pastry cream and fold together with a rubber spatula just until blended.

6. Spread the pastry cream evenly in the cooled tart shell. Arrange the berries casually on top of the cream and serve immediately.

apple cider pie with
toasted-walnut lattice crust

MAKES ONE 9-INCH (22.75CM) PIE, OR 8 TO 10 SERVINGS

Over the years, I've observed that making pies causes a lot of anxiety. If you, too, are afraid, don't be self-conscious, because you aren't alone. I developed a pie dough that is supple, forgiving, and easy to roll out and handle. And a lattice crust really is not as difficult as it sounds. My prefab method will convince you. Rather than weave the lattice on top of the pie filling, I prefer to do it on a sheet of parchment, where I can fiddle with it all I want, slide it into the fridge if it gets too warm or if I need to run out, and then flip it cleanly right onto the pie.

While my mom normally used this filling for her Sunday-night apple crisp, I like it as a pie filling, topped with the lattice crust. The juices are just the right thickness, and the sugar and spices are not so strong that they overwhelm the alluring flavor of the apples.

do aheads

• The apple filling can be prepared as directed in step 1, covered, and refrigerated overnight before proceeding with the recipe.

• The prefab lattice topping can be prepared through step 5, covered, and refrigerated for up to 1 day or frozen for up to 1 month. Just remember to wrap it well and keep it flat. Thaw at room temperature or overnight in the fridge.

3 pounds (1,361 grams) Golden
   Delicious apples, peeled, cored,
   cut into slices 3/4 inch (2cm)
   thick, and the slices halved
   crosswise
2/3 cup (5 fl ounces/146 ml) apple

cider
2/3 cup (5 1/4 ounces/149 grams)
   firmly packed light brown sugar
1 teaspoon ground cinnamon
1/4 teaspoon ground nutmeg
3 tablespoons cornstarch

for the crust:

1 recipe (2 disks) Never-Fail Pie
   Dough (page 244), thawed if
   frozen
2 tablespoons milk

3 tablespoons finely chopped walnuts (no need to toast), mixed
   with 1 tablespoon granulated
   sugar

1. TO MAKE THE FILLING

In a large, heavy pot, combine the apples, all but 2 tablespoons of the
cider, the brown sugar, the cinnamon, and the nutmeg. Stir until well combined. Set the pot over high heat and cook, stirring often, until the sugar
has dissolved and the cider just comes to a boil. Meanwhile, in a small
bowl, combine the cornstarch and the remaining 2 tablespoons apple cider.
Stir until blended and somewhat pasty. Once the cider is boiling, scrape this
paste into the apples. Boil, stirring constantly, until the liquid is thickened
and clear, about 1 minute. The apples won't be cooked at this point; they'll
still be quite crunchy. Remove the pot from the heat and let cool to room
temperature.

2. TO ASSEMBLE THE PIE

Lightly dust the work surface and a rolling pin with flour. Unwrap 1 disk,
place it on the floured surface, and roll out into a 14-inch (35cm) round.
Lift and rotate the dough a quarter turn several times as you roll to prevent
sticking, and dust the surface and the rolling pin with flour as needed. Use
a bench scraper or spatula to loosen the rolled dough as needed. Carefully

roll the dough around the pin and position the pin over a 9-inch (22.75cm) pie plate (I use Pyrex). Unroll the dough onto the pie plate and gently nudge it into the bottom and sides of the plate. Gently but firmly press the dough against the sides and bottom, being careful not to stretch or tear it. Trim the edges, leaving a 3/4-inch (2cm) overhang. Cover loosely with plastic wrap and set aside while you make the lattice top.

3. Roll out the remaining disk into a rectangle slightly larger than 9 by 14 inches (22.75 by 35cm). Trim he dough in an exact 9-by-14-inch (22.75-by-35cm) rectangle. Cut into 12 strips each 14 inches (35cm) long and 3/4 inch (2cm) wide. Line a cookie sheet with parchment. Arrange 6 strips horizontally on the cookie sheet, setting them 3/4 inch (2cm) apart. These are the "bottom" strips. Set aside the remaining 6 strips. They will be the "top" strips.

4. Position the cookie sheet so that the strips are horizontal to you. Starting with the bottom strip nearest you, and working from the right end, fold back every other strip. Slightly right of center, lay down 1 top strip vertically. Unfold the folded strips. Then, working from the left end of the strips, fold back the other 3 bottom strips. Lay a second top strip 3/4 inch (2cm) to the left of the first. Unfold the folded strips. Now fold back alternating strips on the right. Lay a third top strip 3/4 inch (2cm) to the right of the center strip; unfold the strips. Repeat the process on the left and right sides with the remaining strips.

5. Dab a little water between the strips where they overlap and press gently to seal. Cover with plastic wrap and pop the lattice – cookie sheet and all – into the fridge for 15 minutes, be sure to keep it level.

6. Meanwhile, position racks on the lower third and middle rungs of the oven. Set a foil-lined cookie sheet on the lower rack to catch any drippings. Heat the oven to 425 degrees (220°C).

7. Load the cooled apple filling into the pie shell and brush the edge of the bottom crust with water.

8. Remove the lattice from the fridge and uncover. Slide your palm under the parchment and center it under the lattice. Lift the paper and invert the lattice onto the filling, using your palm as a guide to center the lattice on the filling. Press the edges together and trim both crusts, leaving a 3/4-inch (2cm) of overhang. Roll the overhang under itself to shape a high edge that rests on top of the plate rim. Position the thumb and forefinger of one hand on the outside edge of the plate rim and the forefinger of the other hand directly opposite on the inside. Then, pinch-crimp the edge, working your way completely around the rim.

9. Brush the lattice and the edge with the milk and sprinkle the nut-sugar mixture evenly over the top. Bake until the crust is golden and the apples are tender when pierced with the tip of a knife, about 55 minutes. If the topping browns too quickly, loosely cover the pie with foil. Transfer the pie to a rack to cool. Serve warm or at room temperature.

index

Page numbers in **boldface** indicate recipes.